Austerity as Public Mood

Radical Cultural Studies

Series Editors: Fay Brauer, Maggie Humm, Tim Lawrence, Stephen Maddison, Ashwani Sharma and Debra Benita Shaw (Centre for Cultural Studies Research, University of East London, UK)

The Radical Cultural Studies series publishes monographs and edited collections to provide new and radical analyses of the culturopolitics, sociopolitics, aesthetics and ethics of contemporary cultures. The series is designed to stimulate debates across and within disciplines, foster new approaches to cultural studies and assess the radical potential of key ideas and theories.

Austerity as Public Mood

Social Anxieties
and Social Struggles

Kirsten Forkert

ROWMAN & LITTLEFIELD
INTERNATIONAL

London • New York

Published by Rowman & Littlefield International Ltd
6 Tinworth Street, London SE11 5AL
www.rowmaninternational.com

Rowman & Littlefield International Ltd. is an affiliate of Rowman & Littlefield
4501 Forbes Boulevard, Suite 200, Lanham, Maryland 20706, USA
With additional offices in Boulder, New York, Toronto (Canada), and Plymouth (UK)
www.rowman.com

British Library Cataloguing in Publication Data
A catalogue record for this book is available from the British Library

ISBN: HB 978-1-78348-193-4
       PB 978-1-78348-194-1

Library of Congress Cataloging-in-Publication Data Available

ISBN: 978-1-78348-193-4 (cloth: alk. paper)
ISBN: 978-1-78348-195-8 (electronic)
ISBN: 978-1-78348-194-1 (paperback)

∞™ The paper used in this publication meets the minimum requirements of American
National Standard for Information Sciences – Permanence of Paper for Printed Library
Materials, ANSI/NISO Z39.48–1992.

Printed in the United States of America

Contents

Acknowledgements

I would like to thank the support of the Birmingham City University's Faculty Research Investment Scheme, which gave me the time to write this book. I want to thank Debbie Shaw for her careful and insightful editorial work, and the team at Rowman & Littlefield International for making this all happen. Thanks also to those who agreed to be interviewed for this book.

I also want to acknowledge the support of the Economic and Social Research Council (ESRC) in funding the *Mapping Immigration Controversy* project, of which the interview with the immigration advisor in chapter 4 was part (grant number ES/L008971/1). This project involved Principal Investigator Hannah Jones and Co-Investigators Gargi Bhattacharyya, William Davies, Sukhwant Dhaliwal, Yasmin Gunaratnam, Emma Jackson and Roiyah Saltus, as well as the author – and I want to thank all of them, as well as all those who participated in the research. An earlier version of chapter 5 was published in *New Formations* 87, and so I also thank the editors of the issue, Rebecca Bramall and Jeremy Gilbert.

Thanks to all those activists who I have interviewed, for sharing their thoughts and experiences.

I also want to thank those who have helped read parts of this book, and for the ongoing conversations which have shaped my thinking around this book: Vicky Blake, Gemma Commane, the Debt Collective, Rajinder Dudrah, Leslie Faizi, Anne Graefer, John Hamilton, James Holland, Ana Lopes, Jamie Melrose, Eugene Nulman, Saskia O'Hara and Focus E15, David Ridley and Dave Stamp. I also want to thank my fellow activists in the UCU, local campaigners in Lewisham, Birmingham Asylum and Refugee Association and other immigrants and refugee rights campaigners I have worked with over the years. Thanks to the inspiring thinking of Sara Ahmed, Bridget Anderson,

Lauren Berlant, Judith Butler, William Connolly, Stuart Hall, Jo Littler and others who have shaped the book.

Thanks especially to my partner Peter Conlin, whose support has been indispensable and who has also helped me crystallise my thinking around the book. Thanks to my family as well.

This book is dedicated to all those who are campaigning for a future beyond austerity, and to challenge the nostalgic, socially conservative politics which currently shape the public mood.

Introduction

Tightening Our Belts

The seeds for this book were sown when I was finishing my PhD in 2010. It was the aftermath of the financial crisis, and the former Labour administration here in the United Kingdom had bailed out the banks with £141bn, with exposure to liabilities at £1.3tn (Oxfam 2013). The justification was that if they did not do so then it would destroy the global economy (the term 'too big to fail' was frequently used at the time). The public were told that the good times were over and that the hard times were coming, and that we needed to 'tighten our belts'. In order to counter claims by the Conservatives and the press that the Labour Party were profligate spenders, former Chancellor Alistair Darling claimed, rather desperately in retrospect, that Labour would 'cut deeper than Thatcher' (Elliot 2010). Such tough talk did not go far enough to counter these perceptions, as well as more general assumptions around right-wing governments as more fiscally prudent. In May 2010, the Conservative–Liberal Democrat government was elected.

One of the government's first proposals was to treble tuition fees for students in England to £9,000/year, based on the Browne Review,[1] which began under the previous administration. I took part in protests against these proposals, which I will discuss in greater detail in chapter 6. Between 2010 and 2011, my life was split three different ways. Some of it was spent in the unpredictable and exciting spaces of social movements: a large demonstration in London which culminated with a banner drop at the top of the Conservative Party headquarters at Millbank,[2] followed by other large demonstrations with tens and in some cases hundreds of thousands of people; teach-outs (where lessons and discussions took place in public spaces), student occupations and other experiments, although due to other commitments, I could not spend as long on these activities as I wished. Some of my time was spent in the solitary and more reflective experience of thinking and writing. And then

1

finally, some was spent at work: I was juggling two, and, at one point, three, part-time jobs. As the student protests lost momentum after the narrow vote to increase tuition fees, I became involved in local campaigns around saving public services. These developed in response to government plans to cut and privatise these services, as part of an overall policy of austerity.

The term 'age of austerity' was first used in the UK context by former Conservative leader David Cameron at the 2009 Conservative Party conference (Summers 2009). It can be defined as voluntary deflation measures involving deep cuts to public spending but without significant increases in tax, with the goal of restoring competitiveness and giving confidence to financial markets (Blyth 2013a; Oxfam 2013, 2). However, in practice, austerity policies do not have the effect of stabilising economies, reducing debt or promoting growth (Blyth 2013a, 3–4). Instead, economic insecurity and job losses cause people to engage in protective measures, such as cutting back personal spending or taking wage cuts, resulting in shrinking consumer demand and reduced tax revenues (Blyth 2013a, 9–10). In the United Kingdom, the result has been economic stagnation and rising of public debt from 56.6% of GDP in 2009 to 90% of GDP in 2013 (Office of National Statistics 2013a). It was also a policy which resulted in dramatic increases in inequality. Due to changes to tax and welfare, the poorest 10% of the population saw a 38% drop in their income, with the wealthiest 10% only losing 5% (Horton and Reed 2010 cited in Oxfam 2013, 4). At the same time, the wealthiest 1,000 individuals saw their wealth increase by £138bn (Sunday Times Rich List cited in Oxfam 2013, 4).

Austerity measures also included the following significant cuts to public services and privatisation initiatives:

- Introducing an under-occupancy charge widely known as the 'bedroom tax' – all this was introduced between 2011 and 2013 (Social Security Advisory Committee 2014, 9). The bedroom tax involved cutting housing benefits paid to social housing tenants deemed to have an 'extra room' by 14% and two 'extra rooms' by 25% (Shelter 2016)
- Scrapping the Education Maintenance Allowance in England, which paid students from low-income families in England up to £30/week to attend education or training (Taylor 2011)
- The reduction of funding to public libraries of 20%, resulting in the loss of 357 libraries between 2009/2010 and 2013 (Anstice 2015)
- Implementing the Health and Social Care Act, which devolved responsibility for healthcare provision from the national government to local groups of health providers and made it easier for private companies to provide elements of healthcare provision (UK Government 2012)

- Significant funding cuts to Sure Start[3] children's centres, resulting in the closure of 313 between 2010 and 2015, with greatest numbers in recent years (Walker 2016)
- Replacing of Incapacity Benefit (a form of welfare benefit paid to those who are too ill to work) with Employment and Support Allowance 'with more stringent medical tests, greater conditionality and time-limiting of non-means tested entitlement for all but the most severely ill or disabled', including the controversial Work Capability Assessment to decide whether claimants are entitled to sickness benefits (Beatty and Fothergill 2013, 5)
- Introducing a workfare programme requiring unemployed people to do up to 30 hours/week of unwaged work or else lose their benefits of £73.10 (Beatty and Fothergill 2013, 10)
- Scrapping of the Independent Living Fund, which provided funding for disabled people to purchase mobility devices and other supports for independent living, replacing it with a discretionary fund (Disability Rights UK 2016)

Austerity has disproportionately affected those on the lowest incomes, but also has negatively impacted other sections of society, with the exception of the wealthiest. Austerity has led to increases in child poverty, which is expected to rise to 800,000 children (one in four children in the United Kingdom by 2020) (Brewer, Browne and Joyce 2011 cited in Oxfam 2013). Benefit cuts such as those outlined previously have also made people more vulnerable to labour market instability, and have exacerbated in-work poverty. They have also impacted on those already experiencing structural discrimination, particularly women and ethnic minorities who are more likely to be low-paid and in precarious employment (TUC 2015a, Runnymede Trust 2015). As women are more likely to be employed in the public sector, they have experienced greater pay freezes and as users of public services they have been affected by budget cuts, which provoked the Women's Budget Group to call austerity cuts 'regressive'. Disabled people have been particularly affected by the bedroom tax (TUC 2014a), the cuts to the Independent Living Fund, and the controversial Work Capability Assessment tests, which have been carried out by outsourced private companies and have forced severely disabled people and the terminally ill to undergo repeated tests (Lyons 2012).

This book is about the possibilities and the challenges of organising in response to this considerable scale of austerity cuts (figure I.1). It is informed, in certain respects, by the hopefulness of people taking collective action to create change: when they realise that what they thought was private hardship and personal failure is in fact a shared condition; when they discover a sense of agency and voice; and new ways of thinking and acting; when they hold

Figure I.1. Anti-austerity demonstration, London, 2015. *Source:* **the author.**

those in power to account, especially those who are used to taking ordinary citizens for granted; or when they appropriate the spaces within the city that they are kept out of because they are owned by the government or corporations. However, this book is also about trying to understand why the scale of the resistance was not as large as it could have been, and needed to have been to have any significant effect. It is also about examining the failures of imagination which mean that all we can think of is returning to a previous period in history when the cuts had not taken place, or before the Conservatives got into power, or before Thatcherism and so forth rather than imagining and enacting alternatives. Why is that it is so much easier to idealise the past than to come to grips with the present, let alone imagine the future? In considering these questions, this book will explore the relationship between austerity, an inward-looking and nostalgic tendency within political discourse and popular culture, and the hardening of this tendency into right populism.

GUILT AND NOSTALGIA

Throughout the book, I will explore the links between these imaginative failures and an introspective, nostalgic and rather guilt-ridden tendency which I also began to notice around 2010. This tendency has been present within popular culture, politicians' speeches and media commentary and other aspects of the psychosocial landscape. It indicated that austerity was not only a set of economic policies, but 'an enduring commitment to reshape social relations' (Bramall 2016, 2). What does this reshaping of social relations look like, particularly in relation to popular culture? One example of this is the rehabilitation of the 1930s 'Keep Calm and Carry On' posters which became ubiquitous after the financial crisis, and which I will discuss in chapter 1. Another example is the reality television programmes in which people tried to eat or live in the way that previous generations did, and guiltily remarked on their lack of cooking or craft skills. More generally, media commentary seemed to be laced with moral judgements towards contemporary lifestyles: we were eating too many ready meals, buying too much fast fashion or cheap food shipped from halfway around the globe; we were not exercising enough, unlike previous generations, and were addicted to gadgets and social media. The implication was that we have lost our way, and there was a conflation of the excesses of the boom period, the environmental and health consequences of convenience culture, an overgenerous welfare state that undermined the work ethic and the supposed decadence of too much social liberalism (political correctness gone mad, etc.). The response was to get 'back to basics', which austerity provided the opportunity to do. Back to basics meant a simpler time: the post-war era, the Second World War (which was imagined as a time of strong cohesion and solidarity) or even the nineteenth century. It was a time of close-knit communities, 'real jobs' and stable living arrangements.

The questions of *whose* roots we were returning to, and whose cultural memories acted as sources for nostalgia and guilt were not meaningfully discussed, nor were the possibilities that for some the past may have meant exclusion and discrimination rather than social cohesion. The past, in many ways, was being imagined as a white, culturally homogeneous past, and one where gender roles and sexual identities were clearly delineated. Austerity policies coincided with rising anti-immigrant sentiment within political discourse and policy, the media and within public opinion, which will be discussed in greater detail in chapter 4. As public finances were stretched, immigrants became scapegoated as burdens on the welfare state, as 'health' or 'education' tourists and as taking what was not rightfully theirs.

Increasingly, a number of commentators have claimed that mass immigration and a functioning welfare state were fundamentally incompatible (echoing Milton Friedman, but from a xenophobic perspective). One of these is David Goodhart, whose thinking will be discussed in the following chapters; he argues that the public trust necessary to sustaining the welfare state depended on the shared social solidarity and shared values of culturally homogeneous societies (2013). Goodhart also claims to be on the side of history, and that his neo-communitarian and 'post-liberal'[4] views were shared by many working-class people, unlike the liberal metropolitan elite (2014). Goodhart's work can be understood as symptomatic of a broader tendency to position conservative conceptions of community, place and work as an alternative to neoliberal globalisation. He and others had been making similar arguments long before austerity, as will be discussed in chapter 4, but the melancholic and inward-looking climate in the aftermath of the financial crisis gave them a receptive audience. Later, such questioning of the benefits of immigration hardened into the right populism of UKIP[5] and its fellow travellers in other political parties, the vote to leave the European Union, and in the United States, the election of Donald Trump – who campaigned to ban Muslims from the United States and build a wall between the United States and Mexico, which would be paid for by the Mexican government.

To return to my own experience, it was around this time that I found myself the object of both these discourses and their expression in immigration policy as a non-EU citizen (I am a Canadian). I found myself the object of increasingly stricter policies and harsh rhetoric which positioned foreigners as stealer of jobs, burdens on the welfare state and threats to social cohesion. I came to the United Kingdom in 2007 on a student visa within what seemed like a relatively open immigration climate. However, during that same year, former Prime Minister Gordon Brown used the phrase 'British Jobs for British workers' in a Labour Party conference speech (2007). Restrictive policies followed, under both the final days of the Labour administration (desperate to show it was not a 'soft touch' on immigration), and under the Coalition and Conservative majority governments. I was faced with increasing visa fees, and other charges, including having to pay an additional £600/year for healthcare.

At the same time as these developments, I noticed the political rhetoric shift from certain categories of immigrant not being wanted, to all immigrants being problematic, including the white-collar professionals who had previously been seen in more positive terms. This was exemplified by PM Theresa May's speech to the 2015 Conservative Party Conference (as Home Secretary), where she claimed that immigration in general did not benefit UK society and undermined social cohesion (2015). As with Goodhart, cultural difference was framed as the problem. I began to recognise a vicious cycle between austerity cuts, rising inequality, the climate of introspection described earlier and anti-immigrant sentiment. Austerity cuts remove or worsen access to public services. Within everyday experience, this becomes manifest as queues, overstretched services, packed waiting rooms and so forth. The rising inequality makes it evident that some are affected more than others by cuts, although those who are hit the hardest may not be publicly visible, as they may be suffering in the privacy of their homes. The introspective climate and anti-immigrant sentiment (backed up by government rhetoric and policies) identifies scapegoats for austerity, who are framed as taking what is not rightfully theirs, displacing resentments away from those making the decisions in favour of austerity and onto other groups in society.

These groups then become targeted for further austerity cuts and privatisation experiments, as they are seen to lack public sympathy.

To summarise, austerity rhetoric and policies are not only about public finances, but need to be seen within the context of several tendencies within public discourse, popular culture and policy. The first is an inward-looking and melancholic climate marked by a rather guilty sense of having lost our way and living in a broken society, and also marked by nostalgia for earlier moments in history when supposedly we still had our bearings. The second consists of post-liberal arguments about immigration (and, in a more general sense, progressive politics) undermining, and even being incompatible with the welfare state and social cohesion. The third is the manifestation of socially conservative and anti-immigration perspectives within policy initiatives to cut access to public services for problem populations such as the unemployed and immigrants. This means that cuts to public services become not only about saving money, they also carry moral and emotional associations: melancholic longing for a lost sense of community, authentic experience and clear moral purpose; fear of outsiders; anxieties around the effects of globalisation; anger at the 'wrong' people having access to the welfare state, and so forth.

Austerity cuts are ideological, as has been demonstrated by their effects in widening inequality and their disproportionate effects on those who are already marginalised, as discussed earlier. As I will explore throughout this book, the rhetoric used to justify them has drawn on aspects of neoliberal and Right populist ideologies, as well as long-standing prejudices about the deserving and undeserving poor and immigrants as burdens on the welfare state. However, in order to more fully understand how austerity relates to the tendencies I have described earlier, as well as how consent for austerity is secured, I will also need to explore how austerity appeals to emotions. How do pro-austerity arguments and policies mobilise anxiety, guilt, nostalgia, resentment or shame, both public and private?

WHAT IS A 'PUBLIC MOOD'?

This book is called 'austerity as public mood'. But what is a 'mood'? The *Webster English Dictionary* defines a 'mood' as a 'conscious state of mind or predominant emotion', and also as 'a prevailing attitude, a receptive state of mind predisposing to action', and 'a distinctive atmosphere or context'. A mood is thus both individual – about subjectivity – and collective – about politics and the constitution of the public. It is not only about emotion, but also about public opinion and ideology ('a prevailing attitude'). To a certain extent, a mood is also rather undefinable and unexplainable, although we might be able to identify causes in terms of life events. Someone may also be in a particular mood despite their best rational judgement: they just happen to be feeling a particular way. And what of a 'public mood'? A public mood is similar to public opinion. It is also a claim to hegemony: that most people just feel a particular way. In many ways, this is quite similar to Gramscian conceptions of common sense. However, my focus is on how discourses, events and cultural habits (resentments, prejudices, etc.) create a particular affective climate. I am particularly interested in how mood can be mysterious, undefinable and inarguable. This gives it its political power. The common-sense perception is that tapping into the public mood can promise popularity and even electoral success for political parties; conversely to be out of touch with the public mood is to risk irrelevance if not electoral suicide. Claims to the public mood become normative, if not in some cases authoritarian: get with the programme or else risk marginalisation or irrelevance; your views are unpopular so shut up. For example, at the time of writing, the accusation of being out of touch with the public mood is primarily targeted at defenders of progressive politics and, in particular, pro-immigration views, leading to a degree of self-censorship for those holding such views, or worse, desperate attempts to appeal to Right populist politics. At its most pessimistic and paranoid, the public mood becomes as a kind of political *Id*, not so far away from conceptions of the public as mob, as a mass who feels and does not think, who are dangerously close to fascism or violence and cannot be trusted with democratic participation.

The invocation of the public mood is also connected to the framing of the public by public opinion polling and other political marketing techniques as essentially passive vessels for this mood, who could not be reasoned with or convinced (this will be discussed further in chapter 2 in relation to Hall's theories of authoritarian populism). A mood seems to fall outside of rational debate or political ideologies. In this sense, it is the legacy of the civic disengagement which is a result of post-political approaches to governance critiqued during the New Labour period. It was assumed that after the fall of the Soviet Union that ideological conflicts were over, and governance became increasingly technocratic, with citizens increasingly excluded from democratic decision making (Mouffe 2005; Hay 2007). Although the ideological climate has now changed, the exclusion of the public from democratic processes has not, and the cynicism and disengagement resulting from this approach continue to persist. Because the public are not engaged within democratic process or debate, all they can do is express the public mood. The public mood may be a product of demographic categories based on gender, age, social class, ethnicity and so forth, which become treated as fixed and determining factors rather than as social constructs, or sites of political struggle. It is assumed that people of particular backgrounds and socio-economic positions will hold particular attitudes, which are perceived to largely be static. More recently – particularly in the aftermath of the Brexit vote and hardening attitudes on immigration – public mood has been framed in terms of categories of people with varying degrees of comfort or discomfort with social, cultural and technological change (Katwala, Rutter and Rhodes 2016; Ashcroft 2016). The assumption is that it is those who feel anxious (they use the term 'the anxious middle') whose concerns must be addressed (Katwala, Ballinger and Rhodes 2014), more than others who might feel more at ease.

CAN AUSTERITY FUNCTION AS A PUBLIC MOOD?

In this book, I will explore how experiences of austerity become interpreted through long-held prejudices, resentments, moral panics, cultural memories and received ideas which have such a strong cultural familiarity that they just instinctively 'feel right' and are used to judge others and ourselves. Much of this book will explore moralising discourses and their role in constructing a public mood. One of these is around distinctions between the deserving and the undeserving poor, which I will discuss in chapter 3 (in relation to the 'poverty porn' genre and the demonisation of unemployed people) and in chapter 7 (in relation to reactions to a housing campaign by homeless young mothers). In a climate of increasing poverty, inequality and low-paid work, many people are closer to the despised categories than they might think. But judging others who are worse off can be used to affirm our own normality and respectability. Another prevalent moralising discourse exists around normative expectations for what one is expected to achieve in life: for example, full-time employment, property ownership and stable living arrangements. Such norms have become increasingly unachievable within the austerity context, or, as I will discuss in chapter 7, for many people can be attained only through considerable personal debt and sacrifice.

In *Cruel Optimism*, a theorisation of the present moment which has informed this book, Lauren Berlant writes about the crisis between such expectations of the good life in the United States and other industrialised countries in the global North and the 'compromised conditions of possibility' (Berlant 2011, 24) within the context of austerity, neoliberal economics and post-industrial decline. According to Berlant's theorisation, these unattainable ideals of the good life become destructive because 'something you desire is actually an obstacle to your flourishing' (Berlant 2011, 1). Nonetheless these ideals remain very powerful, and difficult to escape even if they are actually failing. In the absence of alternative ways of living or questioning the disconnect between these ideals and their own lived experience, people 'ride the wave of the system of attachment they are used to' even when this system fails them (2011, 28). Working with Brian Massumi's theorisation of affect,

Berlant suggests that affect is not only individual, it is *social:* 'affective atmospheres are shared, not solitary, and . . . bodies are continuously busy judging their environments and responding to the atmospheres in which they find themselves' (2011, 15). This, she argues, operates as a 'refraction' of Williams' 'structures of feeling' (ibid.). Like Berlant's analysis, this book is concerned with the contradiction between the ideals of the past and the lived experience of the present, particularly in the context of the nostalgic, inward-looking discourses described earlier. However, my focus is more sociological than aesthetic and, rather than analyse cultural texts, I will discuss a range of examples within popular culture, policy and social movements. The book will explore the contradictions between the social norms discussed earlier and the lived experiences of austerity, and how these are used to create divisions between insiders and outsiders; it will also explore how such divisions can be challenged.

The term 'public mood' raises questions about who the 'public' is, and whose mood requires attention – in other words, who is the 'public' in the 'public mood'? Elsewhere, I have written about 'whose feelings count' (Forkert, Jackson and Jones 2017), and how the fears, resentments and anxieties of particular sections of society are interpreted by policymakers as indicative of a wider public mood. As I have suggested earlier, at the time of writing it is frequently those with concerns about social change in general and immigration and abuses of the benefits system in particular who are seen as representative of the public mood. Such concerns are frequently presented in emotional terms: discomfort and anxiety about social change and loss of a stable set of social norms which cannot be assuaged by myth-busting or statistics-based arguments (Jones et al. 2017). There is a sense that the auster-ity policies and discourses legitimate emotional responses (e.g., resentment at unemployed people and immigrants) and suggest targets for our anger and fear, and for our pleasure at their misfortune.

Claims to the public mood are thus mobilised by politicians as justifica-tion for pandering to particular resentments, prejudices and anxieties. At the time of writing the invocation of the public mood currently plays a role in the legitimation of Right populist politics. This often manifests itself, typically, as the tactic common to political speeches: describing the conversation on the doorstep with the local constituent, who then claims that there are too many immigrants or too many people abusing the benefits system and something must be done about it, and that nobody is really listening. The conversation on the doorstep and the aggrieved voter who is ignored are invoked as authentic manifestations of the public mood, and the politician, by mentioning this inci-dent, demonstrates he/she is in tune with it – and thus his/her moral authority and electability. Such claims to the public mood thus benefit Donald Trump, Nigel Farage, Marine Le Pen, Viktor Orban and their fellow travellers within mainstream political parties. However, it is important to remember that a public mood may change – and that, like, hegemony, it is not fixed or static. Some of the examples I will discuss at the end offer, in limited ways, hope for shifting a public mood in a different direction – through creating the space for people to reach out to each other, relate to each other in different ways, question pro-austerity norms and arguments, and prefigure alternatives.

In exploring a public mood, I am inspired by theorisations of emotions as *social*, and as shared. Shared emotions produce the harsh moral judgements and scapegoating which will be discussed throughout this book, but also animate the forms of resistance I will examine in later chapters. In addition to Berlant's work, this book is also inspired by Sara Ahmed's work on the cultural politics of emotion (2004), and specifically her question about 'what . . . emotions do?' (Ahmed 2004, 24). Emotions, according to Ahmed, 'circulate between bodies' within an affective economy (2004, 6); they may 'stick' to some objects and slide over others (2004, 8). Ahmed gives the example of a flag – specifically the American flag within the context of the War on Terror – as an object to which emotions stick, connected to its associations of territorial conquest, patriotism and the nation at war (2004, 74). Or, to return to the construction of the public as passive, what power relations are involved in framing the public as predominantly emotional subjects and as not receptive to rational discussions of facts? Ahmed asks us to consider how some subjects, or collectives, are constructed as 'emotional' (2004, 4), and impossible to engage through rational argumentation. I would also add that it is important to consider (particularly in relation to right populism), who claims to speak for these emotional subjects, and to share their feelings (for example, anxieties about immigration and resentments about people on benefits) and see them as worthy of public attention and policy intervention. I am aware that there are also particular limitations to the concept of a public mood, especially its vagueness. It may be too easy to claim that anything is representative, or unrepresentative of a public mood, to argue that certain reactionary tendencies within British society are more dominant than they might be. With these risks in mind, the book is about trying to explore the role a public mood might play in consent for austerity policies, and in the displacing of resentments about the effects of such policies onto scapegoats and outsiders.

How can a public mood be studied? As I have discussed, a mood can seem difficult to define because it might exist within many different places, including everyday life, popular culture, political discourse and social movements. However, it is this diffuse quality which makes it seem ubiquitous, and which gives it its ideological power. This is why the book will cover a range of material on a pilot scale rather than focusing on a particular case study, with each chapter exploring a different dimension of austerity as a public mood.

The material examined in the book ranges from popular culture, social media, policy discourses and grey literature, to interviews with activists within anti-austerity campaigning, trade unions and social movements, to reflections on my own experiences. A range of methodologies are employed, including interviews, online ethnography, policy analysis, along with personal reflections. While not strictly an auto-ethnographic study, the book is also quite autobiographical and personal, particularly the later chapters which have been shaped by my experiences as an activist within the austerity context. The consideration of austerity as a public mood is thus in certain ways a study of my subjective experience. The activists in chapters 5 and 6 I have interviewed are those I have worked with closely on campaigns, and the interviews serve as reflections on our experiences together.

In chapter 1, I will examine the central premise of pro-austerity arguments that debts must be paid, regardless of the sacrifices involved; I will also explore the still-powerful role of the economy-as-household metaphor and its currency within the austerity context. I will also examine the nostalgic and melancholic tendencies that I have outlined here in greater detail. I will examine the underlying belief within these tendencies that we have lost our cultural and moral bearings as a country, and the idea that austerity presents an opportunity to revisit what we have lost. Central to this are the metaphors of *work* and *community* as touchstones for an idealised past that mark what we are lacking in the present. One of the dangers of such narratives, as I will discuss, is their delegitimisation of contemporary experiences of hardship as lacking the dignity and authenticity of those of the past. I will consider these issues in relation to the 'Keep Calm and Carry On' poster, campaigns for citizens to volunteer to clean streets and xenophobic discourses around immigrant labour. I will end the chapter by asking whether buried within nostalgia might be legitimate critiques of neoliberalism, and desires for a better world.

Chapter 2 will explore the historical context of such tendencies through Stuart Hall's theories of authoritarian populism and traditionalism, and their application to the legacy of Thatcherism. Traditionalism, for Hall, was primarily about how the Conservative Party appealed to socially conservative ideas of gender, the family and the nation in order to create divisions between insiders and outsiders. However, it was also about the failures of the Left to challenge such conservatism, and how this limited the political imagination. Authoritarian populism built on Nicos Poulantzas' (2000) theorisation of authoritarian statism, *Power, State, Socialism* (originally published in 1978), which was about the intensification of state control and coercion, as well as the weakening of democratic institutions. Hall developed the concept by arguing that such authoritarian measures were justified through appealing to socially conservative and exclusionary conception of 'the people', against which others were scapegoated as undesirables. I will end the chapter by considering the relevance of these concepts within the austerity context.

Chapters 3 and 4 will focus on the two main targets of austerity discourses: the unemployed and immigrants. Chapter 3 will explore the scapegoating of the unemployed within the austerity context, based on a study of Twitter reactions to the reality television programme *Benefits Street*, which explored the lives of the unemployed residents of a street in Birmingham. Long-standing prejudices towards the unemployed and stereotypes of the undeserving poor, and the moral value placed on work, will be examined within this chapter. I will also consider the persistent ideologies of respectability (Skeggs 1997) and meritocracy (Cross and Littler 2010). I will examine the ways in which the Twitter reactions expressed derision and disgust towards the subjects of the programme, thereby positioning their authors and their audiences as normal and respectable. I will also examine how other Twitter responses challenged such scapegoating and expressed solidarity through humour and parody, and shared testimonials of personal experiences of poverty and unemployment.

Chapter 4 will examine the role of welfare state bordering practices within the austerity context. In response to long-held public perceptions of immigrants as burdens on the welfare state, I will examine how recent immigration legislation has transformed public services into sites of surveillance and the policing of immigration status, with public sector workers playing the role of proxy border agents. Such practices, which have been described as measures to create a 'hostile environment' for irregular immigration, function symbolically to make those whose status is contingent even more precarious, and to reassure British citizens that the scarce resources of the welfare state are being reserved for them and defended against undeserving outsiders. The chapter will draw on interview material with an immigration advisor, in which he discusses his experiences in training public sector workers on immigration legislation, and the attitudes he encountered. Finally, I will examine recent initiatives to bring together anti-austerity and migrants' rights campaigns, and will call for these connections to take place on a much greater scale.

Chapters 5–7 will explore resistance to austerity, and the possibilities and challenges they faced, particularly in shifting a public mood of resignation and defeatism. Chapter 5 will examine a campaign to save a local library in South London, in which I was involved as an activist. It will be based on my own reflections and interviews with three local activists who were also involved in the campaign. In particular, I will examine a split within the campaign which occurred when the local authority[6] decided to outsource library provision to social enterprises and a charity, with volunteers replacing library staff. Some of the activists were opposed in principle to the idea of public services being operated by volunteers, while others became involved as volunteers in the running of the library. This situation will be examined in relation to policy discourses which encouraged greater volunteer involvement in public service provision, using the argument that this would restore a lost sense of community which was missing from both local areas and interaction with public services, and would also enable the creativity and resilience of local residents. The chapter will also more generally examine the limitations of the defensive nature of anti-austerity campaigns.

Chapter 6 will examine the role of trade unions within the current context, based on my own personal experiences as an activist within the University and College Union (UCU) and interviews with activists who have played a leading role within union campaigns. The effects of austerity on higher education have included both the marketisation of education (the introduction of the £9,000 cap on tuition fees playing a major role) and the casualisation of the workforce. The chapter will begin by examining some common narratives around union decline, particularly in relation to post-industrialism and their declining relevance in relation to new social movements. I will argue that the danger of such decline narratives lies in how they frame unions in relation to the melancholic nostalgia critiqued by this book: as guardians of the traditional values and social discipline associated with work-based identities. In order to counter this nostalgia, the chapter will focus on the present and on the thoughts and experiences of union activists who came to trade unionism not out of multigenerational histories, but who were politicised in other ways, such as through the 2010 student protests and the recognition of workplace sexism. I also will discuss how they came to the recognition that the workplace grievances they were experiencing (specifically casualisation and gender inequality) were collective and structural rather than individual, and how they became motivated to take action. I will explore how they interacted with the union's structures and processes, and the imaginative approach they have taken to campaigning and organising, and their approach to interpersonal relations with other activists – and how this presents an alternative approach to the factionalism of the traditional Left.

The final chapter of the book will examine social movement responses to austerity which have departed from some of the conventional approaches associated with single-issue campaigning: specifically, the Debt Collective in the United States, the *Plataforma de Afectados por la Hipoteca* (PAH) in Spain (the Platform for People Affected by Mortgages in Spain) and Focus E15 in the United Kingdom. These campaigns focus on housing problems (e.g., mortgage default, eviction and homelessness) and on household debt as shared experiences of life under austerity. They also involve the occupation of public spaces and buildings: the Debt Collective developed out of the Occupy movement in the United States, and the PAH and Focus E15 have occupied houses to draw attention to the housing crisis in Spain and the United Kingdom. They also, crucially, create spaces for people to share their feelings and concerns about homelessness and debt, and in doing so counter the privatisation of such experiences and the prevalent sense of guilt and shame produced by moralising discourses which more generally marks austerity as a public mood.

These final chapters engage with the question of whether a public mood could be shifted. As I have suggested, it is simply not enough to counter feelings with facts and myth-busting, particularly when austerity appeals to powerful emotions such as guilt and nostalgia. When people feel defeated, resigned and isolated and believe that protest is pointless, then arguments about why the cuts are wrong and defensive campaigns to protect the status quo are not enough. A mood cannot simply be dispelled. Instead, it becomes important to create a counter-mood of solidarity and hope. Such a counter-mood would mean that people would no longer feel alone and would stop blaming themselves or scapegoating others for the difficulties they are experiencing under austerity. A counter-mood would directly challenge the shame that people would feel in sharing experiences of austerity, and would involve the recognition that many of the conditions experienced under austerity are in fact shared. Such a counter-mood can be created through creating spaces for sharing experiences and feelings, and through acts of solidarity, some of which will be discussed in these final chapters. It is through such spaces and acts of solidarity that alternatives to austerity can be built.

NOTES

1. The Browne Review was a 2010 report about higher education funding and finance, entitled 'Securing a sustainable future for higher education'. See https://www.gov.uk/government/uploads/system/uploads/attachment_data/file/422565/bis-10-1208-securing-sustainable-higher-education-browne-report.pdf.

2. Millbank is a building in the Westminster neighbourhood of Central London.

3. The Sure Start initiative was established under former Chancellor of the Exchequer Gordon Brown and established centres in local areas which combined early years' education, day care services and family support.

4. Post-liberalism is a political tendency which emerged in the aftermath of the financial crisis. It was based in critiques of social liberalism and globalisation, and proposed social conservativism and localism as alternatives.

5. The UK Independence Party (UKIP) is a Right populist, socially conservative and anti-immigrant party in the United Kingdom with the goal of the United Kingdom exiting the European Union.

6. A local authority, also known as a council, is a local government organisation which is responsible for local public service provision and governance within a local area

Chapter 1

Austerity and the Appeal of the Past

According to economist Mark Blyth, austerity has become 'standard policy for states in trouble within liberal democracies' (Blyth 2013b, 43), including the United Kingdom.[1] As discussed in my introduction, there have been attempts in the United Kingdom at resistance, but these have not been large enough to change policy or shift public opinion in a significant way. Instead, attitudes towards welfare have hardened, at a time when many people are struggling financially. This was evidenced through the results of the 2015 British Social Attitudes Survey, which has found a long-term trend of declining public support for welfare benefits for the poor – 61% in 1989 and 27% in 2009, remaining low at 30% in 2015 (British Social Attitude Survey 2015).[2] Support for state benefits for unemployed people and single parents was also much lower than for pensioners and disabled people (2015, 1), although, based on reporting by the Crown Prosecution Service, disability hate crime prosecutions increased by 213% (E-Inclusion Europe 2015).

In this chapter, I will examine the prevalence of such attitudes, at a time when jobs are increasingly insecure and precarious. The starting point for this chapter comes out of observing the limitations of the numerous 'myth-buster' pamphlets I handed to passers-by as an activist, and which had been produced by False Economy, the Public and Commercial Services Union, the New Economics Foundation[3] and other organisations. The arguments within these pamphlets were based on statistical evidence of the damage caused to the economy and society by austerity, or emphasised the much greater damage to the public purse caused by tax avoidance than benefit fraud (such as illustrated by the poster in figure 1.1). In doing so, they attempted to shift attention away from the sacrifices that working- and middle-class people might believe they should be making, and towards the costs to public finances of large corporations and the wealthy.

Figure 1.1.   Poster protesting Starbucks avoiding tax, London, 2012. *Source:* **the author.**

The hope was that giving people the facts would empower them to question dominant media myths and challenge austerity. Anecdotally, when I have distributed these pamphlets as an activist or referred to their figures, I have been met with scepticism. No matter how convincing their arguments or how robust the evidence might be, the message of these pamphlets somehow seems implausible.

Why might this be the case? Is it because these perspectives are not widely circulated enough within the media to give them mainstream credibility, or is it that when they are, attempts are made to discredit them? There may be some truth to this speculation, as demonstrated by the angry reactions to Richard Wilkinson and Kate Pickett's book on inequality, *The Spirit Level* (see Booth 2010 and Clark 2010 for a summary and the authors' response). Or is it because pro-austerity arguments resonate more with people than anti-austerity arguments? Is this because claims that there simply is no more money left, that the financial crisis is due to profligate government spending or that the welfare state is a luxury that we can no longer afford somehow convince people despite evidence to the contrary? This chapter approaches this question from a perspective that might seem counter-intuitive at first: it is about trying to understand the appeal of pro-austerity arguments from their *moral* and *emotional* perspective. It is also about how pro-austerity arguments draw on a deep current of nostalgia for previous historical moments such as the Second World War, the post-war period or, in some cases, the Victorian era. These periods are frequently combined into what Owen Hatherley terms 'historical syncretism' (2016, 5), noting that these narratives 'do not have to be historically accurate to be emotionally effective' (2016, 9). It is necessary to grapple with the intuitive moral and emotional appeal of pro-austerity perspectives – to understand how they form a public mood – if we are to understand our current predicament.

I will begin by exploring austerity's intuitive appeal (e.g., through metaphors of the economy as household). I will then examine the conditions of growing precarisation, which make it difficult to imagine a future as one is forced to live constantly in the present (Graefer 2017). Faced with this insecurity and limited resources to imagine or enact change, it becomes easy to see the past as possessing a certainty and authenticity lacking in the present. I will discuss the nostalgic decline narratives that have marked the austerity context, which claim that as a country we have lost our moral and cultural bearings and that austerity provides an opportunity to restore them. Key to these narratives are the metaphors of *work* and *community*, which both look to the past to find these lost bearings, but also, more disturbingly and simultaneously, position sections of society as outsiders who are undeserving of access to the welfare state.

WHY AUSTERITY ISN'T JUST ABOUT ECONOMICS

Austerity's appeal is based at least in part on the common-sense idea of not living beyond our means as individuals and the assumption that an identical logic also applies to macroeconomics. As the economist Mark Blyth argues, 'Ideologically, it is the intuitive appeal of the idea of austerity – of not spending more than you have – that really casts its spell' (2013, 43). The appeal of the metaphor of the economy as household, of staying within your means, is only partly about economics; it is in fact primarily a moral argument. In situations where macroeconomics is perceived as difficult to grasp, the metaphor of economy as household provides a reassuring simplicity and ordinariness. According to this logic, the economy is not about complex financial operations; it is about personal budgeting. This resonates with everyday experience, as many people can remember having to forgo small luxuries in order to save money. A working-class or middle-class subject is broadly assumed in such a metaphor, although living within one's means can mean something very different depending on one's income. The economy-as-household as metaphor is so powerful because it assumes that public debt is no different from owing money to a friend or relative. In *Debt: The First 5,000 Years* (2011b), David Graeber recounts the experience of trying to explain why structural adjustment programmes for developing nations would do more harm than good, and was met with the response by an NGO representative that 'surely one has to pay one's debts' (2011b, 4). As Graeber argues:

> The reason [the debt myth] is so powerful is that it's not actually an economic statement: it's a moral statement. After all, isn't paying one's debts what morality is supposed to be all about? Giving people what is due them. Accepting one's responsibilities. Fulfilling one's obligations to others, just as one would expect them to fulfil their obligations to you. What could be a more obvious example of shirking one's responsibilities than reneging on a promise, or refusing to pay a debt? It was that very apparent self-evidence, I realised, that could make the statement so insidious. This was the kind of line that could make terrible things appear utterly bland and unremarkable. (ibid.)

Such metaphors not only render the complex easily comprehensible but also evoke the certainties of an older social order, exemplified by former Prime Minister Margaret Thatcher's statement that 'any woman who understands the problems of running a home will be nearer to understanding the problems of running a country' (BBC 2013). If public finances can be simplified to a question of everyday morality, then the division between those who are 'good' and 'bad' becomes deceptively simple as well – as it becomes about who follows the rules or pays one's debts and who does not.

As Judith Butler and Athena Athanasiou observe, 'there is nothing merely economic about economics' (2013, 39). Arguments in support of austerity are not only technical questions about public finances or the economy; they also draw on deep-seated feelings, social mores, old habits, unquestioned prejudices and long-held cultural memories. Politicians and commentators treat the financial crisis as an opportunity to entrench neoliberal policies and practices, never letting a serious crisis go to waste (Klein 2008; Mirowski 2013); such feelings and habits serve as important tools for them. However, the economy as household and other familiar metaphors could also be the instinctive common-sense ideas that we reach for when it is difficult to imagine other explanations or possibilities. These then begin to be taken for granted as truths within the context of what Michel De Certeau terms 'the recited society' which is 'defined by stories (*recits*), the fables constituted by our advertising and informational media, by citations of stories and by the interminable recitation of stories' (2011, 186). Such metaphors and narratives take on the weight of truths because we have heard them so many times, and because they fit in with other pre-existing narratives.

Austerity also goes beyond how we might interpret changes in the economy; it equally reshapes our everyday experiences, our hopes for the future and our perceptions of the past in relation to the present, particularly during a time of declining prospects. It could even be considered a 'structure of feeling' (Williams 2011). As I pointed out earlier in relation to Lauren Berlant's (2011) argument, austerity places limits on our capacities to achieve our aspirations, and, in some cases, makes the contradictions between these aspirations and the reality particularly stark. These contradictions can be exploited within pro-austerity arguments and rhetoric, particularly when ideals of the 'good life' or neoliberal self-reliance are not critically examined. Austerity also redefines what we perceive as luxuries to be sacrificed during hard times and what we deem to be necessities. It both draws on and produces a *habitus* around a diminishing sense of entitlement to public services, and increasingly precarious employment. It is also about redefining who we deem valuable to society as well as those aspects of ourselves we deem to be valuable. Conversely austerity also frames who we see as expendable, as the question of which public services to cut is often by definition about who we see as less important to society. And, most fundamentally, it is about how we perceive our interdependency, our own vulnerability as well as the vulnerability of others.

AUSTERITY, PRECARISATION AND TIME

I will now discuss the interaction between pro-austerity rhetoric and the conditions of job insecurity and financial uncertainty in which such rhetoric is received. Judith Butler and Athena Athanasiou characterise these conditions as 'precarisation', defined as the exposing of a 'targeted demographic to unemployment or to radically unpredictable swings between employment and unemployment, producing poverty and insecurity about an economic future, but also interpellating that population as expendable, if not fully abandoned' (2013, 143). Within the context of austerity, precarisation does not only affect those who are obviously destitute, but is something many people experience to a certain extent. According to the Skills and Employment survey, 52% of UK workers were worried about their jobs in 2012 (Felstead et al. 2015); the Trades Union Congress (TUC)[4] report that between 2010 and 2012, the number of temporary, casual jobs increased by 89,000, and the number of workers involuntarily on temporary contracts (meaning they would rather be on permanent contracts) had doubled (TUC 2013). The number of people aged 20–34 years living with their parents has increased by 25% since 1996 (Office of National Statistics 2014). This suggests a normalisation of the idea that one's job, wages or living conditions are never truly secure.

Bridget Anderson argues that those in precarious situations are forced to live in the present rather than being able to plan for the future, arguing that 'time matters' – in terms of the length of employment contract, and the irregularity of employment (2007, 5). Drawing on the work of Dimitris Papadopoulos and Vassilis Tsianos, Anderson frames precarity as a form of exploitation that takes place through temporal conditioning (Anderson 2007, 6). She argues that 'chaotic and unpredictable working times undermine other social identities' (Anderson 2013, 5–6) such as relationships, family, friendships and democratic participation. For Anderson, precarious work is a key part of the 'insecurity and uncertainty about tomorrow that testifies the return of mass vulnerability' (Castel 2005 cited in Anderson 2007, 5). If one is continually living in the present, then imagining any kind of alternative future or the ability to take action is severely limited, with disturbing implications for democracy. Austerity, too, is premised on present sacrifice as a condition for a deferred, more prosperous and stable future.

In *The Fragility of Things* (2013), William Connolly argues that living under financial uncertainty undermines the time and space to engage critically with larger political issues, including the consequences of austerity. Exhaustion and pre-occupation with day-to-day issues make it difficult to have the time to think and consider alternatives to the status quo. He says:

> If you are stuck in circumstances in which it takes Herculean efforts to get through the day – doing low income work, obeying an authoritarian boss, buying clothes for the children, dealing with school issues, paying the rent or mortgage, fixing the car, negotiating with a spouse, paying taxes – it is not easy to pay close attention to larger political issues. Indeed, you may wish that these issues would take care of themselves. (2013, 24)

This means that those who may not necessarily agree with neoliberal ideology 'may become predisposed to the myth of the rational market in part because the pressures of daily life encourage them to seek comfort in ideological formations that promise automatic rationality' (2013, 25). This means that people, including those experiencing hardships under neoliberalism, may reject state interventions such as welfare or healthcare provision.

In other words, those most in need of alternatives to the current system do not have the space to meaningfully engage with and develop them. Previous research has drawn attention to the significant role taken by the 'new middle class' in new social movements (Crossley 2003; Bagguley 1995; Rootes 1986), highlighting the role of access to higher education, family and other resources which make it possible to be politically active. These dynamics are exacerbated under austerity conditions, as time and resources for people to be able to develop the alternatives to challenge it are taken away. Increasing inequality also limits who can be involved in public debates and campaigns on alternatives. This then potentially plays into Right populist accusations about anti-austerity campaigns being dominated by 'metropolitan elites'.

AUSTERITY MELANCHOLIA

When one does not have the space or time to resist or consider alternatives because of preoccupations with day-to-day survival and not being able to plan one's time, then claims to restore an orderly society can have an immediate intuitive and emotional appeal, particularly when this orderly society is based on cultural memories of the past. In 'How the Conservatives Can Win Again' (2015), Phil Burton-Cartledge argues that the Conservative Party develops policies which produce insecurity on a material level, but then simultaneously present themselves as the providers of stability:

> 'Long-term economic plan', 'Northern powerhouse', 'securing a better future', 'competence vs. chaos', 'strong leadership', it was all flim-flam but they successfully appealed to (atomised) voters' need to believe something better, something more tangible and stable was just around the corner. Yet as the Tories flattered the aspirations they stuck knitting needles deep into the insecurities. (Burton-Cartledge 2015)

The Conservatives were not only claiming to restore stability in public finances; they also appealed to socially conservative values as providing *moral certainty* in response to social anxieties caused by *material insecurity*. Pro-austerity narratives often involve a degree of introspection (directly or indirectly) about how society has lost its way, and promise to restore a lost social order – or, when it is practically impossible to do so, to mourn the *loss* of social order. Examples of this include the decline narratives about 'Broken Britain', used by *The Sun* newspaper[5] and the Conservative Party to describe social disintegration, and former Prime Minister David Cameron's comments about 'strivers vs. skivers', in which he pitted those in work against the unemployed, blaming an overly generous welfare system. Such narratives both condemn a society in decline, and draw on the cultural memory of earlier periods in history when similar decline narratives were used (e.g., the 1970s, which will be discussed in the next chapter). Within such narratives, idealised conceptions of the Second World War and the immediate post-war era frequently come to stand in for the thrift, discipline and moral certainty seen as lacking in the present (Bramall 2013; Jensen 2013; Hatherley 2016). If the future appears bleak, 'primed to resemble an enterprise zone full of call centres on the edge of a business park on the M4'[6] (Hatherley 2016, 4) and we feel powerless to create something better, then the past can restore a lost moral compass, and offer some lessons about how society should be. However, as it is essentially a backward-looking and rather guilt-ridden view, this sort of austerity-driven introspection can also limit our capacity to imagine the future (as it will never live up to the ideals of the mythical past).

This backward-looking aspect of austerity discourses could be interpreted as a form of melancholia, which Paul Gilroy has examined as a 'depressed reaction that inhibit[s] any capacity for responsible reconstructive practice' (2004, 107). Drawing on the work of the German social psychologists Alexander and Margarete Mitscherlich on the German public's melancholic longing for the power of the Nazi regime after the death of Hitler (ibid.), Gilroy argues that the United Kingdom is experiencing a condition of 'postcolonial melancholia', which is a form of mourning which is marked by continual anxieties about British culture being in decline and which prevents a critical examination of the legacy of colonialism (2004, 162). There are connections between postcolonial melancholia and austerity's idealisation of the past, particularly the post-war era. In part this is because of an unwillingness to examine the role of the Empire in post-war prosperity, and particularly the basis of this prosperity in exploitation of other countries. Austerity and postcolonial melancholia also share 'the need to get back to the place or moment before the country lost its moral and cultural bearings' and an 'underlying hunger for reorientation' (2004, 97), with the Blitz Spirit[7] invoked as the last moment when the country still had these moral and cultural bearings. Gilroy also theorises postcolonial melancholia as a backlash against 'the perceived dangers of pluralism and . . . the irreversible fact of multiculture' (ibid.). More generally, Gilroy's characterisation of melancholia as a depressed reaction that inhibits reconstructive practice can apply to the introspection and nostalgia associated with austerity. Instead of trying to come to terms with the current situation – which includes the legacy of colonialism and the lived reality of multiculturalism and post-industrialism, and trying to work through alternatives to neoliberalism within this context – the tendency is instead to turn to the past to provide the moral and cultural certainties which are perceived as lacking in the present. Anxieties about decline and nostalgia for a lost sense of certainty (which must now be restored) coalesce around the figures of *work* and *community*. Claims that a sense of community has been lost and that austerity offers the opportunity to restore it come together with anxieties about work, supported by nostalgia for 'real', authentic jobs, as well as xenophobic responses to immigrant labour. Thus anxiety and nostalgia are mobilised as a *public mood* to invalidate contemporary experience, making it all the more difficult to come to grips with current conditions.

AUSTERITY, NEO-COMMUNITARIANISM AND SOCIALLY CONSERVATIVE VALUES

In the following section, I will explore narratives around restoring lost community within the austerity context. In *The Ministry of Nostalgia* (2016),

Owen Hatherley examines the rehabilitation of the 'Keep Calm and Carry On' poster. This poster was originally designed as propaganda for the Ministry of Information[8] in 1939, but never circulated publicly. It was rediscovered in a bookshop in 2000, and became much more widespread after the recession. Hatherley explores the more disturbing variants of 'Keep Calm': street posters by the London Metropolitan Police in 2009 which used a similar design and layout but with slogans reading 'We'd like to give you a good talking to' and 'anything you say may be taken down and used as evidence' (Hatherley 2016, 35); one by the Ministry of Justice reading 'have your say on how criminals pay back' (Hatherley 2016, 37) and a poster from one of Britain's privatised energy companies reading 'pay bills and carry on' (Hatherley 2016, 40), used to advertise PayPoints, machines for people on insecure incomes to pay energy bills with cash. Hatherley sees the poster's rehabilitation as both the affirmation of a national stereotype (the 'stiff upper lip') and a 'manufactured nostalgia for the protective, watchful eye of public institutions' (2016, 33). Given current imperatives to dismantle the welfare state, there is a particular irony in such imagery. As *Guardian* columnist Zoe Williams points out:

> The word 'austerity' conveys an atmosphere that is the exact opposite of the society it actually creates: blitz spirit, togetherness, community, waste-not-want-not (the results of the spending cuts have, contrariwise, been mutual suspicion, alienation, and a huge amount of want). (Williams 2015)

However, the examples that Hatherley describes are about the authoritarian, exclusionary and punitive aspects of the welfare state or the privatised companies that now carry out these functions, rather than economic redistribution or support for those in need.

In *The Cultural Politics of Austerity* (2013), Rebecca Bramall examines a broadcast of *BBC Newsnight* on 24 February 2009 as a 'representative instance' in which the term 'the age of austerity' was used to describe impending and inevitable public spending cuts which would change our lives (2013, 19). Guests reflected on comparisons between the present moment and the Second World War, frequently invoking the need for 'community spirit', 'solidarity' and 'the need to reassess misplaced values' (ibid.). Kirstie Allsopp, one of the *Newsnight* guests, since has become a 'self-styled champion of the philosophy of "make-do-and-mend"' (Bramall 2013, 20). Allsopp has also become a spokesperson for the anti-littering campaign Keep Britain Tidy, in which she argues that clean streets are intrinsic to pride in one's community, calling for 'litter picks in every school' in order to train children in lost civic virtues (Allsopp 2015). Another significant moment in the early development of the austerity narrative – which also literally involved cleaning the streets – was the #riotcleanup campaign, a social media-generated volunteer campaign to clean up the streets of Clapham, London, after the August 2011 riots. Sofia Himmelblau characterises this as a 'strikingly middle-class, broadly white effort . . . to sweep issues of inequality under the carpet of a simulated Big Society[9] photo-op' (Himmelblau 2011). Former London Mayor Boris Johnson was also photographed wielding a broom 'in solidarity with concerned citizens', and one of the volunteers wore a T-shirt bearing the slogan 'looters are scum' (Tyler 2013, 181). As Himmelblau notes, the #riotcleanup created rhetorical divisions between the 'real' Londoners and therefore their opposite, 'inauthentic' Londoners, who were also framed as non-citizens (Himmelblau 2011). It is not difficult to imagine who these inauthentic Londoners might be – for example, the poor, sex workers, the homeless, racialised people, immigrants – which is where the metaphor of cleaning up the streets takes on more disturbing associations. This foreshadows the amplification of exclusionary and xenophobic politics which would develop later on during the crisis, and which will be explored in chapter 4 in relation to anti-immigration politics.

Imperatives to restore a lost sense of community, and the sense that austerity provides the opportunity for this restoration, are present, not only within popular culture but also within political discourse. One example of this is the Blue Labour project, which is an initiative connected to the British Labour Party to reclaim social conservatism on the Left (see Glasman et al. 2011; Davis 2011; Geary and Pabst 2015). This will be discussed in greater detail in the following chapter. Similar perspectives were expressed in *Red Tory* (2009), by Phillip Blond, director of the ResPublica think tank. He evoked the experience of previous generations, arguing that there is truth to claims that 'children really were polite, that people really did know their neighbours, and that, yes, whole families really did stay together and form lasting bonds with their relations' (Blond 2009, 2), and that 'by denying their memories we are denying ourselves . . . a better and nobler recent history' (Blond 2009, 2–3). His proposals to restore this lost sense of community (underpinning the 'Big Society' concept) involve transferring public services to mutual and social enterprises, which would be run by volunteers (2009, 232–234). Such initiatives, he argued, promise to restore 'a shared commitment to moral and social norms' (2009, 238). As will be discussed in chapter 5, this approach was taken on board by the Nesta think tank in their proposals for public sector reform.

There have been precedents, such as attempts under New Labour to look to civil society organisations as a resource. Bob Jessop terms this 'neo-communitarianism' in relation to expectations for the voluntary sector and 'the social economy' to take responsibility for economic development and social cohesion. He refers to the role of 'grassroots (or bottom-up) social and economic mobilisation in developing and implementing economic strategies' (Jessop 2002, 463), although he does not specifically discuss the mobilisation of nostalgic discourses of community to support neo-communitarianism. Will Davies has also examined neo-communitarianism in the context of behavioural science and 'nudge' theory within policymaking (2012). He argues that within such approaches, 'neoliberalism is accused [by neo-communitarian thinkers such as David Goodhart, Maurice Glasman and Philip Blond] of being built on an unrealistically empty theory of the individual, as provided by neo-classical economics' (Davies 2012, 772). Neo-communitarian approaches may have a basis in legitimate critiques of neoliberalism as overly focused on individual aspiration at the expense of the collective, and of neoliberal policies which have led to the destruction and impoverishment of some communities. However, the neo-communitarian response, on a practical level, is about the 'survival of neoliberalism rather than its replacement', such as through behaviour interventions designed to reduce dependence on the welfare state (2012, 773).

This narrative of recovering a lost sense of community also underpins the arguments of 'post-liberal' commentators such as David Goodhart, who in *British Dream* (2013) argues that immigration undermines the social solidarity necessary for sustaining the welfare state. How does this connect to austerity? It is not only that immigrants are perceived by Goodhart to create pressure on underfunded public services (an assertion made without much evidence). There is also a perception that more 'cohesive' societies – in other words more homogeneous ones – are also more resilient ones, better able to resist the shocks created by cuts to public services, producing volunteers willing to fill the gaps. This perception has informed some policymakers. For example, Newham Council (a local authority within London with one of the most ethnically diverse populations in Europe) implemented the *Community Resilience Strategy* which framed community relationships and shared values as intrinsic to the success of both the local residents and the borough as a whole (Newham Council 2011). In the process, they cut 72% of funding for translation services, and required 'British values' to be taught in schools (Nye 2012).

WHO BELONGS IN AUSTERITY BRITAIN?

Within the context of austerity, discussions about community are ultimately about marking whose place in society is secure and whose is contingent, designating who is seen to be deserving of access to public services and whose support can be cut with little public outcry. Drawing on Ulrich Beck's concept of the risk society, Sara Ahmed argues that in insecure times, conceptions of community become defensive in response to a perceived risk (Beck

1992 cited in Ahmed 2004, 72). The designation of insiders and outsiders is done through asserting socially conservative values in relation to conceptions of vulnerability versus toughness, and in terms of nativist and xenophobic conceptions of national identity. Notably, the rhetoric around deservingness, citizenship and poverty is often framed in gendered terms. The undeserving are often presented in terms of excessive masculinity or femininity, such as the criminal, or 'the trafficking victim, or the single mother who has too many children in order to claim welfare benefits, reflecting value judgements about 'the right kind of motherhood' (Anderson 2013, 4). It is not only individuals who are gendered; the nation state itself is also framed in highly gendered terms in terms of its relationship to outsiders. For example, the government is routinely accused by the tabloid press of being a 'soft touch' on immigration or unemployment benefits, using language normally used to describe a vulnerable, naïve person as well as a 'feminised and disabled body' (Tyler 2013, 88). To prove they are not soft or weak in the face of such accusations, politicians must demonstrate their toughness on benefits claimants in the face of this perceived 'softness'. Due to its welfarist legacy, the Labour Party has been particularly vulnerable to this charge and so has taken rather desperate measures to prove its toughness. For example, former Labour Work and Pensions minister Rachel Reeves MP claimed that the Labour Party was 'not the party of people on benefits', demonstrating insensitivity to those who had lost their jobs as a result of austerity cuts and the recession (Gentleman 2015). This was also evident in the Labour Party's response to a 2015 vote to put a cap on benefits. Former leader Harriet Harman advised its MPs to abstain from the vote on the 2015 Welfare Reform and Work Bill (BBC 2015a). The purpose of the Bill was to limit benefits overall to £20,000 for households outside London and limit child tax credit[10] to the first two children (BBC 2015b). Harman cited 'voter concerns' about large families on benefits (ibid.), without examining the basis of such concerns – evidence perhaps of a perceived need to act in keeping with a public mood where one is obliged to demonstrate a masculine 'toughness' in attitudes towards benefits claimants.

This imperative for both individuals and states to 'get tough' predates austerity, but austerity has entrenched a public mood marked by masculinist conceptions of vulnerability and interdependency as shameful. According to William Connolly, this means that the welfare state itself becomes inevitably associated with weakness, dependency and personal failure, which he frames as the 'feminisation' of the welfare state (2013, 24):

> corporate elites, sports heroes, financial wizards and military leaders project
> images of independence, mastery and virility that can make them attractive
> models of identification, whereas state welfare programs, market regulations,
> retirement schemes and health care, while essential to life, may remind too

many of the very fragilities, vulnerabilities, susceptibilities and dependencies they strive to deny or forget. (ibid.)

Connolly argues that this 'double logic of masculinisation of market icons and feminisation of state supports and regulatory activities takes a toll on the polity, particularly when it is over-coded with race and immigration issues' (ibid.). Vulnerability is rejected through the rhetoric and application of policies which claim to 'get tough'. But what is toughness in this context? Toughness is about affirming autonomy and appeals to the self-reliance of the neoliberal subject who does not depend on the welfare state or on others, but it is also about the moral certainties and polarised language of 'law and order' discourses: hang em' and flog em', pull up the drawbridge, send them back. It refers to tough decisions about who deserves to belong and who does not, and the rationing of resources and, in some cases rights, to those perceived as deserving. It is the apparent decisiveness of drawing lines and creating boundaries between sections of society. The stoicism evoked by the 'Keep Calm and Carry On' posters can possibly be seen as a milder version of what Hatherley terms *'nostalgia for the state of being repressed* – solid, public-spirited, as opposed to the depoliticised, hysterical and privatised reality of Britain over the last thirty years' (2016, 21). Both the imperatives to be tough and nostalgia for earlier periods of history (when supposedly people were tougher) are often expressed through the metaphor of work, taken to literally mean employment, but also referring to other aspects of everyday experience involving toil and sacrifice. This will be discussed in the following section.

STRIVERS VERSUS SKIVERS: AUSTERITY AND WORK

Moralising discourses about work long predate austerity, and in fact can be seen as endemic to discussions of working life. Drawing on the historian Johann Huizinga, Richard Sennett explores the 'absolute moral value placed on work' within the nineteenth century (Sennett 2004, 109). This belief was incorporated into the early welfare state, influencing the distinctions made between the paupers on poor relief and the working poor, and the moral judgements passed on the paupers as 'not simply poor but degraded, their character corrupted and their will sapped through reliance on charity' (Fraser and Gordon, cited in Sennett 2004, 109). According to Sennett, 'belief in work itself as the single most important source of both mutual respect and self-respect' united socialists and capitalists (ibid.). In the late twentieth century, moralising around work was prevalent in welfare reform discourses. These discourses positioned work as the only way out of poverty, penalised the unemployed for being out of work and framed unemployment as a personal, rather than structural, problem. Most recently, within the austerity context, moralising discourses around work have underpinned punitive policies such as the 2015 Welfare and Work Bill, which penalises not only the unemployed but also those in low-paid and part-time work (Butler and Arnett 2015). This follows on the introduction of Universal Credit in 2012, which required low-paid part-time workers in receipt of in-work benefits to be available and actively seeking and prepared for better-paid work (Child Poverty Action Group 2012). These reforms were based on the conviction that a proper job is a full-time permanent job, not the part-time, casualised work or self-employment which, according to research by the TUC, has accounted for two out of five jobs created since 2010 (TUC 2014b).

Nostalgia is common in many discussions of working life. In *Nostalgia for Permanence at Work* (2007) Tim Strangleman explores a prevalent sense of nostalgia in interviews with railway workers, in which there is a mourning for the loss of 'real work' and 'real workers' as older workers leave and are replaced by (mostly younger) workers who are perceived to lack commitment (Strangleman 2007, 91). Notably, contemporary work is not critiqued by his respondents for being exploitative, but for being *inauthentic*. This reflects a wider tendency within popular culture to frame authenticity as represented by residual forms of employment, such as artisanal labour or more recently industrial labour. Nostalgia and desires for authenticity continue to inflect discussions of work within the austerity context, such as through arguments for bringing back manufacturing. For example, former Chancellor George Osborne MP appealed, in his 2011 Budget Speech, for 'a Britain carried aloft by the march of the makers' based in manufacturing (UK Government 2011). There have also been calls on the Left to restore the post-war Fordist economy (see Gilbert 2013 for a critique).

However, behind such desires for authentic work is a legitimate critique of contemporary working life. As David Graeber argues in *Bullshit Jobs*, entire industries have been created with questionable social use (he names corporate law, telemarketing, financial services and PR, for example) (Graeber 2013). Graeber points to an underlying awareness that socially and culturally valuable work is undervalued. He illustrates this with the example of the poet and musician he knew as a school friend who, faced with high debts and the birth of his daughter, ended up, as the friend put it, 'taking the default choice of so many directionless folk: law school' (ibid.) and became a corporate lawyer. According to Graeber, he was 'the first to admit that his job was utterly meaningless and contributed nothing to the world' (ibid.). But this recognition can lead to a political impasse around *what is to be done*: 'How can one even begin to speak of dignity in labour when one secretly feels one's job should not exist?' (ibid.). Awareness of one's implication within systems which produce meaningless jobs, combined with a sense of powerlessness, can produce a guilty impasse. In response, it can be tempting, rather than campaigning for better conditions in low-paid precarious work (e.g., the recent fast-food protests in the United States), to romanticise earlier periods in history such as the Fordist era, forgetting that these too had their share of bad and meaningless jobs, and that much of this period was a difficult one for women and ethnic minorities (to be discussed further in chapter 6).

Nostalgia for older types of work and the ideal of authentic jobs are also mobilised within xenophobic discourses around labour migration and benefits, where it is assumed that immigrants doing low-skilled jobs encourage working-class British people to live on welfare benefits rather than engaging with the labour market (Holehouse 2012, cited in Anderson 2013, 71). According to this perspective, jobs are assumed to be in scarce supply and should be prioritised for local residents (who have the duty to take them up); it is assumed that a fixed number of jobs are available and the role of migration in job creation is ignored, a perception termed by economists as the 'lump of labour fallacy' (Krugman 2003). As Bridget Anderson argues in *Us vs. Them*, 'the Migrant is contrasted, not only with the Benefit Scrounger, but also with the British Worker, whose predicament as unemployed reveals the mercenary nature both of those employers who do not reserve jobs for the national labour force, and of the migrants they employ who take jobs that are not rightfully theirs' (Anderson 2013, 71). This contrast was implied in the 2011 statement by former PM David Cameron that 'immigration and welfare reform are two sides of the same coin' (Cameron 2011 cited in Anderson 2013, 75). Anderson asks, rhetorically, what might constitute a British job within the context of multinational corporations, outsourcing and subcontracting (2013, 74). Nationalist discourses position a 'British job' as 'by virtue of its Britishness, a decent one' (Anderson 2013, 76). A British job, through this nostalgic lens, is a good job, a stable and well-paid job for life, imagined to be held by a male breadwinner. It is a job for an organisation or company that produces goods and services for the British public, rather than a subcontractor or multinational corporation. This vision is also far away from the experience of work in the United Kingdom as 'not necessarily secure or well protected' (Anderson 2013, 77). In this context, it 'contains a claim for decent, non-alienated and secure work that is a far cry from the kinds of jobs that have proliferated in the UK over the past two decades' (ibid.). According to the Office of National Statistics, 1% of UK-based businesses in 2013 were foreign-owned but contributed 28% to UK GDP, particularly larger companies with 250+ employees (Office of National Statistics 2013b), meaning that there are questions to be asked about how 'British' the economy really is. However, the 'Britishness' of a job does not guarantee security or decent conditions. Nostalgic, nationalistic visions of work call for returning to a time before globalisation and mass immigration when work was restricted to an idealised moral community (Anderson 2013, 77). They also naturalise competition between workers which is conducive to resentments and moral judgements (the 'bad workers' as competing and undermining the chances of the 'good [British] workers') and does not fundamentally address the issue of poor wages and conditions, and how these have worsened under austerity, as the TUC figures reveal.

Beyond the workplace, metaphors of work have long been used to channel resentments and frustrations towards those positioned as outsiders, who are seen to be taking advantage of the drudgery and sacrifice of others. In the 1970s, as Stuart Hall et al. suggested in *Policing the Crisis*, the metaphor of 'hard work' and the figure of the scrounger were used against outsiders (with little evidence, and even in some cases directed towards people who were in work) as a way of expressing anxieties about social change (Hall et al. 1978, 156–157). Abstracted from the experience of employment, 'hard work' can be mobilised to talk about many aspects of everyday experience. Within the context of austerity, the hard work and everyday sacrifice is not only about the drudgery of bad jobs; it is about the hardship of austerity: making do with less, giving up everyday pleasures and, in some cases, everyday necessities. As Jo Littler suggests, invoking the importance of 'hard work' also elides class distinctions, which is why 'million/billionaires, celebrities and children at elite private fee-paying schools' can all claim that they 'work hard' (Littler 2013, 67), ignoring or suppressing the question of why some forms of hard work are rewarded more than others, or why some must experience more hardship than others. Within the context of austerity cuts, the relative lack of a strong labour movement (which would make collective responses both conceivable and practically possible) or public debate about what good jobs should be, the material conditions of employment are ignored and work becomes valued specifically for its normative aspects, particularly the '*social relations of work*' (Anderson 2013, 77). In line with older arguments about the moral value of work, work is seen to provide discipline and routine, and signify belonging to the mainstream of society. The metaphor of work becomes mobilised to distinguish the 'strivers' or 'hardworking families' from the 'skivers', and to articulate resentments against those who are seen to be taking advantage of the hardworking majority. One particular irony of austerity is that as the material conditions of work are being made increasingly difficult and precarious, full-time stable employment increasingly becomes fetishised as a social norm and a marker of belonging.

USING AN IDEALISED PAST TO INVALIDATE THE PRESENT

I have discussed the role of nostalgic metaphors of community and work within moralising discourses, both before the financial crisis and during the current period of austerity. Such discourses appeal to the certainties associated with previous periods in history, which are imagined as a moment before the country lost its bearings. In this sense, they are melancholic, in that they turn to nostalgia rather than coming to grips with the conditions of the present and the legacy of the past. These metaphors are also mobilised within punitive discourses and policies. I will now discuss a further consequence of austerity nostalgia: the mobilisation of idealised conceptions of the past to invalidate contemporary experience. One common example of this is the claim that present-day experiences of hardship are trivial compared to the past. *Telegraph* economics commentator James Bartholomew writes that:

> Overall, the typical person in modern poverty has *access to a mobile phone* and lives in a household with *a television, an inside lavatory, electricity and probably access to the internet.* By all means, observers can call this poverty. But it would have been unrecognisable to Flora Thompson [author of *The Lark Rises to Candleford*]. (Bartholomew 2015, my italics)

Mobile phones, flat-screen televisions and other gadgets are held to illustrate how low-income people and particularly those on benefits do not really experience the hardship of previous generations; this also implies that they are spoilt and addicted to technology (e.g., Bowditch 2006; Gavin 2011; for a critique see McInerny 2012). Bartholomew evokes the cultural memory of a time when such gadgets were still luxury items, ignoring the fact that they have since become more accessible as they are cheap, are widely available and can be bought on monthly instalment plans or on credit. This availability means that in real terms they are no longer a luxury. Flat-screen televisions have now also largely replaced the obsolete cathode ray tube televisions and are thus ubiquitous (Evans 2009). Nor is purchasing consumer items on credit a recent phenomenon as buying furniture through instalment plans was common during the post-war period; it was seen as a respectable and even a prudent activity in a period of rising wages (Trentmann 2016). Even if his implication is that unemployed people should enter the workforce to better themselves, Bartholomew ignores the fact that internet access has now become indispensable to the job search (Nominet Trust 2012). His moralising is based on the perception of *consumerism* as rendering present-day poverty illegitimate. He implies that people spend beyond their means (on gadgets and other luxuries), but also that consumerism confounds long-held expectations of the poor as figures of frugal, virtuous, dignified suffering. The low-income consumer as debased figure is strongly classed (see for example Jones 2017) but it is also gendered in certain respects, positioning the female consumer as Other to the male worker. This idea of consumer culture as feminine in opposition to 'authentic' masculine culture predates the financial crisis (Huyssen 1986; Fiske 1989); in the 1960s, popular psychology blamed the 1960s counterculture on the post-war consumer society and the lack of a strong father figure in parenting (Ehrenreich 1989).

Bartholomew does not only mention gadgets, but also electricity and an indoor toilet, evoking cultural memories of pre-welfare state and even possibly nineteenth-century experiences of poverty as *deprivation*, different from present-day poverty as marked by stretched finances, over-indebtedness, reliance on payday loans and food banks and so forth (Lansley and Mack 2015). In the United Kingdom, the experience of living without electricity or an indoor toilet is one that the majority of people living today do not remember, and thus it is all too easy to mythologise. By mentioning Flora Thompson's novel, Bartholomew also evokes a pastoral and picturesque conception of poverty, one that had dignity because it involved certain forms of material hardship, unlike today's degraded and inauthentic experiences. More generally popular culture at the time of writing is laden with guilty and wistful pronouncements about how previous generations were tougher and more resilient than us, had better craft skills, looked after each other and had a stronger sense of community. This produces a public mood in which we feel our current lives and experiences are somehow inadequate.

This underlying narrative is widespread, particularly in BBC reality television programmes in which participants learn cooking or craft skills supposedly possessed by previous generations, and which are seen to be markers of authentic experience (e.g., *Eat Well for Less* or *The Great British Sewing Bee*). In other series, participants reveal their incapacity for life in specific historical periods. *24 Hours in the Past*, for instance, plunges participants and, by extension, the viewer into Victorian 'reality' as the standard by which all experiences of poverty are measured. As audience members, we are meant to relate to the guilty responses of the participants, as they find themselves unable to use tools or carry out household tasks which were once commonplace. Guilt then is part of the affective landscape of austerity. Like shame (to be discussed in chapter 7) guilt is individualising and disempowering.

If the past is seen to possess an authenticity and *gravitas* absent in the present, then those subjects associated with the past (e.g., pensioners) are also seen to possess a moral authority which younger generations do not have. They also have been rewarded by policymakers, who have courted 'the grey vote' through a succession of measures which have led retirees to increase their income by 5.1%, while that of working households decreased by 6.4% between 2007/2008 and 2011/2012 (Office of National Statistics, cited in Intergenerational Foundation 2015). People in their twenties saw their incomes decrease by 12% (Institute for Fiscal Studies cited in Intergenerational Foundation 2015), and they have also been penalised with a raft of policy measures including the increase of higher education tuition fees to £9,000 in 2010, and most recently the cutting of maintenance for poorer students, and the exclusion of workers under twenty-five years from the 'living wage' (McVeigh and Helm 2015). However, there seems to be a consensus about the perception of older groups as more deserving, including among the young. Research carried out by Ipsos-Mori (cited in O'Leary 2014) suggests widespread perceptions 'that the elderly are vulnerable, through no fault of their own, and that they have earned entitlements through contributions over time' (O'Leary 2014).

The idealisation of the past is not only used to discredit present-day experiences of poverty and justify austerity policies. It also casts a long shadow over anti-austerity social movements. As Craig McVegas has pointed out, the anti-austerity movement has been 'characterised by this vague nostalgia for the post-war consensus or the "Spirit of '45" or the full employment society' (2014). Janina Kehr has also explored the role of 'biopolitical nostalgia' (defined as an imagined past of healthcare provision) in campaigns to save the health service in the United Kingdom and Spain (2014). Such an approach to the post-war welfare state tends to ignore the contradictions of social policy at the time, including the exclusion of working women, lone parents and immigrants, who had to campaign for access to welfare entitlements (Clarke and Gewirtz 2001). This then is part of a disempowering narrative which asserts that *the present can never be as good as the past*.

New social movements of the twentieth century – and more recent and current forms of resistance which will be discussed in chapter 7 – are seen, in this context, to be less historically significant. Writing about Ken Loach's *Spirit of 45* film about the history of the welfare state and its decline, Owen Hatherley points to the 'whiteness of the film' (meaning the lack of representation of ethnic minority speakers), its ignoring of the contribution of immigrants in the building of the welfare state and the legacy of colonialism, and its use of 'an iconography so firmly rooted in a past that so much of the contemporary working class had nothing to do with' (2016, 53). This presentation of the history of the welfare state thus offers little to social movements fighting contemporary austerity and its effects. Such a disconnect between a mythologised past and contemporary struggles carries particular dangers of demobilisation and disempowerment. Without being able to refer to a history of struggle which has some affective resonance with current concerns, and to which those currently fighting austerity can actually relate, it can be all too easy to fall back on narratives of guilt and nostalgia provided by the prevailing public mood.

CONCLUSION: NOSTALGIA AS SUBVERTED DESIRES FOR A BETTER WORLD?

I began this chapter by examining the appeal of simple and familiar ideas such as the economy as household or 'paying one's debts'. These ideas are readily received by people who do not have the time, space and mental energy to think otherwise about the financial crisis and its aftermath or to consider workable alternatives to austerity. Instead of grappling with the realities of the present, nostalgic discourses present an immediate appeal because of the certainty and continuity they provide. Central to this nostalgic perspective are the metaphors of work and community – which are both used to create a decline narrative, sharpen divisions between insiders and outsiders, and focus resentments towards outsiders. As Paul Gilroy suggests, nostalgia and decline narratives may function as a form of 'melancholia' which prevents us from constructively dealing with the situation at hand. They also delegitimise contemporary experiences of hardship which are seen as less real or authentic.

However, buried deep inside these discourses may be legitimate concerns about the effects of neoliberalism on livelihoods and communities, the devastation of working-class communities by deindustrialisation and outsourcing, the insecurity caused by the reduction and privatisation of the social safety net, and the dominance of neoliberal aspiration and entrepreneurship of the self at the expense of other values. In 'The Just's Umbrella', Ruth Levitas argues that we need to consider neo-communitarian projects such as The Big Society in relation to genuine concerns, rather than dismissing them entirely as false consciousness (2012, 332). She notes that 'only such an approach explains why discourses such as the Big Society have purchase among some of those whose interests are not served by Coalition policies' (2012, 330). This reflects a situation when such genuine concerns are disconnected from working-class self-organisation and social movements (past and present) which would enable working constructively towards an alternative.

In the absence of material conditions which could create self-organisation, resilience and sociality, it becomes difficult to conceive of alternatives to austerity, or to develop the collective agency to articulate them and put them into action. The situation is exacerbated when such material conditions are largely missing from mainstream debates. When they cannot be channelled towards alternatives, legitimate concerns about the effects of neoliberalism instead lead to nostalgic arguments about lost authenticity and cultural and moral decline, or divisive arguments blaming the 'wrong people' (the outsiders, the undeserving, the unrespectable) and positioning the presence of these people as standing between present conditions and a better society. As it becomes difficult to imagine the future, this better society is seen within idealised conceptions of the past. As will be discussed in later chapters, this is how politicians can frame some very divisive politics as a perverse form of 'social justice', and themselves as conviction politicians.

NOTES

1. Cuts to welfare have also taken place during the 'good times'; for example, the Blair administration cut benefits to disabled people only two years after being elected, citing the need to balance 'rights and responsibilities' (BBC News 1999).

2. The survey's authors have suggested that the 3% rise between 2009 and 2015 may be due to both either increasing sympathy for those who might have lost their jobs as a result of recession, or, perhaps, hardening attitudes towards those who rely on the state (British Social Attitudes Survey 2015, 3).

3. False Economy is an information/resource service about cuts to public services, supported by several trade unions. The Public and Commercial Services Union is a national trade union representing civil servants. The New Economics Foundation is a Left economics think tank.

4. The TUC is an umbrella organisation for trade unions in the United Kingdom.

5. *The Sun* newspaper is a daily tabloid newspaper in the United Kingdom and Ireland; it is known for right-wing views and inflammatory headlines.

6. The M4 is a motorway that runs between London and South Wales.

7. The Blitz Spirit refers to a sense of community and solidarity as well as stereotypical British stoicism in the face of the Second World War.

8. The Ministry of Information was the central UK government department responsible for publicity and propaganda during the Second World War, and was in existence between 1939 and 1946. See http://www.nationalarchives.gov.uk/theartof war/inf3.htm.

9. The Big Society was a political ideology developed by thinkers close to the 2010–2015 Conservative–Liberal Democrat coalition government, and is based around 'integrating the free market with a theory of social solidarity based on hierarchy and voluntarism'. See Matthew Scott (2011). 'Reflections on "The Big Society"'. *Community Development Journal* 46 (1), 132–137.

10. Child tax credits are a subsidy paid to low-income families in the United Kingdom.

Chapter 2

Authoritarian Populism, Traditionalism and Austerity

In the previous chapter, I discussed the intuitive appeal of austerity policies through the framing of the economy in moral and emotive terms. Some of these include the metaphor of the economy as household and gendered language around 'hardness' and 'softness'. I also discussed nostalgic and melancholic evocations of previous moments in history such as the Second World War or the post-war era, in which, it is claimed, we lived more authentic lives, worked at real jobs and lived within cohesive communities. Austerity, within this context, promises to take us 'back to basics', restoring authenticity to our lives and countering the excesses of the boom era, the post-industrial economy and a social liberalism that had gone too far. The chapter also explored divisions between deserving and undeserving, as certain sections of society have been framed as taking the scarce resources of the welfare state from those who really need and deserve it. Social and cultural conservatism become used to define who is an insider and an outsider, which is where austerity policies and rhetoric meet narrow and exclusionary concepts of community and national identity.

I will now explore these themes through Stuart Hall's concepts of 'authoritarian populism' and 'traditionalism', which he developed to interpret and theorise the legacy of Thatcherism, Blairism and, to a lesser extent, the Conservatives following 2010 (although comments on the Coalition government were limited due to Hall's illness and death in 2013). These concepts enable us to understand some of the continuities over the past forty years, including how austerity has built on discourses of what was then termed the New Right: appeals to nostalgic conceptions of work and community to provide moral certainty in the face of social change, and the positioning of the unemployed and immigrants as outsiders. Hall's thinking also provides insights into the continuing impasses for the Left in confronting these and presenting alternatives. Although Hall does not theorise emotion explicitly, he argues that politicians appealed to lived experience and moral feelings, and in doing so both drew on and perpetuated common-sense prejudices. He also warns that the Left ignored these tactics at their peril. There are therefore close connections between authoritarian populism, traditionalism and the concept of public mood in terms of the appeals to hegemony, and the claims to speak for the majority of popular opinion, but also in terms of the appeal to feelings – particularly fear, anxiety and resentment. In 'The Neoliberal Revolution' (2011), Hall remarks that one of the ways that ideology works best is by 'suturing contradictory lines of argument and emotional invest-ments' – creating what Ernesto Laclau (and Chantal Mouffe) termed 'systems of equivalence'. Successful ideologies bring together 'the contradictory ele-ments of common-sense, popular life and consciousness' (Laclau and Mouffe 1985 cited in Hall 2011). Hall understands this in terms of the role of socially conservative values within neoliberalism: how 'market/free enterprise/private property discourse persists cheek by jowl with older conservative attachments to nation, racial homogeneity, Empire and tradition' (ibid.). There are conti-nuities between the phases of neoliberalism about which Hall was writing and the current austerity context.

I will outline the development of these concepts through Hall's analysis of a developing law-and-order discourse in *Policing the Crisis* (1978) and then through a series of articles on Thatcherism which were published in *Marxism Today* throughout the 1980s and 1990s, then (following closure of *Marxism Today*) several articles which considered the cultural politics around the Coalition Government. Due to his death, Hall did not specifically write about the Conservative majority government of 2015, but his ideas will be considered within that context. It is beyond the scope of this chapter to pro-duce a comprehensive overview or an extensive contextualisation of Hall's work (see, among others, Morley and Chen 1996; Gilroy, McRobbie and Grossberg 2000; Rojek 2003). Instead I will focus on some of Hall's attempts to understand how Thatcher and other politicians used the rhetoric of law and order to appeal to 'common-sense ideas, . . . personal experience and specific incidents' (1978, 124). Hall also remarks on the belief that 'suffering is good for us' (1988, 166) – which has particular resonances in the contemporary discourse of austerity and, as discussed in the previous chapter, in the roman-ticising of past experiences of poverty as authentic *suffering*.

TRADITIONALISM

Published in 1978, *Policing the Crisis* took as its starting point the dispro-portionate sentencing of three young men who attacked and robbed a man outside a pub in Birmingham. This coincided with the entry of the term 'mugging' into UK media discourse. The term had been in use in the United States during the 1960s and 1970s, and was used within that context to raise the spectre of ungovernable inner cities (populated by black 'muggers') as part of a backlash towards the Civil Rights movement and their white liberal sympathisers. This also connected with Nixon's rhetoric around the socially conservative 'silent majority' who were opposed to the 1960s counterculture, Civil Rights movement and anti-war movement (28), as well as his appeal to discourses framing intellectuals as an out-of-touch elite (152–153). This narrative continues to be very powerful in the present (e.g., see Ehrenreich 1989; Frank 2004).

In the United Kingdom, as in the United States, an important focal point for these anxieties was the post-war consumer society which had led to changes in the way of life that people had been used to, as this seemed to be the diametrical opposite of the thrift and sacrifice of comfort encouraged during the Depression and the Second World War. Consumerism was perceived as causing the loss of traditional values, and not all of society could enjoy its rewards (156–157). In particular, the petty bourgeoisie (what Hall terms the 'lumpen bourgeoisie') drew limited benefits from the post-war boom, but nonetheless still maintained a certain moral authority as the guardians of tradition; furthermore, they saw their own anxieties as representing those of the nation (162–63). Although the specific causes of these social anxieties were slightly different in the United States and the United Kingdom, there were enough similarities for this to resonate on both sides of the Atlantic. In the United Kingdom, social anxieties were then projected onto 'outsiders': youth, students and black people (Hall et al. 1978, 142). In particular, black and Asian people became symbols for the 'pain and powerlessness' of socially conservative white British people who were alienated by the social change of the 1960s and experienced it as 'a succession of dislocations: in housing, neighbourhood, family, sex, recreation, law and order' (Hall et al. 1978, 160). These social anxieties were frequently expressed through calls for harsh forms of punishment for criminals and others constructed as deviant.

Drawing on Gramscian conceptions of the power bloc,[1] Hall framed 'traditionalism' as a cross-class consensus (1978, 139), although he also argued elsewhere that traditionalism was experienced differently by different social classes (1978, 140). Similar to the discussion in the previous chapter, *work* as a metaphor was central to traditionalism, as it brought together a variety of ideas, feelings and lived experiences: work as literally meaning employment and thus non-dependence on the state (which was where it connected to the scrounger discourse), but also work as drudgery. Work was also invoked for its normative functions, as providing routine and social discipline (getting to work on time, dressing smartly, etc.) as well as the work involved in conforming to societal norms, including those connected with the consumer society. For middle-class people, respectability took a competitive form, 'keeping up with the Joneses' (1978, 141), and was linked to self-control, self-reliance, self-sacrifice, hierarchy and authority (1978, 43). For working-class people, this was connected to work as the means to a respectable life, particularly skilled employment as performed by the male breadwinner. At the same time, work also shaped the relationship to and interpretation of crime, as crime was set against work defined as arduous toil (1978, 142). Hall argued that a 'real objective material reality' was distortedly expressed within the scrounger discourse, in that for many people, 'life-long commitment to hard work' was the only route 'to a minimal degree of security and material comfort' (1978, 142).

'Traditionalism' mobilised these metaphors of work, as well as feelings of resentment and anxiety about social change by framing benefits claimants and others seen to deviate from social norms as taking advantage of the hard work and sacrifices of the majority (work as meaning employment, self-discipline and the work of compliance with social norms, as discussed in chapter 1). Benefits claimants were resented for their reliance on public money and because they were seemingly spared the experience of drudgery. They, and others who did not conform to social norms, were resented because they were seen to be rejecting the *work* involved in social conformity (e.g., the repression of pleasure and individual self-expression). Hall explored this in 'Living with the Crisis', originally published in 1978 (1988a) and 'The Great Moving Right Show' (1988b), originally published in 1979, which were both republished in *The Hard Road to Renewal* (1988). 'Living with the Crisis' was based on a 13 June 1975 *New Statesman* article by Conservative advisor, Sir Keith Joseph, which positioned the 'traditional family of modest size, moderate habits, thrift and self-reliance' against a host of disreputable and deviant others, particularly lone mothers from working-class backgrounds who were seen to be producing too many children, accounting for 'a third of all births'.[2] The article also praised Christian morality campaigner Mary Whitehouse (1988a, 27). Hall saw the article as indicative of a growing social conservatism within political discourse typified by both anti-benefits rhetoric and anti-abortion campaigns, in which the Labour Party in part colluded (ibid.). 'The Great Moving Right Show' examined the figure of the 'scrounger' as a 'new folk devil' (1988b, 47), and the framing of claimants and, by extension, anyone who benefitted from the welfare state, as 'soft' and 'dependent' as opposed to what was seen as the self-reliant and personally reliable British citizen, with this independence and self-reliance framed as an intrinsic national characteristic (ibid.). In 'Gramsci and Us' (1988e), Hall also discussed how Thatcher – in a tactic borrowed by later austerity-era politicians (see last chapter) called on the public to be tough; to put up with hardship and sacrifice: 'she said, iron times, back to the wall, stiff upper lip, get moving, on your bike, dig in' (1988e, 166). Such rhetoric affirmed national stereotypes (the 'stiff upper lip') and thus national identity. Simultaneously, it called on the public to be resourceful, disciplined and tough, and to identify with toughness and resourcefulness as intrinsically positive traits.

Hall drew attention to the language of 'hardness' versus 'softness' in Thatcher's rhetoric, although he did not explicitly theorise this in terms of gender. However, gender in relation to traditionalism was explored more fully in 'Popular Democratic vs. Authoritarian Populism' (1988c), which focused on the 'economy as household' metaphor mobilised by the Conservatives in the 1980s. The individualising and moralising implications of this metaphor have been discussed in the previous chapter; however, it is worth flagging up here its suggestions of traditional gender roles. Hall examined how such metaphors positioned women as:

> connotatively identified with the keeper of traditional wisdoms, and guardian of conventional popular morality; but this composite 'she' is, at the same time, the 'practical one' – the one who knows the 'value of money' and the 'impact of rising prices in the shop': that is, the figure through which the economic and monetarist themes of Thatcherism can be made to connect with the empirical experience of the everyday life of ordinary folk. (1988c, 145)

These associations of women with the domestic sphere were also remarked on by Hall in 'No Light at the End of the Tunnel' (1988d), in relation to Thatcherism's fusing of traditional values with neoliberal economics:

> The language of the market as opportunity, computer technology as power, of financial 'big bangs' and competitive frontiers to conquer, is a discourse clearly addressed to Thatcherite men (or the Thatcherite 'man' in all of us). The language of moral discipline, law and order, sexual conventionalism and 'one (white) nation' is clearly a language for the female guardians of the national hearth (the little Thatcherite 'woman' in us all). (1988d, 85–86)

This division of roles resonated with aspects of everyday experience and popular culture which positioned women's place as the home. Traditional gender roles as represented by the rhetoric of 'hardness' and 'softness' as well as gendered divisions of labour provide an immediately accessible vocabulary for understanding one's place within neoliberalism. They function as a way of mapping and reconfiguring older values and social norms for the neoliberal moment, providing emotional and moral certainties in the face of social and economic change.

I have discussed Hall's critiques of traditionalism as it was mobilised by the Conservatives in the service of 'authoritarian populism', whereby governments justify authoritarian policies by appealing to divisive and exclusionary conceptions of the people, which I will discuss in further detail later in this chapter. I should also point out that Hall was also highly critical of traditionalism within the Labour movement and the Left. Traditionalism on the Right, as discussed, focused on the creation of moral panics, the capitalisation on fear and anxiety towards social change, and the affirmation of socially conservative ideas of respectability, both emerging from and reinforcing certain forms of popular 'common sense' (in Gramscian terms). However, Hall's critiques of traditionalism on the Left centred on crude and dogmatic forms of Marxism, unthinking nostalgia for Keynesian economic policies and Fordist industrial capitalism, and lack of engagement with or even resistance towards new social movements, particularly those relating to race, gender and sexual equality. Hall argued this forcefully in 'Gramsci and Us' (1988e), in which he proclaimed the death of 'Socialist Man', the title of a well-known speech by Isaac Deutscher (1967), and a term commonly used within the Left at the time to refer, sometimes ironically, to the necessary personality traits for living within a future socialist society. For Hall, 'Socialist Man' exemplified the asceticism and patriarchal values of the orthodox Left, as well as its inability to account for the plurality of interests in contemporary society (1988e, 170). He also argued that traditionalism 'has a deep and profound hold inside the socialist movement, inside the labour movement, inside the working class itself', and that 'that is why and where racism and sexism lurk' (1988e, 194). Following on from this, Hall argued that a socialist politics which did not challenge discrimination against women or ethnic minorities would make limited gains. He also claimed that 'if you have working people committed to the old ways, the old relations, the old values, the old feelings' then they would ultimately be unable to transform society (ibid.). As Michael Rustin has noted, there was a sense that Hall saw the 'unthinking conservatism of the Left' as the cause of its failure (1989, 9), and felt that the real possibilities for social change were to be found elsewhere. Related to this, Hall has also been critiqued for ignoring the struggles for race and gender equality within the labour movement and the wider Left (Coates 2013). Bearing in mind these critiques, many of the issues that Hall raised continue to be valid. As will be discussed in greater detail in chapters 5 and 6, my experience (as a woman and an ethnic minority) of both anti-austerity campaigns and trade union activism is that patriarchal ideas of leadership continue to persist, as well as nostalgic conceptions of class which do not reflect many aspects of contemporary experience. As this book is concerned with public mood, it is also worth briefly reflecting on Hall's evocative phrase, 'the old feelings'. Although Hall did not elaborate on this phrase (it was intended as a provocation), I understand it to mean the reliance on those social structures and value systems which were being challenged by new social movements such as the gendered division of labour or ideas of social solidarity based on shared ethnicity, and the feelings of emotional certainty these provided, at least for those who benefitted. Such unresolved issues continue to limit the imaginative capacities of Left politics.

AUTHORITARIAN POPULISM

Traditionalism, particularly around ideas of work, family and community, is also closely connected to another related concept, 'authoritarian populism'. Authoritarian populism draws significantly on Nicos Poulantzas' concept of 'authoritarian statism' in *State, Power, Socialism*, originally published in 1978 (2000). Poulantzas defines authoritarian statism as:

> intensified state control over every sphere of socio-economic life combined with radical decline of the institutions of political democracy and with draconian and multiform curtailment of so-called formal liberties, whose reality is being discovered now that they are going overboard. (2000, 203)

Poulantzas theorises authoritarian statism as symptomatic of both the crisis of the state and the crisis of capitalism, remarking that 'wild animals are most dangerous when they are wounded' (2000, 204), as well as the sharpening of contradictions within the historical bloc (particularly between the *grand bourgeoisie* and the petty bourgeoisie, largely attributed to the decline in living standards experienced by the latter (2000, 211). As Ian Bruff argues, his most potent lesson for the Left was that authoritarian statism was 'the reality which emerged from the ruins of the Welfare State myth' (Poulantzas 2000 cited in Bruff 2014). Authoritarian statism involves the concentration of power within the executive and administrative domains of government. This is linked to the consolidation of a government and business elite, increasingly drawn from the same educational background. Poulantzas uses the example of France's exclusive and insular *Grand Ecoles* (2000, 225), but parallels could be drawn with Oxford and Cambridge in the UK context, or the Ivy League in the United States. This process also involves the weakening of political parties and the distancing of party leaders from rank and file, as citizens are increasingly excluded from decision-making processes. Instead, politicians appeal to the public through 'administrative networks and techniques' such as opinion polls and political marketing, and the use of the mass media (2000, 229), a process which creates disaffection with political parties and democratic institutions in general. This process of disengagement, according to Poulantzas, allows those in positions of power to become even less accountable (2000, 231). Simultaneously, individual citizens also become subject to greater regulation and control (2000, 219–220).

Authoritarian statism, according to Poulantzas, has a self-perpetuating logic, in terms of the normalising of authoritarianism within the lives and experiences of citizens, legitimating the introduction of yet more authoritarian measures (2000, 227). Poulantzas' examples focus on processes of decentralisation in 1970s France which ultimately resulted in greater central control (ibid.). I would also suggest that the bordering practices which I will discuss in greater detail in chapter 4 would serve as examples of this process, in that they institutionalise expectations for public, private and voluntary sector workers to be responsible for checking immigration status – thus normalising banks, hospitals and so forth as sites of border control. Despite his emphasis on state control, Poulantzas is careful to distinguish between authoritarian statism and totalitarianism or fascism (2000, 205) as authoritarian statism does not actually involve the dismantling of the institutions of liberal democracy, even as they are marginalised and weakened. However, he acknowledges that 'every democratic form of capitalist state carries totalitarian tendencies' (2000, 209). At the time of writing, the phenomena described earlier (political disengagement, unaccountable governments and other failings of parliamentary democracy) are now being discussed in relation to the EU referendum vote and the election of Donald Trump. However, the relevance of Poulantzas' analysis indicates the historical roots of this situation can be traced to the late twentieth century.

Hall drew on the concept of 'authoritarian statism' to interpret Thatcherism's 'law and order' language and policies, aggressive approach to industrial disputes and inflammatory and divisive rhetoric around immigration and race. As discussed, more generally Hall saw the support for Thatcherism and the backlash against the 1960s counterculture and the unresolved contradictions of the post-war settlement as intrinsic to what he saw as the 'drift towards a law and order society', as outlined in 'Living with the Crisis' (1988a). Authoritarian populism is about the techniques through which consent for authoritarian statism was secured, as well as a description of the emotional character of political disengagement. The executive control and weakening of democratic structures, as well as the security measures theorised by Poulantzas, are perceived to provide the necessary discipline and leadership for restoring social order but also respond to, and in some cases amplify, social anxieties about loss of control – which then in turn require more discipline. Hall's highlighting of the populist dimension comes from a critique of Poulantzas' assumption that these developments are state-led and top-down, and thus ignoring social struggles and non-state actors (Hall 1985, 116–118).

For Hall, what makes authoritarian populism specifically *populist* is its consolidation of conceptions of 'the people' along socially conservative lines (consistent with 'traditionalism') to the exclusion of trade unionists, black people, immigrants, lone parents, working mothers and others. Hall also argues that the success of Powellism[3] and its adoption within mainstream politics (despite Powell's resignation and subsequent pariah status) successfully established links between race, immigration control and 'the image of the nation, the British people and the destruction of "our culture, our way of life"' within mainstream public discourse (1988b, 55). This positioning of certain people as effectively outside the body politic justified targeting them with law-and-order measures, as a socially acceptable response to a society perceived to be out of control:

> [The government] attempted to impose a new regime of social discipline and leadership 'from above' in a society experienced as rudderless and out of control. However, the 'populist' part of the strategy required that this move to new forms of social authority and regulation 'above' should be rooted in popular fears and anxieties 'below'. (1988d, 84)

The concept of authoritarian populism enables us to consider links and interactions between unaccountable government, authoritarian state tactics, political disengagement and disaffection, and the framing of particular sections of society as outsiders. In other words, it helps us understand how public moods are constructed, and the relationship between public moods and government policy. Lacking public sympathy, outsiders become targeted by inflammatory political rhetoric blaming them for the breakdown of society as well as authoritarian state measures. Such rhetoric and policies then allow politicians to demonstrate decisive 'leadership' and moral conviction to restore the social order. It is questionable whether such 'tough' measures actually mitigate political disaffection or simply exacerbate it, as the public perceives this as a cynical performative politics (Jones et al. 2017) in which the goal of policy is to demonstrate that something is being done, regardless of outcome.

Authoritarian populism also enables us to understand the continuities between a moment such as the late 1970s or 1980s and the present, particularly as the scapegoats have changed little. Witness the demonisation of the 'undeserving poor' in the scrounger discourse (see chapter 3) or arguments similar to those outlined in Powell's infamous speech, in which he expressed fears about 'unrecognisable communities' or white British people becoming marginalised subordinates. Although such anxieties may not always be expressed through biological definitions of race, as demonstrated by the current hostility towards white Eastern Europeans, the basic argument remains the same. Authoritarian populism also has particular resonances with austerity politics and policy. As will be discussed in chapters 5 and 7, austerity policies involve the closing down of democratic forums and processes for citizens to make their voices heard, particularly when it involves challenging decisions to cut public services. As I have discussed in the previous chapter, austerity policies are justified through blaming of certain categories of people as burdens on the welfare state, which then makes it justifiable to cut resources or privatise public services they use, such as the plans, at the time of writing, to outsource the provision of the Equality Advisory and Support Services helpline[4] to the G4S security firm[5] (Bowcott 2016).

At the time when it was first proposed, the concept of 'authoritarian populism' and more generally Hall's approach was critiqued by Jessop et al. (1984; 1985) for a number of issues, notably the privileging of culture and ideology at the expense of the economy (1984, 87), and as reflecting a pessimistic and defeatist interpretation which assumed the hegemony of Thatcherism, the stability of the power bloc, and the unified character of public opinion including those who might tactically vote Conservative without fully having signed up to Thatcherite ideology (Jessop et al. 1984, 43). However, they later admitted that Thatcherism had in fact convinced many middle-class voters that 'popular capitalism' was in their best interests (1987, 119). Hall claimed in his response to Jessop et al. that authoritarian populism was never intended as an overarching concept (1985, 154) and admitted that it did not account for why some elements of public opinion were incorporated into official political discourse more than others (1985, 152). The concept does have particular limitations, notably around theorising resistance, although Hall writes about resistance within the context of culture and everyday experience elsewhere (e.g., Hall 1990; Hall and Jefferson 1993; Morley and Chen 1996). Hall also makes some rather sweeping statements such that 'social democracy has finished' and 'the welfare state has gone forever' (1988e, 166). While these were intended as provocations to a nostalgic and traditionalist 1980s Left, they also could be interpreted as a wholesale rejection of practices perceived to be on the 'wrong side of history', lending credence to the (mostly unjustified) charge that Hall's thinking justified the rise of New Labour. Reflecting on this in 2012, Hall admits that:

> There is a tiny kernel of truth in the assertion that [*Marxism Today*] created Blairism, in the sense that the 'new times' stuff was addressing the change of the whole terrain. But what we recommended was that you needed a project on the left of the same breadth and depth as Thatcherism. (Derbyshire 2012)

However, as I will demonstrate in the following section, Hall also identified Thatcherist tendencies in New Labour.

NEW LABOUR AND THE TRANSFORMATION OF TRADITIONALISM AND AUTHORITARIAN POPULISM

In the following section, I will consider how some of the underlying principles of 'authoritarian populism' and 'traditionalism' informed Hall's analysis of New Labour, notably in 'The Great Moving Nowhere Show' (1998) and

'New Labour's Double Shuffle' (2005). While the modernising impulses within New Labour could be interpreted as a reaction against what Hall called the 'traditionalism' of the orthodox Left, in many ways traditionalism was implicit in how New Labour appealed to the public. The focus on appealing to voters in marginal Conservative constituencies and the construct of 'Middle England',[6] which Hall critiques in the 'The Great Moving Nowhere Show' (1998), serves as an example of this approach. Hall creates a rather parodic characterisation of 'Middle England', which simultaneously evokes both Thatcher's address to the public and Nixon's 'silent majority':

> Middle England is a place of the mind, an imagined community,[7] always located somewhere south or in the centre of the country, never north – though Mr Mandelson[8] has recently put in a claim for Hartlepool Man. Middle England is peopled by skilled, clerical or supervisory grade home-owners, never manual workers or public sector professionals. It is committedly suburban, anti-city, family-centred, devoted to self-reliance and respectability. Its cultural icons, he argues, are Neighbourhood Watch, Gordon's Gin, Enid Blyton.[9] Ford Mondeo, Hyacinth Bucket,[10] *The Antiques Roadshow*.[11] Nescafe Gold Blend. Acacia Avenue,[12] Scouts and Brownies'. 'Nigel Kennedy and the Salvation Army.' Its voice is the *Daily Mail*.
>
> (1998)

The class position of this constituency is ambiguous: it seems both solidly middle class and simultaneously evokes the 'lumpen bourgeoisie' of *Policing the Crisis*, but most of all it is socially and culturally conservative. Hall argued that shortly after their 1997 electoral victory, much of New Labour's rhetoric replaced 'Middle England' with 'The People' whose desires must be flattered: 'wooed rather than represented' (1998, 13). Later he also drew attention to the role of 'spin'[13] in persuading the public (2005, 329). The appeal to emotion (flattering and wooing) is significant in essentially treating citizens as passive consumers rather than active agents in democracy, to be addressed, as Poulantzas observed, through political marketing techniques to gauge the 'public mood'. This is also a public whose prejudices should be pandered to rather than challenged. Ultimately, Hall considered this to be a public for which [The Labour Party] holds 'a profound contempt' (2005, 321), who supposedly did not know what was best for them, and perhaps whose worldviews many Labour politicians disagreed with, but who nonetheless they felt compelled to appeal to, perhaps because they begrudgingly saw them as representing the public mood. This also reflected a 'two-step shuffle' for the Labour Party between a dominant tendency – neoliberalism – and a subordinate tendency – social democracy (2005, 329), with 'spin' used to 'square the impossible circle' (ibid.). Many of the same divisions between insiders and outsiders constructed by Thatcherist political discourse persisted under New Labour, likely a result of the attempt to appeal to marginal constituencies, while taking it for granted that those who had historically voted Labour would continue to do so. Hall remarked on how 'The People' were defined by New Labour, in many ways, by who they were not: 'the "working classes" or the "underclasses" or the "chattering classes" or manual workers or lone parents or black families or trade unionists or public sector workers, or Labour Party rank-and-file members' (1998, 14). Much of society was ironically excluded from this definition.

In order to appeal to the constituency of marginal Conservative voters, New Labour mobilised the scrounger discourse and the 're-moralisation of the work ethic, obsession with deserving/undeserving poor, [and] introduction of workfare measures' (1998, 12). In doing so, they simultaneously appealed to older prejudices about the unemployed, and neoliberal expectations for the self-reliant, entrepreneurial subject – or possibly a reconfiguration of these older prejudices for a neoliberal era. Hall also identified a range of authoritarian policies under New Labour which mobilised state intervention for socially conservative aims: 'the top-down, managerialist approach of centralised control' and 'the rich panoply of the "audit culture", including "moralistic shaming", and "the novel, contradictory strategy of tough love"' (2005, 331). This approach was represented by policies which were directed at controlling the local population, such as anti-social behaviour orders (ASBOs[14]) and the proliferation of CCTV cameras for the purposes of surveillance. It was also made manifest through a militarist and interventionist approach to foreign policy where a hawkish toughness could be demonstrated, including complicity with rendition and torture (2011, 714) and military intervention in Iraq.

The underlying principles within 'authoritarian populism' and 'traditionalism' were also present in Hall's critiques of the Coalition Conservative–Liberal Democrat Government, in 'The Neoliberal Revolution' (2011) and 'We Have to Talk about Englishness' (2012), published shortly before his death in 2013. If, according to Hall, New Labour's version of the silent majority was 'Middle England' or 'The People', then 'community' was the term mobilised by the Cameron Conservatives to describe, largely, the same, imagined group of people. Within the context of austerity, citizens are expected to volunteer to compensate for cuts in public service provision, which Hall critiques as 'the lure of localism' in terms of how unpaid volunteer labour is framed as empowering citizens and local communities (2011, 720). Hall also notes the Conservatives' appropriation of 1960s rhetoric about 'shift[ing] power to the people', while simultaneously undermining the structures of local democracy (2011, 721). Hall remarks that 'the Left, which feels positively about volunteering, community involvement and participation – and who doesn't? – finds itself once again triangulated into uncertainty' (ibid.).

Aspects of 'traditionalism' are also present in Hall's critique of nationalism within the Labour Party (expressed particularly, at the time, through the Blue

Labour tendency).[15] In 'We Have to Talk about Englishness' (Derbyshire 2012), Hall accuses John Cruddas, one of the Blue Labour architects, of 'raiding the past, out of context' (ibid.). Here Hall refers to Blue Labour's appeals to the early history of the labour movement as a source of national pride, especially nineteenth-century friendly societies which provided support in the absence of the welfare state (Glasman et al. 2011). In the article, Hall questions whether nationalism could be reclaimed for the Left. Despite the influence of Gramscian thinking on his ideas, he does not interpret the concept of the 'national-popular' to specifically mean Left patriotism, but rather frames it as a contested territory, emphasising the *popular* much more than the *national* (Hall 1981). This is a position Hall has taken for a long time; unlike others who wrote for *Marxism Today*, such as Eric Hobsbawm (e.g., 1996), Hall does not make claims for a Left nationalism. It is notable that in the aftermath of the 2014 Scottish independence referendum, the rise in popularity of the UK Independence Party (UKIP)[16] and the subsequent vote for the United Kingdom to leave the European Union calls for reclaiming English nationalism for the Left, particularly to appeal to disillusioned working-class voters, have become louder (e.g., Jones 2015; Garton Ash 2016; Denham and Kenny 2016), although such calls have been numerous. Hall points out that Englishness is a contested terrain and is deeply implicated in histories of colonialism, making any attempt to reclaim it for the Left a rather difficult task (Derbyshire 2012). He also questions the extent to which affinities with the radical aspects of English history can be manufactured to create a progressive conception of English nationalism (and in fact Blue Labour was one of the more socially conservative versions), pointing out that radical English traditions (examples mentioned in the Blue Labour book include the Levellers and the Chartists) could not be simply revived 'at will' (ibid.). Although Hall does not explicitly name this concern, I feel it is important to question who might feel an instinctive, spontaneous connection to radical English history and who may not, or what it means to base a conception of national identity on such culturally specific references. Who might be excluded by such expectations to identify with English history, and might such exclusions betray what is ultimately an ethnically specific conception of Englishness which is incompatible with a diverse globalised society? There has yet to be a satisfactory answer to Hall's questions.

ARE 'TRADITIONALISM' AND 'AUTHORITARIAN POPULISM' STILL RELEVANT AS CONCEPTS?

At this point in time, aspects of the new social movements of the twentieth century have been institutionalised and even taken for granted. For example, gay marriage was adopted under the Liberal Democrat/Conservative coalition, and there is a certain degree of acceptance of race and gender equality, as enshrined in the 2010 Equality Act.[17] Simultaneously, elements of progressive politics have been appropriated by neoliberal actors to frame the empowerment of women or ethnic minorities narrowly as individual advancement for exceptional individuals within a meritocratic system.[18] However, the painful irony is that neoliberalism, and especially austerity cuts, entrench pre-existing socio-economic hierarchies as they disproportionately target those who are already lacking resources, notably women, young people, ethnic minorities and the disabled (Runnymede Trust 2015; TUC 2014a; TUC 2015b; Women's Budget Group 2016; Belfield et al. 2016). Organisations for monitoring discrimination, such as the Equality and Human Rights Commission, have had their resources cut (Disability News Service 2016). This has been justified by rhetoric framing some people as legitimately entitled to rights and stretched public resources, while others are perceived as both social threats and undeserving of these resources. Witness the rhetoric around 'hardworking families' (a term with heteronormative associations) versus the familiar scapegoats of the unemployed and immigrants, with racially minoritised British citizens sometimes being lumped in with them. Such rhetoric justifies British and European governments in restricting rights and access to the welfare state for immigrants and asylum seekers. Initiatives have been introduced to monitor and survey Muslim communities, positioning migrants and ethnic minorities as dangerous to gender and sexual equality within the context of Islamophobia and the War on Terror and its aftermath (Puar 2007). The current conjuncture is thus marked by the mainstreaming and institutionalisation of progressive politics, at the same time as anxieties are expressed by some about how these gains have 'gone too far', amid the intensification of racism, xenophobia and nativist and exclusionary conceptions of national identity, in connection with the austerity rhetoric which frames particular sections of society as undeserving. This can be interpreted through Hall's theorisation of ideology as suturing together contradictory ideas and emotional investments (2011). But could the current moment specifically be interpreted in terms of traditionalism and authoritarian populism?

I will now dwell on the increasing prevalence of nativist and socially conservative conceptions of the British public, as this is where both concepts remain relevant, particularly in the pitting of sections of society against each other. The common narrative is that equality legislation and mass immigration have damaged the prospects, but also the identity of the 'white working class', producing resentment and a sense of abandonment. This can also be understood in terms of continuities with Powellism as well as the authoritarian tendencies Hall identified within Thatcherism and New Labour, while also representing a backlash against the institutionalisation of progressive politics (traditionalism). Notably, the 'white working class', as it has been constructed (e.g., Collins 2004; Goodwin and Ford 2014), is not a proletariat in the Marxist sense as they do not possess the ability to withdraw their labour power. Rather, their threat is seen to consist specifically of political disengagement and the channelling of resentment and anger into support for the far right, such as, UKIP and their far-right equivalents elsewhere. For example, Matthew Goodwin and Rob Ford frame UKIP's support as 'concentrated among older, blue-collar workers, with little education and few skills: a group who have been "left behind" by the economic and social transformation of Britain in recent decades, and pushed to the margin as the main parties have converged on the centre ground' – a characterisation similar to Hall's 'lumpen bourgeoisie', minus his critical reflexivity. This same group is characterised as 'angry and disaffected working-class Britons of all political backgrounds, who have lost faith in a political system that ceased to represent them long ago' (2014, 270). In *British Dream*, anti-immigration commentator David Goodhart expressed a similar perspective in this rather curious passage:

> One of the challenges to our immigration story is how to allow older poorer white people a safe space in which to express a sense of loss, and homesickness for the past, without this mood becoming destructively pessimistic or spilling over into racism. (Goodhart 2013, 256)

Goodhart's views will be discussed in further detail in chapter 4. However, here it is worth considering the framing of the white working class as powerless, residual (age is highlighted to emphasise this) and unable to control their emotions – which is where such characterisations ultimately reveal their patronising tone.

And what emotions are being named as representing a public mood? There is a sense of loss and homesickness, and certainly a sense of abandonment. But the predominant emotion invoked is actually *resentment*. In 'Towards a Sociology of Resentment' (2008), Vron Ware draws on German sociologist Max Scheler's formulation of Nietzsche*'s ressentiment* in relation to revenge, and in particular his argument that 'revenge tends to be transformed into *ressentiment* the more it is directed against lasting situations which are felt to be "injurious" but beyond one's control – in other words, the more the injury is experienced as a destiny' (Bershady 1992 cited in Ware 2008). This is not about challenging inequality or injustice (as within the formulation of resentment, social movements are pointless), but instead identifying with a sense of grievance, and *resenting* other groups in society. Within the politics of resentment, the 'white working class' is framed as guided by emotions rather than making conscious decisions; they are 'driven' (note the passive voice) to far-right politics rather than actively choosing them (Hanley 2008), in need of therapeutic safe spaces to express their pain and loss, lest this turn into something more dangerous. Nonetheless, this section of society is perceived as possessing a particular moral authority; there is a sense that their pain and loss *matter* more than the pain and loss experienced by others, such as young people, immigrants or working-class people who are not white. This recalls Hall's comments that I discussed at the beginning of the chapter about the moral authority of the petty bourgeoisie, but also more generally the moral authority of traditionalism: of those who were associated with another time and another, more authentic and legitimate set of values and experiences.

The vote to leave the European Union and the replacing of David Cameron with Theresa May as UK Prime Minister, as well as the election of Donald Trump as US president, have also increased the sense, within mainstream political debate, that this section of society has been previously ignored and abandoned (but their time has now come) but also that they represent the majority. For example, in a speech on the morning of the 24th of June 2016, former UKIP leader Nigel Farage called the vote to leave the European Union 'a victory for ordinary, decent people' (Hobolt 2016) and PM Theresa May's first public statement as Prime Minister was pitched at those who are 'just about managing' (Gov.UK 2016). Exactly who is being addressed? It could be argued that everyone thinks they are decent, or that everyone may feel they are 'just about managing' at some point in their lives, including the very wealthy. However, as much as these interpellations are about speaking to everyone, they are also about who they are *not* addressing. It is implied in Farage's speech that those who voted to remain in the European Union, including the majority of young and ethnic minority voters, as well as EU citizens who did not even have the right to vote in the EU referendum, are not decent, and are in fact tainted by an indecent cosmopolitanism. May is not speaking to those who cannot manage and must rely on significant state support, nor is she speaking to the vilified 'liberal metropolitan elite'. Significantly, she is appealing to the 'just about managing' primarily on the level of values and identities rather than economic interests. In the 2016 Conservative Party Conference speech, she said she understood their concerns, in contrast to the liberal elite: 'they find your patriotism distasteful, your concerns about immigration parochial, your views about crime illiberal, your attachment to your job security inconvenient' (May 2016). At another point in the speech, she again attacked the liberal elite with the words: 'if you think you are a citizen of the world, you are a citizen of nowhere' (ibid.). Ironically, at the time of writing, the Conservative government's cuts to benefits and other continued austerity measures will actually make life for those who are 'just about managing' more difficult (Helm and Inman 2016).

May's authoritarian tendencies, which were present in her tenure as Home Secretary (during which she implemented some very harsh immigration policies, expanded the role of state surveillance and exempted the government from public scrutiny), seem set to continue now that she is Prime Minister. And, crucially, her authoritarianism is being justified by populist rhetoric. Populism, according to Dutch political scientist Cas Mudde, is a 'thin-centred ideology' that can easily incorporate these elements which seemingly come from opposite ends of the political spectrum; its 'empty heart can easily incorporate and refashion disparate ideological elements and issues along a crucial central distinction' (2007 cited in Lentin and Titley 2011, 117). Populism 'considers society to be ultimately separated into two homogeneous and antagonistic groups, the "pure people" vs the "corrupt elite", and which argues that politics should be an expression of the *volonté generale* [general will] of the people' (ibid). This is why, within the context of both austerity and xenophobic populist politics, it becomes easy for politicians to claim they are simultaneously on the side of the people and against the corrupt elite by cracking down on immigrants. The corruption of the elite is blamed for mass immigration, and the elite are framed as vaguely foreign (as not paying tax, as living transnational rather than local lives). However, it is unclear, even at the time of writing, to what extent the constituencies addressed by May actually constitute a power bloc. As Will Davies notes in 'Home Office Rules', the cultural coalition of 'working-class Brexiters, pensioners, *Daily Mail* readers and traditionalists' barely holds together and may have contradictory interests' (Davies 2016).

Stuart Hall's earlier critiques of traditionalism on the Left could also well be applied to the guilty and conflicted response of the Labour Party to the unfolding situation. One example of this was a branded mug produced during the 2015 General Election campaign with a slogan reading 'controls on immigration' as one of the Labour Party's five key election promises, which was controversial among its own activists (Bush 2015). In the aftermath of the EU referendum, there were calls from Labour Party MPs to make the ending of free movement within the EU a 'red line' in the Brexit negotiations in order to reconnect with core working-class voters (Reeves 2016). The decision of the party leadership to pose no significant challenge to the government in the parliamentary debate to trigger Article 50 (the legislative mechanism to leave the EU) for fear of alienating Eurosceptic voters could be interpreted in similar terms. Hall would have critiqued such nostalgic politics on the Left, as he had the previous incarnations discussed earlier in this chapter. Hall's response to Jeremy Corbyn as leader of the Labour Party would have likely been ambivalent. He would have welcomed the decisive rejection of the New Labour orthodoxy and an opportunity to transform the party into a genuinely democratic, member-led organisation, after so many years of managerialism and spin. Bearing in mind the critiques of Hall's silence on social movements in the 1980s, he would have welcomed some of the early experimentation of Momentum[19] as a bold initiative for democratic engagement, although he would have little patience for the sectarian infighting that plagued the organisation later on. Hall would have possibly seen the Labour Party's confused position on the Brexit vote as possibly another example of a 'double shuffle' between those who voted to leave the European Union and those who voted to remain. However, he would have acknowledged that the conditions were different from New Labour's electoral manoeuvring, and that the party was genuinely in a bind. According to exit polling, two-thirds of Labour voters voted to remain in the European Union (Moore 2016), but the majority of constituencies represented by Labour MPs voted to leave (Hanretty 2016). This indicates both the complexities of the situation and the challenges facing progressive politics. Hall would have also likely understood these impasses as reflecting wider unresolved issues and imaginative failures around the role of the state, so that Keynesianism and protectionist economics seemed like the only viable alternative to austerity. He would have recognised the challenges of mapping these onto a globalised, diverse society (as illustrated by Hatherley's critique of *Spirit of '45* in the previous chapter).

Such impasses were also recognised by Ian Bruff, who, in his theorisation of 'authoritarian neoliberalism', attempts to build on Hall's thinking. Bruff examines impasses around the tendency of the Left to present the state as safeguarding citizens' rights against neoliberal market forces. He argues that it is difficult to envision such a role for the state when it plays an active role in implementing austerity measures or undermining the right to protest (2012; 2014). Returning to the discussion in chapter 1 of the gendering of the welfare state as a vulnerable 'soft touch', such authoritarian and securitarian approaches can be understood as a compensatory move to demonstrate toughness and invulnerability – an approach which will never be enough to satisfy Right populist critics. This makes it more difficult for those on the Left to unreservedly champion the state as inherently more democratic than the market (2012, 115), because one cannot be confident that it would not abuse its power. This also means that radical, anti-establishment narratives about the crisis from the Right become much more immediate and accessible than those from the Left (2014, 126) – as exemplified by the phenomena described earlier.

CONCLUSION: HALL'S WORK AS AN IMAGINATIVE RESOURCE

Because he passed away in 2013, Stuart Hall did not comment on these recent developments. However, in 'The Urgent Legacy of Stuart Hall', Jeremy Gilbert asks how his thinking could be applied to the current situation. Gilbert argues that Hall would have warned against the tendency on the Left to turn to social conservatism, localism and communitarianism as a reaction to New Labour's embrace of neoliberal globalisation. He would have been critical of those advocating such an approach as 'demonstrating a widespread inability to see any progressive potential at all in current cultural trends, shaped as they are by the emergence of new communication technologies and by historically unprecedented levels of global mobility and migration' (Gilbert 2014). The relationship to New Labour notwithstanding, Hall would have looked to the utopian possibilities within these phenomena rather than perceiving them as a threat. This is why his passing marks the loss of a progressive voice, particularly at a moment when socially conservative and communitarian approaches seem to be increasingly dominant, and where alternatives seem difficult to imagine. Hall's thinking and his legacy also serve as imaginative resources for developing alternatives, as much as his critiques help us understand the impasses of the Left.

Authoritarian populism and traditionalism remain useful concepts, particularly in terms of understanding the development of a public mood based around appeals to nostalgic visions of the past, and the pitting of sections of society against each other, with some positioned outside the body politic and – in the context of austerity – undeserving of state resources. Hall's thinking also serves as an important caution for the Left against the dangers of reclaiming traditionalist conceptions of nation, identity or community to appeal to working-class voters. These concepts also have their limitations, one of them being the unsuitability for theorising resistance. However, they still have their value because many of the same impasses remain, particularly around the role of the state and the definition of the public, which have become particularly fraught within the austerity, and now post-Brexit context. These impasses and attempts to overcome them will be discussed in the chapters that follow.

NOTES

1. A power bloc, also known as a historical bloc, was theorised by Antonio Gramsci in *The Prison Notebooks* as a unity between the structure and superstructure, meaning an alliance of class forces around a set of hegemonic ideas.

2. Prejudices around poor people having too many children are at the heart of long-held beliefs about working-class people being genetically inferior and were associated with both Malthusianism and eugenics.

3. Enoch Powell was a British Conservative Party politician who became infamous for an inflammatory anti-immigration speech made in 1968 to the West Midlands Area Conservative Political Centre, which became later known as the 'Rivers of Blood' speech. The speech scapegoated immigrants for destroying social cohesion. Powell was immediately sacked from the Conservative Party for inciting racial hatred, but the speech was very popular with the British public at the time.

4. The Equality Advisory and Support Services helpline is a national helpline for victims of discrimination.

5. Group 4 Security (G4S) is a multinational security company, currently the largest in the world. It has been awarded many contracts for outsourced public service provision, including prison services, immigration detention centres, welfare, hospitals and so forth. They have been controversial for their operation of detention centres, human rights abuse and allegations of fraud.

6. 'Middle England' is a colloquial term used to refer to middle-class and lower-middle class white people in England with socially conservative views. Similar to 'Middle America' in the United States, Middle Englanders are frequently positioned against ethnic and sexual minorities, as well as liberal metropolitans. 'Middle England' is also seen as crucial to winning elections.

7. The term was coined by Benedict Anderson (1983) to theorise national identity.

8. Peter Mandelson is a Labour Peer in the House of Lords and was MP for Hartlepool from 1992 to 2004, and also held a number of Cabinet positions. He was close to former PM Tony Blair and is seen to be one of the architects of the New Labour regime. Mandelson was especially known for the 1998 declaration that 'New Labour is intensely relaxed about people getting filthy rich, as long as they pay their taxes'.

9. Enid Blyton was a famous children's writer in the United Kingdom who wrote between the 1930s and 1960s.

10. Hyacinth Bucket was a character on the 1990s situation comedy *Keeping Up with Appearances*.

11. *Antiques Roadshow* is a British television programme where antique appraisers travel to different regions to appraise the value of antiques brought in by local people.

12. Acacia Avenue is a shorthand cliché for the average suburban street.

13. The term 'spin', meaning media manipulation, did not become commonly used until the New Labour era. It was critiqued by the Leveson Inquiry (2012) as causing damage to democracy.

14. Anti-Social Behaviour Orders were civil orders against behaviour which was deemed to be 'anti-social', including: 'drunken or threatening behaviour; vandalism and graffiti; and playing loud music at night'. They were replaced by injunctions and criminal behaviour orders in 2014.

15. Blue Labour is a tendency within the Labour Party in the United Kingdom which is based in the conviction that working-class voters who have become estranged from the Labour Party can be won back through socially conservative policies and rhetoric.

16. The UK Independence Party (UKIP) is a Right populist, Eurosceptic political party, with an emphasis on lowering immigration and socially conservative values. Its economic policies are at times libertarian and other times protectionist in relation to trade.

17. The 2010 Equality Act combined acts and regulations, forming the basis of anti-discrimination law in the United Kingdom.

18. For critiques see Gill 2002, Gill 2007, McRobbie 2008, Fraser 2013, although see the critique of Fraser by Bhandar and Ferreira Da Silva 2013 on the exclusion of black Feminism from such analyses and the experience of ethnic minority and working-class women as well as those based in the global South.

19. Momentum is a political organisation founded by Jon Lansman which seeks to build on the enthusiasm around the campaign for Jeremy Corbyn's leadership. See http://www.peoplesmomentum.com/.

Chapter 3

The Mediatisation of Austerity and the Case of *Benefits Street*

This chapter will examine judgement and derision towards the unemployed as an aspect of the public mood. Judging present-day poverty as lacking dignity and authenticity as compared to the past is an element of this, as is the metaphor of work as a marker of normality and belonging to mainstream society. Here I will focus on the ideologies of *respectability* and *meritocracy*, which are important given their connection to one's sense of self-worth and the perception within neoliberal ideology that one's lot in life is due to ability rather than socioeconomic privilege. There is much at stake in these ideologies; to lose faith in meritocracy means facing some uncomfortable and difficult questions about power and privilege, and to lose respectability risks losing one's self-worth. Within the austerity context, both meritocracy and respectability come under pressure due to the decline in living standards and social mobility (Dorling 2013).

The simple division between being either in work or unemployed and on benefits is not entirely accurate at a time when employment does not necessarily mean not making use of the benefits system. TUC research showed that in 2014, five million families earned less than the living wage and relied on in-work benefits and tax credits to make ends meet (TUC 2014c).[1] However, the apparent simplicity of such a division has a particular immediacy in creating a distinction between strivers and scroungers, affirming familiar narratives around respectability and meritocracy. I am interested in the perpetuation of these distinctions and also how it feels to be judged through them. In this chapter, I will explore the role of media representations in perpetuating divisive narratives; I will also examine how these narratives are affirmed or challenged in online debate.

Benefits Street was a fly-on-the-wall documentary about the residents of James Turner Street, a street in the Winson Green neighbourhood of Birmingham, United Kingdom, where, it was claimed, almost everyone was unemployed. It averaged over 5.1 million viewers (Deans 2014) and was controversial due to its depiction of the street's residents. Its representation of the unemployed made it a topical reference point for commentators and policymakers to assert their position on benefits, such as by claiming the programme dared to tell the 'ugly truth' about welfare dependency, justifying 'tough' responses. It also provoked many highly emotive reactions on social media. I am focusing on *Benefits Street* and the reactions surrounding it because of the ways in which it provoked people to perform their belonging and respectability through deriding and judging others. I will also discuss the resistance provoked by the programme and how people challenged or refused the striver/scrounger distinction.

RESPECTABILITY

In her influential study *Formations of Class and Gender,* Beverley Skeggs argues that the classification by and of the working classes into 'rough' and 'respectable' has a long history (1997, 3). The idea of 'respectability' has of course existed for a long time (famously termed by Friedrich Engels as 'a most repulsive thing', 'a false consciousness bred into the bones of the workers' (1953 cited in Skeggs 1997, 3). As a concept, it is so deeply entrenched within modern liberal societies that to lose respectability is to have little social value or legitimacy (ibid.). As Richard Sennett observes, the related concept of 'respect' has been central to liberal conceptions of the subject as an autonomous individual who is not dependent on others, with dependency likened to a state of immaturity (2004, 103). Both the integrity of the body (as in conceptions of universal human rights) and the dignity of labour are perceived as the sources of respect (2004, 57).

Distinctions between 'respectable' and 'unrespectable' become prominent where understandings of class are particularly fraught. Skeggs observes that most people do not see themselves as 'middle class' in the United Kingdom because of the term's associations with snobbery;[2] however, nonetheless people still want to distinguish themselves from others who are perceived as lower status, as 'trash' (2012, 278). When class solidarity is absent, social inequalities become characterised as moral positions, and values traditionally associated with the experience of a particular class become disassociated from their original context and are appropriated (e.g., by right-wing politicians) for the purposes of social conservatism. Drawing on Thomas Frank's critique of right populism, *What's the Matter with America?* (2004), Skeggs and Wood argue that 'part of the Right's rhetorical appeal was to detach already formed moral values such as unpretentiousness, authenticity, hard work, and loyalty from the conditions of their original production (working class life), and re-attach them to the interests of an imaginary safe and secure, prosperous right-wing nation through the promise of respect and respectability' (2012, 282).

This has particular salience within the austerity context, where it has become more difficult to achieve conventional markers of respectability, such as holding a permanent, full-time job or owning property. As discussed in chapter 1, these markers of respectability continue to persist as social norms despite their unattainability (Berlant 2011), and due to the pressures of life under neoliberalism, people do not have the time or resources to develop a systemic analysis of their conditions (Connolly 2013). Because there is already such an emotional investment in markers of respectability, there is a sense that to give them up, one is left with nothing.

Faced with this situation, an obvious and predictable response is to claim respectability by judging or deriding others as unrespectable, mobilising the immediately accessible 'scrounger' discourse. For example, commentators have observed the resurgence of the idea that the poor need to be taught correct behaviour, as disability rights activist Frances Ryan observes:

> We are sliding back to the notion that suffering helps the soul, that the underclass – be it the unemployed, the disabled, or chronically ill – need to be trained in order to behave. And, as almost a secondary consequence, their punishment cuts the welfare bill down. A bonus all round. (Ryan 2015)

This discourse has even been internalised by those on benefits, indicating the extent to which resentment towards those on benefits has become normalised as part of the public mood. For example, research by the Joseph Rowntree Housing Trust explores how benefits claimants scapegoat other claimants:

> the disabled man thinks it's wrong the drug user down the road gets methadone. The drug user is outraged that the large family next door gets a spare room and hopes they are hit by bedroom tax. The large family is sick of elderly people getting big houses they don't need. The elderly woman hopes these large families are forced to stop having kids once the money dries up. (Brady 2013)

Others note the operation of a politics of shame in the tendency for the poor to blame themselves for their own hardship, while simultaneously affording the 'well-to-do' an opportunity for self-righteous defamation' (Seabrook 2014). As mentioned, distinctions between the deserving and undeserving poor and conceptions of respectability have existed for a long time, but there is a particular cruelty to these vindictive responses evidenced by the shame felt by people who feel their situation is entirely their own personal responsibility, particularly when they lack the resources or alternative value systems to challenge this. This can be in part understood as resulting from the ideological work done by individualised notions of success and failure within neoliberalism, and the related rhetoric of 'meritocracy' and 'aspiration', and how these reinforce older conceptions of respectability.

MERITOCRACY AND THE INDIVIDUALISATION OF SUCCESS AND FAILURE

According to geographer Danny Dorling, social mobility has declined for the past thirty years; for those earning less than the average income it is now worse than it was in 1983 (Dorling 2013). The 2012 Poverty and Social Exclusion report (which measured inequality between 1983 and 2012) found that between 1983 and 2012, the wealthiest people became even wealthier while increasing numbers of people worried about money, felt shameful about their economic situations, lived in substandard housing – and – most recently, highlighted by the growing presence of food banks – were unable to feed themselves (PSE 2012). Meanwhile, unpaid internships and other forms of 'opportunity hoarding' ensure that children from wealthier backgrounds are more likely to enter well-paid jobs than children from less privileged backgrounds, including those who achieve better grades in school (McKnight 2015). However, despite this situation, the Coalition and Conservative majority governments have tended to frame poverty largely in terms of the (now discredited) transmission of poverty from one generation to another. This has manifested itself through a focus on poor parenting skills and the identification of 'troubled families', which David Gordon traces back to 'the Victorian "residuum" through theories of pauperism, social problem groups and multiple problem families to the underclass arguments of today' (Gordon 2011, 5). These theories originally were based in the eugenics movement. However, after the Second World War, eugenics became discredited and the emphasis shifted to the 'cultures of poverty' thesis. This thesis is based on the assumption that there is 'a significantly large, stable and relatively homogenous group of "poor" people in order for a culture to develop that is different from the culture of the rest of society'; this assumption has persisted to this day, despite not being substantiated by any scientific evidence (ibid.). Notably, this perspective has not been limited to right-wing policymakers; it was also the driving force behind punitive New Labour policies that were designed to manage 'failed citizen parents' through limiting financial and/or material aid. The belief was that these sanctions would force citizens to 'take responsibility' for their own welfare by finding work and 'be . . . more aspirational' for their children (Jensen 2013, 62). There was also a streak of social conservatism in some of New Labour's social policies demonstrated by their emphasis on 'community' and 'family', and the blaming of lone parents for crime and other social problems (Lavalette and Mooney 1999). This reveals continuities in terms of the perception of low-income parents as bad parents, as well as 'rough' versus 'respectable' distinctions.

Despite, or possibly because of this situation, the rhetoric of 'meritocracy' remains prevalent within political discourse, as in former Prime Minister David Cameron's 'Aspiration Nation' speech: 'We are building an Aspiration Nation. A country where it's not who you know, or where you're from; but who you are and where you're determined to go' (Cameron 2013 cited in Littler 2013). According to this rhetoric, 'talent' and 'effort' should be sufficient to be successful, regardless of one's social position (Littler 2013, 52). Jo Littler argues that the idea that we *should* live in a 'meritocracy' has become integral to 'contemporary structures of feeling', as it has become common sense across the political spectrum as well as within popular culture and education (ibid.). The rhetoric of meritocracy is also based in the assumption that we have moved on from the "bad old days" of deference and inherited privilege. Who wouldn't want to believe that we now live in a meritocratic society, and does giving up on the hope of this mean returning to that dark past?

As meritocracy is about individual, rather than collective, success, it is premised on a hierarchical and competitive system, which by nature creates winners and losers. According to Littler, 'unrealised talent is therefore both the necessary and structural condition of its existence' (Littler 2013, 54). Success is thus assumed to be the result of talent and effort rather than entrenched privilege; in this sense, while meritocracy acknowledges 'the need for social mobility' it simultaneously obscures social and economic inequality (Littler 2013, 55). To return to the discussion about harsh moral judgements, the converse of the celebration of individual talent and effort is the disparaging of those who do not succeed, as their failure is assumed to be their own fault. This connects to meritocracy's 'validation of upper-middle class values as norms to aspire to and its rendering of working-class cultures as abject'; as 'all movement must happen upwards', working-class culture becomes something to flee from, a signifier of lack of effort and ambition (ibid.). The discourse of meritocracy thus justifies the vilification of the poor and the unemployed, as their situation is seen to be the result of individual personal failings rather than structural conditions. This is how neoliberal individualism rehabilitates and perpetuates old prejudices about the undeserving poor, which now includes within the criteria for respectability the expectation that one be aspirational.

REALITY TELEVISION AS THE SCENE FOR DIVISIVE POLITICS

I will now explore the reality television genre as a site for the staging of social anxieties and moral judgements around social mobility and class, and for affirming or challenging narratives around meritocracy and respectability. In doing so, I am using Beverley Skeggs' and Helen Wood's framing of television as 'intervention' rather than 'representation' because of its emphasis on affect and reaction rather than on determined meaning (Bratich 2007 cited in Skeggs and Wood 2012, 11). There is a sense that reality television *does things* in the world; in Judith Butler's theorisation, it is *performative* (Butler 1990 cited in Skeggs and Wood 2012, 24). Reality television also has a particular value for policymakers because of its claim, as a documentary genre, to represent the 'truth'.

Reality television programmes such as *Benefits Street* and the Twitter reactions (to be discussed later) thus become key sites for articulating norms of belonging and unbelonging. In this sense, they operate as what Nick Couldry has termed 'media rituals', arguing that 'rituals can intensify conflict and exclusion as much as restoring unity and shared values' (2002, 137). In 'From Media Events to Ritual to Communicative Form', Eric Rothenbuhler argues that 'one aspect of rituals is that there is a process of codification – where people start to feel that there are expectations about how one should behave, and what sorts of cultural forms need to be produced' (2009, 66–67). In this case, the expression of scorn, outrage and derision as appropriate responses to poverty and unemployment (or representations of this) are activities that bring people together in affirming a sense of respectability, and in distinguishing them from those who are not respectable.

Reality television as a genre also has particular resonances with the question of meritocracy because reality stars are frequently criticised famous for being famous. Thus, it raises questions about achievement, worth and criteria for a proper career or a good family, and how these are gendered and classed. For example, in *Reacting to Reality Television*, Wood and Skeggs draw on findings of an audience study[3] of female reality television viewers, which found that the working-class respondents thought that the reality television stars did well for themselves, but that the middle-class respondents saw them as getting something for nothing, and therefore not deserving their success (2012, 203). Working-class respondents also judged the aspirational working-class women in *Wife Swap* as pretentious and 'non-caring' bad mothers (2012, 180).

It is in the sub-genre of 'poverty porn' reality television where such reactions and judgements have become particularly intense in either affirming people within the category of respectability or cruelly rejecting them. According to Tracey Jensen, the term 'poverty porn' has uncertain origins, but she notes that it was first used to critique fictional representations of the developing world, notably the film *Slumdog Millionaire*'s depiction of India. More recently it has been used to characterise post-recession representations of poverty as entertainment (Jensen 2014, 5). *Benefits Street* is part of this apparently popular formula of reality programmes about benefits and the welfare state which achieved a high profile in 2013–2014, including *We Pay for Your Benefits* (BBC1), *Benefits Britain 1949* (Channel 4), *Skint* (Channel 4), *On Benefits and Proud* (Channel 5) and continuing with programmes such as *Britain's Hardest Worker* (to be discussed later on).

Benefits Street followed the lives of the residents of James Turner Street in Birmingham, particularly Deirdre Kelly ('White Dee'), a former office worker on long-term disability benefits, who looks after many people in the neighbourhood. She was characterised in the final chat show episode by *Telegraph* columnist Alison Pearson as 'a one-woman Citizens' Advice Bureau'. Fungi, Dee's friend who engaged in substance use and, in the programme, suffered a series of mishaps, often called on her for help. To set the stage, the first episode began with one of the local residents pointing out all the houses on the street where people were unemployed, which turned out to be most of them. The residents engaged in benefits fraud, shoplifting, selling small items door to door and doing odd jobs; they contended with struggles with the benefits system, the electricity being cut off, children being taken into care and so forth. The programme confirmed many of the stereotypes of the unemployed as feckless, bad parents, involved in criminal activity and so forth. While some of these activities (e.g., the selling of items door to door) might from another perspective be seen as resourceful and inventive examples of entrepreneurialism, they were presented as dubious activities on this programme. There were rare moments of compassion. As Helen Wood observes in her analysis of the programme: 'Dee's caring for the hapless addict Fungi, the violent exploitation of migrant workers, Mark's efforts to get help from the food bank with the wrong paperwork, the door-to-door sales of 50p items to those who's benefits have been stopped' (Wood 2014). However, these perspectives were overshadowed by the repetitive images of 'the constant smoking, the sitting (in houses or on sofas in the road), the shouting, the drinking and so forth that get distilled and used as evidence to support the rhetoric of the lazy "scrounger"' (ibid.). The programme finished with a chat show panel discussion – which did not engage with the politics of representation, or require the filmmakers or the audience to consider their responsibility in the perpetuation of the scrounger stereotype, but left the participants to defend their personal situations and the conditions of benefits claimants in general (ibid.).

CONTROVERSIES

In the following section, I will not focus on the details of the programme itself, but on the reactions and wider controversies around it, as these issues spilled beyond the screen into wider public debate. Much of the controversy around the programme focused on allegations of misrepresentation. Residents of James Turner Street claimed that they were told that the show was supposed to be about 'neighbourly togetherness and community spirit' – only to find out later that it was called 'Benefits Street'. One local resident stated that 'we opened our doors and hearts to them and they violated us and abused our trust' (Stuart 2014). A couple were filmed for the programme, but when it was found that they were in work, they were not included in the final edit (Saul 2014). Nine hundred complaints were made to the media regulator Ofcom about the programme's depiction of criminal activities and its representation of children, although the regulator later ruled that these did not warrant further investigation (Sweeney 2014). While an extensive discussion of media ethics is outside the framework of this chapter, *Benefits Street* raises many questions about the politics of representation and the uses of controversy to reinforce, rather than challenge, stereotypes. Despite the claims of its creators to 'provoke debate', there was no real attempt at reflection on their social responsibility (Wood 2014), the representation of the participants or the role of audiences in the consumption of such stereotypes.

The programme also featured prominently in political debates on benefits. In the House of Commons, Conservative MP Philip Davies posed the following question:

> Has the Secretary of State managed to watch programmes such as 'Benefits Street' and 'On Benefits & Proud'? If so, has he, like me, been struck by the number of people on them who manage to combine complaining about welfare reform with being able to afford to buy copious amounts of cigarettes, have lots of tattoos, and watch Sky TV on the obligatory widescreen television? Does he understand the concerns and irritation of many people who go to work every day and pay their taxes but cannot afford those kinds of luxuries? (Hansard 13 January 2014)

In response, *Mirror* columnist Ros Wynne-Jones described how, in Davies' constituency of Shipley (which she termed the 'real Benefits Street'), a man had frozen to death, unable to heat his home properly because his benefits had been stopped. She accused Davies of 'gloating' (Wynne-Jones 2015). Iain Duncan Smith MP, Secretary of State for Work and Pensions, referred to the programme as justification for benefit cuts, arguing that it demonstrated how the previous Labour administration had been out of touch with the reality of 'communities which for the most part remain out of sight' (Wintour 2014). He claimed to be on 'a crusade to rescue Benefits Street Britain' through welfare reform (Dominiczak 2014). Such rhetoric affirms the stereotypes with which this book has thus far been concerned. Gadgets (e.g., the obligatory reference to the widescreen television) are seen to be luxuries that people should not have, because poverty should be *suffering* and *deprivation*. Smith's comment about unemployed people being 'out of sight' and ignored by the Labour Party evokes the familiar trope of the out-of-touch liberals who are 'soft' because they are insulated from the difficult truths about the poor, which television programmes such as *Benefits Street* reveal. It is authoritarian populist rhetoric – tough welfare measures justified by speaking for 'the people'. Notably it is assumed that these 'feckless poor' are not part of the audience; it is we, the respectable, who are being interpellated. Such statements reassure us that we are *normal* as they simultaneously stoke our outrage at the unemployed.

In addition to these controversies, *Benefits Street* also provoked some very strong online reactions, which will be the focus of the next section. I am using Skeggs' and Wood's theorisation of 'reacting' as 'something immediate and instantaneous and residing in bodily form, in order to be felt', and as 'the interaction between opposing forces, propelling elements to different sides' (2012, 5). Beyond the interpretation and making meaning from media texts studied by audience research, 'reacting' captures the emotional dimension of audiences' relationship to media. They are working with emotion as the codification and translation of affect into ideas (Deleuze 1978), and using this to explore the relationships between audiences and texts, but also between people (Skeggs and Wood 2012, 6). It is thus useful for considering the relationship of audiences to the *Benefits Street* characters and to each other on social media.

I will now turn to the Twitter reactions to *Benefits Street*, based on a pilot study of a sample of fifty tweets from the nights when the show was broadcast, using the #benefitsstreet hashtag, in which I studied their content and their emotional tone. Many of the tweets derided and vilified the people on the programme, affirming stereotypes of the unemployed as lazy, stupid, bad parents and as squandering taxpayers' money on objects of conspicuous consumption like flat-screen televisions or other gadgets. There was also a sense that expressing such judgements was enjoyable. Such responses were encouraged by the programme, which periodically flashed the #benefitsstreet hashtag on the screen.

Not surprisingly, many of the tweets in the sample expressed disgust and derision directed at the people on the programme, and, on the 13th of January and 27th of January, this was the most common sentiment expressed. However, on the 20th of January and the 17th of February, more of the tweets expressed disgust and outrage at the government for implementing cuts, and on the 10th of February, outrage was directed at public attitudes towards the unemployed. Drawing on Judith Butler's concept of performative speech acts, Sara Ahmed explores the performative utterance of disgust, arguing that 'it works precisely by citing norms and conventions that already exist' (Butler cited in Ahmed 2004). She argues that:

> The speech act is always spoken to others, whose shared witnessing of the disgusting thing is required for the affect to have an effect. In other words, the subject asks others to repeat the condemnation implicit in the speech act itself. Such a shared witnessing is required for speech acts to be generative, that is, for therefore the attribution of disgust to an object or other to stick to others. (Ahmed 2004, 94)

It is useful then to apply this to the derision expressed and the consequent affirmation of stereotypes in the tweets. The tweets involve the performative articulation of a sense of respectability and normality, sharing it with followers and retweeters. These reactions can be seen as performative utterances where, through deriding or expressing outrage at others, one both articulates a shared norm and positions one's self as belonging to it, among an audience of those who are also performing respectability. According to Belinda Morrissey and Susan Yell, the simplicity of Twitter as social media allows its participants 'the feeling of being in the same time as those they follow, regardless of their geographical distance' (2016, 37). They also argue that 'the very nature of the medium, and the spare nature of the conversation it encourages, . . . creates its extraordinary affective intensity' (ibid.). Therefore, we can say that the performative nature of the tweets and the affective intensity of the communication contribute to the development of, and also affirm, a *public mood* defined by a shared sense of outrage against the unemployed. However, the ambiguity of the tweets in my small sample suggests that there is room within social media for other perspectives. Many were equally outraged by the exploitative nature of the programme and the stereotyping of the James Turner Street residents. I will return to this towards the end of the chapter.

TROLLING OR PRO-AUSTERITY COMMON SENSE?

The next section will examine these reactions to *Benefits Street* in terms of online culture. Can we interpret the crueller responses as a form of trolling or rather as an online expression of pro-austerity common sense? According to Emma Jane, the literature on trolling has historically tended to focus on defining it as a technological problem or a social problem, or is more pragmatically focused on how to respond to e-bile within online learning or business contexts, rather than considering its ethical ramifications (Jane 2014, 538). Other literature has tended towards techno-libertarianism, presenting trolls as 'misunderstood tricksters' or as 'engaged in laudable and savvy resistance to mainstream media norms' (Lange 2006 and Philips 2011 cited in Jane 2012). These perspectives pay much less attention to or express concern towards its victims (Jane 2012, 539). However, Jane suggests that such communication is not an aberration, but could be the norm, citing Jaron Lanier's comments that 'the culture of sadism on-line . . . has gone mainstream' and that trolling 'is not a string of isolated incidents, but the status quo in the online world' (2010 cited in Jane 2012, 540). She argues that 'the internet and technology-based interactions no longer constitute occasional adjuncts of off-line existence, but have become dominant – and integrated – parts of contemporary existence itself' (Jane 2012, 542). The editors of *Fibreculture*'s 2014 special issue on trolling acknowledge that 'spreadability, instantaneity, labyrinthine backchannels and nodal proliferations do not inevitably secure a pluralist conversation – they are also used to fortify privilege' (2014, 8).

It is this fortification of privilege that I wish to explore. How do expressions of online bile operate as a norm rather than an exception? In particular, how do these responses assert distinctions between those who are respectable and those who are not, and then expose those who fall on the wrong side of the line to moral judgements and derision? In 'What Trolling Can Teach Us about Race' (2014), Tanner Higgin argues that the internet, as a site of political fantasy, nurtures what Vincent Mosco calls 'the central myths of our time: the end of history, the end of geography and the end of politics' (2005 cited in Higgin 2014). She points out that:

> the unifying thread behind all three dominant myths is an illusory freedom whether it be from past violence, market borders, or cultural politics. Not coincidentally, all of these freedoms are especially desirable for free market loving white men of able means looking to escape responsibility for persistent, institutionalized oppression. (Higgin 2014, 140)

Similarly, in *This Is Why We Can't Have Nice Things* (2016), Whitney Phillips argues that trolling is 'born out of and embedded within the dominant institutions and tropes, which are every bit as damaging as the trolls' most disruptive behaviours' (2016, 11). I am taking on board the idea of trolling as an intrinsic aspect of everyday experience and embedded within dominant institutions and tropes rather than as aberration or 'glitch' (Nakamura 2013), or an activity that is essentially a form of deviant behaviour carried out by badly behaved individuals (which is what the term 'trolling' implies). Rather than a manifestation of hate speech (although anonymity enables some of the more extreme responses), these reactions can be interpreted as a banal – if cruel – online expression of status quo values. These reactions also reflect how some of the pleasures of the internet can maintain dominant social hierarchies (of race, gender, class ability sexuality). Within the context of austerity, they justify benefit cuts as the people who receive them are seen to be undeserving of public money. Such reactions are ultimately about experiencing pleasure and humour at the expense of the powerless – in this case those on the sharp end of austerity – and reinforcing perceptions that they deserve their fate as well as any ridicule they receive. In this sense these online reactions cement a public mood, to the extent that it feels *right,* it feels socially acceptable to judge and deride people in this way, rather than asking questions about the structural conditions of poverty, or why cuts are being made that affect the poorest.

BAD HABITS AND RECKLESS LIFESTYLES

Many of the reactions on Twitter had a rather smug and derisive tone, laughing at what they perceived as the stupidity of the James Turner Street residents:

> I must be the unluckiest guy in the world . . . Or the biggest retard on the estate lol #benefitsstreet.
>
> (10 February 2014)

> Boys at college doin there GCSE[4]'s [*sic*] and thinking they're the dons[5]! #future #stars #off #benefitsstreet
>
> (27 January 2014)

Other comments were about lifestyle: smoking in particular was seen as evidence of poor health, reckless spending and bad etiquette:

> The way that guy smokes on Benefits Street. OMGGGGG #benefitsstreet.
>
> (10 February 2014)

> #benefitsstreet begging for food with a pack of 20 cigs in their hand #priorities
>
> (27 January 2014)

The hashtag #priorities was being used to indicate that people had the wrong priorities – in this case referring to lifestyle choices, as well as the familiar trope of bad parenting:

> Callin his daughter for the 1st time in a yr, dropped his phone n his beer n picked up his beer n drank it 1st #priorites [*sic*] #benefitsstreet.
>
> (27 January 2014)

Reactions on Twitter were not confined to the programme itself; there were even attempts to look at James Turner Street on Google Street View. One tweet circulated a photograph from Google Street View of a woman eating in front of her house:

> Ginge off benefits street on google maps eating McDonald's in her garden #BenefitsStreet pic.twitter.com/G4YikX2uPM
>
> (27 January 2014)

It was assumed that the woman was eating fast food from McDonalds, although the photograph was not close enough to identify what she was eating. This reveals how easy it is to project assumptions (e.g., the eating of unhealthy fast food) and moralise around bad lifestyles, which, implicitly, are a burden on the NHS (and thus the taxpayer, justifying the sense of outrage). There is also a sense of pleasure in expressing this outrage, and in the confirming of stereotypes.

BAD PARENTING

Bad parenting was one of the most common references in the sample. There were many comments about reporting parents to Social Services, and epithets such as 'feral', 'hideous' and 'so-called parents'. Notably, 'socialism' is blamed in one of the comments as encouraging irresponsible behaviour – suggesting the welfare state is itself to blame. However, in other cases the welfare state (as represented by Social Services) is called on to intervene in what is seen to be an unacceptable situation. This reveals contradictory perceptions of the welfare state as both encouraging feckless behaviour and as intervening to stop it:

> I hope social services go round that horrid woman's house tomorrow. Dragging the poor 5 yr old around and swearing at him #benefitsstreet.
>
> (8 March 2014)

> I don't blame the feckless, feral benefits parasites of #benefitsstreet. I blame the socialism that put them there. It is evil.
>
> (10 February 2014)

> why aren't those hideous, so called parents known to social services! Those poor children are neglected!! #benefitsstreet
>
> (8 March 2014)

These sorts of reactions belong to a long history of portrayals of poor and working-class mothers as bad parents. This includes not only poverty porn but also mainstream media representations of 'poor parenting'. Morally correct parenting has been normalised by the phenomenon of instructional reality television programmes, in which people are shown by television presenters how to live better lives. An early example of this was *Supernanny,* a programme that ran on *Channel 4* between 2004 and 2010, featuring professional nanny Jo Frost. Frost helped families who were struggling with parenting, showing them how to discipline their children. The programme focused on the role of the mother as primarily responsible for maintaining order in the household, with any failings seen to be her personal fault. As Rebecca Feasey argues, rather than the misbehaving children, it is the 'lenient, weak and fragile maternal figure that is the family problem that needs to be re-educated' (2011). Working-class mothers who were struggling financially and lacked the time and resources to 'educate [their children] inventively, entertain them and inspire them creatively' were slated by the programme for particular scorn. There was little acknowledgement of the material challenges they were facing (ibid.). This further normalised the notion of working-class people as bad parents (Jensen 2013, 62). Emotional responses such as scorn and derision, which were mobilised by *Supernanny,* easily become transferred to other programmes such as *Benefits Street,* as part of the broader public mood in which it is socially acceptable to judge the poor and unemployed.

GENDERED, CLASSED PERSONAL ATTACKS

By far, the cruellest Twitter attacks were directed at the main character, White Dee. There was much attention paid to her appearance, specifically her weight and the size of her breasts, as well as speculation about whether or not she wore a bra.

> Can't wait to see white D's saggy double G's later. Hope fungi gets a starring role he's been pushed aside by the Romanians #benefitsstreet (20 February 2014).
>
> Would you shag White Dee? #benefitsstreet well we know u would!! #cupids. . . #grabagranny (27 January 2014)
>
> Final episode of #benefitsstreet and white [dee] still doesn't have a bra (10 February 2014)!!!

The gendered aspect of these online reactions is worth closer attention. In *Formations of Class and Gender* (1997), Skeggs explores how the body and bodily dispositions carry markers of social class (1997, 82). In focus group discussions with working-class women in the North West, class, gender and the self-regulation of the body were frequent themes, as well as fear of downward mobility (the term used for this was 'letting go') (ibid.). Skeggs argues that 'fat signifies immovability; social mobility, [the focus group respondents] maintain, is less likely in a fat body' (1997, 83). The focus group respondents also suggested that 'the working-class body which is signalled through fat is the one that has given up the hope of ever improving, of becoming middle class' (ibid.). Within the online responses to *Benefits Street*, White Dee became an embodiment of the woman who has 'let herself go' ('the saggy double G's'), thus deserving to be made an object of scorn.

Angela McRobbie examines the disappearance of sympathetic portrayals of the working-class mother in 'Feminism, the Family and the New Mediated Maternalism' (2013), which explains attitudes towards White Dee. She notes that the 'strong, working-class mother, the kind of stalwart of the community which [Richard] Hoggart described so vividly and before him DH Lawrence . . . has almost gone from the popular imagination' (McRobbie 2013, 125). Instead, mothers are now either exemplary (2013, 120), the 'active (i.e. en route to the gym), sexually confident [mother]' or else they are shameful and abject: 'the slovenly and benefit-dependent "underclass" single mother, the UK equivalent of the US "welfare queen"' (ibid.). McRobbie sees this as symptomatic of a wider political shift in which 'social democracy is in decline, . . . welfare is widely targeted as wasteful and . . . there are fewer voices in politics, media or in public policy fields defending these principles' (2013, 125). There are a few residual traces of positive portrayals of working-class women in the scenes of Dee helping other local residents (the 'one-woman Citizen's Advice Bureau'), but none of these provoked any reactions in the Twitter sample (as will be discussed, resistance took the form of general critiques of the show rather than sympathy with the characters).

SCHADENFREUDE

Some of the tweets expressed a palpable form of pleasure in judging and making fun of White Dee and the other residents of *Benefits Street*. This derision and disgust could be understood in terms of what Sianne Ngai calls 'ugly feelings' (Ngai 2005). Ngai's book of the same title (2005) explores banal emotions or 'minor affects' such as envy or irritation, rather than more dramatic emotions such as anger or fear. These emotions, as Ngai argues, are amoral and non-cathartic, and do not offer therapeutic release (2005, 6). Bad feelings are worthy of attention because they function as a diagnostic for conditions of blocked agency, inaction (Ngai 2005, 21) and social powerlessness (Ngai 2005, 30). She argues that these emotions do not solve the problems of disempowerment, but can help us better understand it as a social phenomenon. Thus, the emotional responses highlighted by the Twitter reactions can help us understand how they are expressed within conditions of individualised atomisation and a lack of collective agency for meaningfully challenging inequality, in the face of increasing precarity and the persistence of social norms about meritocracy and respectability. As one's hold on these social norms becomes more tenuous, the distancing activities performed in the tweets described serve a reassuring and even pleasurable purpose – affirming one's belonging to the category of respectable people.

There is another, related pleasure expressed through these reactions, which is a form of *schadenfreude* – pleasure in the misfortune of others, particularly those who have become public figures, whose lives thus become open to scrutiny. The inhabitants of James Turner Street thus become subject to what Steve Cross and Jo Littler call 'celebrity schadenfreude' (2010) – which is pleasure at the misfortune of celebrities. The James Turner Street residents, through participating in the programme, became celebrities and were thus treated as fair game. They argue that:

> A widespread popular hostility to celebrities undoubtedly exists. It emerges 'outside', or between the cracks, of 'professionally'-produced media culture (everyday banter, email jokes, bitchy blogs), but also within those not so hallowed spaces themselves (snide comments in newspaper columns, 'revealing insights' in magazines devoted to celebrity lives).
>
> (2010, 396)

I would add to this that social media, and particularly Twitter, is a key site for celebrity schadenfreude.

Cross and Littler argue that celebrity schadenfreude is the result of a thwarted desire for equality that is unable to think of it as anything other than 'levelling through humiliation' (2010, 397). This is about a hierarchy of misery in which everyone must suffer, and any gains, including collective ones, are conceived of in individualised terms, as getting 'special treatment'. Cross and Littler attribute this to a contradiction or slippage between the intrinsic value of self-worth, and the worth of the self under capitalism (2010, 406), as well as contradictions between desires for equality and fears of it (ibid.). This is why the issue of deserving one's fame and success becomes so important – if one is seen to be undeserving then scorn and derision become appropriate responses, and the idea of someone who is not respectable being famous provokes particular outrage and scandal. As Cross and Littler argue:

> the tensions between such performances of being 'one of us' and conspicuous displays of wealth is held in check so long as worth is earned and so long as the celebrity function as an emblem of making it, in other words, as emblematic of *aspiration*. Losses of wealth, health, looks, career collapses, everyday misfortunes can be celebrated and enjoyed in direct proportion to their apparent deservedness. (2010, 406–407)

Cross and Littler argue that celebrity schadenfreude is quite common within tabloid culture, such as the glee displayed towards female celebrities who do not look their best or whose lives are falling apart (2010, 411). They also point out that the boisterous address of tabloid culture, rather than being used to challenge power, is frequently deployed towards conservative ends such as anti-democratic populism and 'increased commodification rather than enhanced political enfranchisement' (Carey 1988 and Turner 1997 cited in Cross and Littler 2010, 411). Right-wing tabloid discourses (as opposed to Left tabloid discourses, as the authors point out) are not opposed to the principle of privileges being granted, but are merely angry that they have been granted to the wrong people (2010, 411). As mentioned, reality stars such as the residents of James Turner Street, with their dubious claim to fame, are particularly susceptible as targets. If they do not deserve their celebrity status, then the act of taking them down becomes not only morally justified but also pleasurable (which is possibly another way the attacks on White Dee can be interpreted).

NEWSJACKING AND OTHER COUNTER-RESPONSES

However not all online responses to *Benefits Street* consisted of derision or moral judgement. Many of the responses – in fact slightly greater than the number of derisive comments – were critical of benefit cuts and the demonisation of the unemployed. Because of the publicity surrounding the television series, many campaigners saw the programme as an opportunity to raise public awareness around poverty and unemployment. The visibility of the event meant there was a sense of something being at stake, in part due to an increasing awareness of how programmes such as *Benefits Street* were used to justify benefit cuts. There were thus many attempts to newsjack the #benefitsstreet hashtag to raise concerns around in-work poverty, the bedroom tax, cuts to disability benefits and so on:

> #Bedroomtax Meacher calls Dickensian #poverty #hoc with two thirds disabled and 90% with no smaller properties available #benefitsstreet.

Other responses on Twitter specifically responded to the programme as a negative representation of the unemployed. For example, the disability rights group Disabled People Protest held a Twitter demo against *Benefits Street*'s producer, Love Productions:

> Monday 13th Twitter Demo against Love Productions supporting Street Demo against #BenefitsStreetshar.es/9PQIT via @Dis_PPL_Protest (13 January 2014) http://dftr.org.uk/BenefitsStreet/songbird.php

These tweets reflect an awareness of how disabled people are being demonised by the media and politicians as 'scroungers', and how programmes such as *Benefits Street* contribute to this. Some of these tweets intervened to make the point about the disproportionate over-representation of the feckless poor and the under-representation of white-collar crimes (leading to the well-documented misperceptions about benefits costing more to the taxpayer than tax fraud) – and in doing so challenging the very distinction of respectable versus unrespectable. Others used #benefitsstreet to redirect attention to tax fraud, corporate greed and cronyism:

> 177 MPs who voted for #BedroomTax[6] claim up to £25,000 each in accommodation expenses #BenefitsBritain #BenefitsStreet pic.twitter.com/JyWA4xamXT
> (17 February 2014)

COUNTER-PLEASURES

Some of the tweets also expressed subversive counter-pleasures: subverting dominant messages through parody and redirecting attention away from the powerless and towards the powerful. One example of this was through the use of photoshopped spoofs such as the following tweet which made fun of controversial right-wing commentator Katie Hopkins by comparing her to a Margaret Thatcher puppet from the 1980s comedy programme *Spitting Image:*

> Finally worked out who KTHopkins looks like #spittingimage #benefitsstreet pic.twitter.com/mwEtbyRQXB

This was also highlighted in the spoof site *Parasite Street* which was also advertised via Twitter, a site about an expensive street in Mayfair, London, which was inhabited by a cast of unsavoury multimillionaire characters: Sir Philip Green, chair of the Arcadia group and controversial for his tax arrangements; Richard Ricci, former head of Barclays Bank investment banking during the Libor scandal; Charles Gow, a buy-to-let landlord who bought and sold council properties back to local authorities at inflated prices and Philip Clarke, the CEO of the supermarket chain Tesco, who refuses to pay staff the Living Wage.[7]

Some of the tweets in the sample expressed scorn and anger at audiences who believe the scrounger hype.

> #benefitsstreet haters, you are simply boring, because you are simply ignorant. Poor little #Sheeple
>
> (10 February 2014)

> Never watched #benefitsstreet but it brings some vile tweets from the arseholes of the judgemental bigots doesn't it? #morons

This response was about judging the audience of the programme (ironically by calling them judgemental), calling them 'bigots', 'morons' and 'sheep' – and the language being used here is quite strong, as in the use of the term 'vile' and 'arseholes' – an indication of the emotionally loaded nature of the debate. This is ironic as it could be argued that these reactions express the same scorn and derision towards the Twitter users who judge the *Benefits Street* characters (similar to commenters below the line who correct the grammar of other commenters). There is something unsatisfyingly predictable and 'tit for tat' about such responses. Similar to those they critique, such reactions could also function as assertions of superiority and they are also intended to bring together others who feel superior. It is worth returning to Ngai again, and her observations about the ambivalence of ugly feelings (2005, 5). These feelings can be mobilised for different political purposes and do not exclusively belong to the Left or the Right, but there are questions about whether such responses generate new types of feelings or questions, or just affirm pre-existing camps.

However, another, less obvious, but equally significant, response was the sharing of personal testimonies and poems. Openly revealing one's experience of poverty or life on benefits is a courageous and self-revealing act – courageous because it means risking the online ridicule, judgement and scorn directed at the James Turner Street residents. It also humanises the debate to a certain extent and problematises distinctions between the deserving and undeserving.

> I wrote this after a prog similar to #benefitsstreet but it applies here too. 'On Benefits & Working' http://underoccupied.net/2013/11/22/on-benefits-and-working/ (10 February 2014).

This blog post is written by someone who is living on benefits as he is caring for his severely disabled grandson. He shares his personal testimony about the experience but also talks about the fact that most people who are on benefits are actually in work – thereby challenging the stereotype of people on benefits being unemployed.

Another shared a poem entitled 'Benefits-land', using the #Benefitsstreet hashtag.

> Please read & RT. . . . Benefits-land? #poem http://po.st/JiKSVw #BenefitsStreet #BenefitsBritain (17 February 2014)

The poem included the following lines:

> I once stood in a line,
> I too signed to get mine.

And:

> Love thy neighbour?
> Not on my street!

This structure called society,
Is falling like a house of cards. (Slimstone 2014)

Given the divisiveness of the debate on benefits, this is a courageous expression of vulnerability, as it involves making visible one's dependency on the benefits system, and acknowledging that one is not entirely a self-made individual (although it could be argued that the convention of online anonymity may shield one from this). These tweets also function as defences of the benefits system itself. In *Dispossession* (2013), Judith Butler and Athena Athanasiou call for a performative politics that is connected to an acknowledgement of one's vulnerability and interdependency (which I also understand to mean the welfare state). I interpret this as making one's vulnerability public and breaking the taboos of shame that have become associated with public discourse on benefits. This will be discussed in the final chapter in greater detail. However, it is worth flagging up the subversive pleasures in letting go of the pressure to be respectable and the fear that one might be judged or ridiculed if one's life choices or lifestyle is found to be lacking. In the context of austerity, such pleasures challenge the distinctions between the respectable and unrespectable which underpin the existing system. It is making one's vulnerability public, and risking opening one's self up to online scorn, derision and personal attacks. Online personal attacks have been highlighted by feminist media scholars in particular in connection to 'networked misogyny', particularly following a string of high-profile trolling cases (Banet-Weiser and Miltner 2016) (Morrissey and Yell 2016), but other forms of discrimination and judgement, including attacks on the unemployed, are also worthy of consideration. This is what makes Slimstone's admission courageous.

DEVELOPMENTS SINCE *BENEFITS STREET:* POVERTY PORN AS A CONTROVERSIAL AND SUCCESSFUL GENRE

At the time of writing, it has been a year and a half since the airing of the *Benefits Street* programme. The production company, Love Productions, has become increasingly controversial, as they became associated with exploitative filmmaking and misrepresentations of local residents. A second season was filmed in 2014 in Stockton-on-Tees, which was met with a counter-campaign by local residents entitled 'Positively Stockton-on-Tees (psst)' (Valios 2015), and was condemned by the council, community groups and local MP Alex Cunningham (McNeal 2014). The following year, their attempt to film *Immigration Street* (following a similar formula of reality television featuring controversial subjects) led to a large-scale backlash by Southampton residents that forced the production company to reduce the series from six episodes to one (Sherwin 2015).

The poverty porn subgenre has become more controversial, leading programmes, such as *Skint* (which had been in existence since 2004), to attract protests (which had not taken place in the past). When KEO Films attempted to film a season in Grimsby, for instance, they were met with protests by local residents (Burrell 2014); local MP Austin Mitchell called Channel 4 'deplorable and dishonest', and accused the station of 'poverty tourism' (Methven 2014). However, despite such controversy, there have been other examples of the genre, indicating it continues to be lucrative. In 2015, the BBC announced that it would begin filming a programmed entitled *Britain's Hardest Worker*, in which unemployed people would compete for low-paid part-time jobs and undergo a series of tasks and challenges, with the 'least productive' eliminated. The prize was a cash sum equivalent to year's income on a living wage outside of London (£15,000). The news of the filming provoked some angry responses on Twitter, particularly those using the #povertyporn hashtag:

> Julie Smith@lazyjoolz
> BBC #povertyporn hunger game style reality show for low paid http://ind.pn/1FDlEi5 Is this real or something cooked up in episode of W1A? (28 May 2015)
> @BBCOne @bbctrust @bbcpress @TwentyTwentyTV I'm not paying a licence fee so you can make more #povertyporn (28 May 2015)
> John Dyer-Causton@JohnDyerCauston
> BBC's new reality TV show: Benefits Street meets The Hunger Games http://ind.pn/1FDlEi5 #schadenfreude #povertyporn (28 May 2015)

These responses make references to *The Hunger Games*, the dystopian science fiction film involving poor people participating in a televised death-match – and reflecting the perceived cruelty of the programme. There are also questions raised about the responsibility of the BBC as a public service broadcaster, and who the BBC speaks for, and who is excluded (a question which has been asked many times, but it is notable that it is being asked yet again). A petition was launched on Change.org, which received nearly 30,000 signatures and called on the BBC to abandon the programme. Some of the comments included:

> There is too much exploitation of the disenfranchised and impoverished. Perhaps my fears about the break-up of the BBC are misplaced – it is already beyond saving if it commissions such immoral crap.
> This disgusting and divisive 'concept' shouldn't have passed the 'ideas' stage let alone actually be produced. Even worse is the fact this is with public money. (28 May 2015)
> The BBC has become more and more crass in its output in recent years. This is a new low for the public broadcaster – insulting the very people who fund it.

> The producers take us for fools if they think we accept their programme as a 'serious social experiment'. As if it will lead anywhere or contribute meaningfully to any debate about low pay – it's a cheap game show with a paltry prize that won't change anybody's life for the better. (29 May 2015)

The popularity of poverty porn has thus led to questions being raised about the role of public service broadcasters such as the BBC. Equally, questions have been raised about the impacts on communities where filming takes place. For example, White Dee was forced to move away from the neighbourhood due to her mixed-race children receiving online threats (McKinney 2014). In an interview with *The Guardian*, she claimed that the programme had destructive effects on the neighbourhood: 'This documentary turned our street into a tourist attraction. They turned us into figures of hate' (Press Association 2015). The petition and the protests against *Britain's Hardest Worker* as well as subsequent episodes of *Benefits Street* and *Immigration Street* also suggest a challenge to libertarian conceptions of controversy as provoking debate, particularly when it is used to reinforce stereotypes and existing power hierarchies and attack the vulnerable.

CONCLUSION: TWITTER AS A SITE FOR AFFIRMING OR CHALLENGING AUSTERITY

I have explored the role of concepts of respectability and meritocracy in debates about welfare, and the scorn and judgement directed towards the unemployed (those perceived to be failures) as the other side of the celebration of individual success. I have examined how these concepts have played out through the reactions and controversies surrounding *Benefits Street,* which is significant as a reality television programme for the claims it makes on the truth. In particular, the online reactions to the programme have demonstrated the positions taken in relation to the benefits debate. This is a space where one can engage in punitive discourses about how benefits recipients are lazy, undisciplined, bad parents and so on. These reactions can possibly be interpreted as expressions of denial of one's own precarity: *it won't happen to me*. Following Ahmed, they can also be seen as performative utterances which reinforce norms and divisions between insiders and outsiders. They can also involve particular pleasures: schadenfreude towards those on the sharp end of austerity or in the affirmation of one's own respectability through judging and deriding others who are worse off. Given the anonymity of much participatory and social media (many of these comments were posted under pseudonyms), it is very easy to do this with few consequences. However, Twitter can also be the site for challenging stereotypes, staging protests and engaging in subversive parodies. It can also be a space for demonstrating one's solidarity – through personal testimonies that show that those affected by benefit cuts are not alone, that talking about the experience of being on welfare is not shameful, and through challenging easy stereotypes and scapegoating. In many ways, it is through these responses, these processes of identification and dis-identification, as much as arguments about economics, and in these sorts of online contexts, that austerity as public mood can be affirmed or challenged.

NOTES

1. In the United Kingdom, some benefits and tax credits are paid to people who are in work, but are low pay. See https://www.citizensadvice.org.uk/benefits/in-work-or-looking-for-work/benefits-and-tax-credits-for-people-in-work/.

2. The term 'middle class' as it is used in the United Kingdom is possibly closer to the upper class in the North American context, where the term 'middle class' is more commonly used to describe the situation of most ordinary people.

3. The research consisted of focus groups carried out with forty women in South London between 2005 and 2008. Using a Bourdieuisan framework around forms of capital, Skeggs and Wood identified the class position of the women through in-depth interviews in which questions were asked about a range of issues, education, social position, work, housing, consumption habits, taste and so forth. (Skeggs and Wood 2012, 113–114).

4. The General Certificate of Secondary Education (GCSE) is a secondary school qualification.

5. A don is the head of a college at Oxford or Cambridge.

6. The Bedroom Tax is a cut in housing benefit (a subsidy paid to those who do not earn enough to cover housing costs) to those living in social housing who are deemed to have a 'spare bedroom'. See http://england.shelter.org.uk/get_advice/housing_benefit_and_local_housing_allowance/changes_to_housing_benefit/bedroom_tax.

7. The Living Wage is calculated every year by the Living Wage Foundation to reflect the wages which would be necessary for employees to make a living, beyond the minimum wage. The Living Wage Foundation runs an accreditation scheme for employers who pay the Living Wage.

Chapter 4

Immigration, Austerity
and the Welfare State

This chapter will consider controversies and tensions around immigration and the welfare state which have become increasingly fraught within the austerity context. I will examine the normalisation of bordering practices as incorporated into the institutions of the welfare state. These have become sites of surveillance and policing, creating the expectation for public sector workers to act as proxy border agents, and for immigrants to feel their access to public services is precarious and contingent. In order to consider these issues, I will draw on material from an interview I conducted with an immigration advisor (whom I have given a pseudonym)[1] conducted as part of the Mapping Immigration Controversies project, who discussed his experiences of anti-immigration views in his interactions with public sector workers and was the only respondent in the project who specifically discussed these issues. This material will be used to examine the convergence between neoliberal conceptions of the self-reliant subject and nostalgic conceptions of national identity.

The wider context for this discussion is a series of legislative changes which led to restricting non-European immigrants' access to the welfare state (specifically the 2014 and 2015/2016 Immigration Acts). This legislation has outsourced immigration controls to public and voluntary sector institutions, and even private individuals (e.g., landlords), placing a duty on them to report irregular immigrants to the authorities or else face fines and other sanctions. These policy measures have been justified by moral panics around 'benefit tourism',[2] immigrants' perceived reliance on welfare benefits or the United Kingdom's supposedly generous benefits system as a 'draw' (BBC 2016). These moral panics also played an important role in the vote to leave the European Union, despite the fact that the numbers they refer to are statistically insignificant (Migrants Rights Network 2016).

The persistent belief that immigrants are a drain on the system resists statistics-based arguments about the economic contribution of immigrants or the fact that they are working and paying tax, or are less likely to depend on benefits than British citizens (Keen and Turner 2016). These beliefs may therefore be more symptomatic of an increasingly xenophobic public mood, and one in which immigrants are resented for taking what is not supposedly theirs. As Sally Davison and George Shire argue in 'Race, Migration and Neoliberalism', common-sense anti-immigration narratives frame immigrants as unentitled to normal services and benefits even if they have paid tax all their lives, and are also located within a wider stance that seeks to characterise the welfare state in terms of people 'taking' things (2015, 91). Davison and Shire's analysis is based on the reaction of former Secretary of State for Work and Pensions Iain Duncan Smith, MP, to a report by the academics Christian Dustmann and Tomaso Frattini on immigration from the EU to the United Kingdom 2001–2011 (2013). Dustmann and Frattini found that immigrants paid more in tax than they received in benefits and made a positive contribution to public finances, contrary to claims that they were a burden on the taxpayer (ibid.). Speaking on the Andrew Marr television chat show, Smith refuted Dustmann and Frattini's claims, arguing immigrants would begin 'taking' from the system when they reached retirement age (Davison and Shire 2015, 91). Smith ignored the fact that by that point, they would have contributed to the public purse over many years, and that pensions are essentially deferred pay. Smith also claimed that the arrival of people who spoke little English would create problems for local public services (ibid.).

So why is it so easy, and even intuitive, to make such apparently illogical claims? Why is it thought that people who work and pay tax are burdens on the welfare state, simply because of where they were born? Why do facts and statistics demonstrating the contrary fail to convince? In a more general sense, Smith's comments reflect the neoliberal common sense of welfare benefits as a privilege rather than a right, which judges those who rely on them as shameful. This viewpoint has become entrenched within public debate over several government administrations, and has become an element in creating the public mood. It is also important to remember that Smith himself was the architect of some controversial and punitive welfare reforms, including workfare schemes and cuts to support for disabled people (Black Triangle Campaign 2016). As Davison and Shire suggest, comments such as Smith's can be interpreted as reflecting neoliberalism at its starkest: the ideals of 'a worker with no rights and no social or familial existence' (2015, 92), 'cheap overseas labour [that] can be even cheaper if workers can be denied the usual rights of citizens (and even better if they could be blamed for the underfunding of public services and lack of affordable housing)' (ibid.). Precarity has been discussed throughout this book as a widespread condition of economic insecurity, and in terms of an increasingly fragile social safety net. It is important to highlight both how immigration regulations are an additional source of precarity for immigrants, and also how they become scapegoated for the precarity experienced by British citizens.

At the same time as they perpetuate principles of neoliberal economics, Smith's comments are also consistent with entrenched prejudices about immigrants as not belonging to British society and thus lacking any legitimate entitlement to the welfare state. Such viewpoints mobilise feelings and moral judgements around the definition of the welfare state and its purpose. Crucial to this are questions around who is seen to contribute to the welfare state or benefit from it, and – more importantly – who should have access. These questions have become particularly vexed within both the context of globalisation and austerity cuts. They are also emotionally loaded as they are about anger, fear and resentment, and the impulse to protect entitlements against those who do not deserve them. Similar to the moral judgements and feelings mobilised against the unemployed and single mothers by *Benefits Street* (as discussed in the previous chapter), in this case resentment and suspicion are directed towards those born outside the United Kingdom, with their accessing of public services framed as taking what is not rightfully theirs.

THE INTEGRATION OF BORDERS INTO THE WELFARE STATE

Although there is no space to give a comprehensive overview of the history of the welfare state and immigration regulation in the United Kingdom (but for useful introduction see Saggar 1992; Spencer 2002; Panayi 2014), I will give a brief overview of immigration reforms as they have specifically related to access to the welfare state. Citizens from Commonwealth countries had access to the UK labour market prior to 1962, as many were employed to fill labour shortages, including for the National Health Service (NHS) and other aspects of the expanding post-war welfare state. However, there was a marked contradiction between the image presented externally as open to the world, and the imperatives to exclude citizens of former British colonies, particularly Africans and Asians (Spencer 1997 cited in Geuntner et al. 2016) – with obvious ironies around those recruited to staff the welfare state being unable to enjoy its benefits. The 1962 Commonwealth Immigrants Act, then the 1971 Immigration Act restricted access to the UK labour market (Spencer 2012, 26). The 1981 Nationality Act then redefined British citizenship 'more narrowly to match those who now had the right to live in the UK and creat[ed] subcategories of citizenship for many who did not' (Spencer 2012, 28). The principle of No Recourse to Public Funds banned immigrants from outside of the EU who were working and residing in the United Kingdom from accessing any welfare provisions, including unemployment benefits, childcare benefits and access to social housing (the category of 'public funds' was not clearly defined). In the 1980s, this principle was first applied to non-EU spouses of British citizens, then subsequently expanded to other categories of new immigrants (Taylor 1989; Geuntner et al. 2012; Southall Black Sisters 2016). Further restrictions on immigrants' entitlement to welfare benefits were imposed throughout the 1990s by both Labour and Conservative governments (Geuntner et al. 2012). A key election pledge of the Conservative–Liberal Democrat Coalition Government (2010–2015) and the Conservative majority government (in power as of 2015) was to cut net migration to the 'tens of thousands', although this goal has not been achieved to date (net migration at the time of writing stands at 323,000; see Office of National Statistics 2016). To this end they enacted a series of policies to discourage immigrants from coming to the United Kingdom. This was mostly targeted at non-EU citizens as, at the time of writing, EU citizens were historically protected by European legislation and thus their numbers could not be restricted (UK Government 2013).

One of these initiatives was the 2014 Immigration Act, which, as former Home Secretary (currently Prime Minister) Theresa May stated in an interview with the *Telegraph* newspaper, was intended to create a 'hostile environment' for irregular immigrants (Kircup and Winnett 2012). Notably, one of the elements of the Act was to require immigrants other than asylum seekers staying in the United Kingdom for more than six months to play a healthcare levy in addition to their visa fees, despite already paying for the NHS through taxes and National Insurance contributions in the same way as UK citizens. Those not classified as 'ordinarily resident' (meaning visitors and those with irregular status) were already being charged for emergency treatment (Geuntner et al. 2016, 8). These developments, which were about the limitation or privatisation of access to the NHS, can be understood as a response to the perception of immigrants as a burden on the welfare state – in line with Smith's comments – despite the lack of evidence of a serious problem (FullFact 2013). Instead, they involved the *creation* of a problem of 'health tourism' requiring tough policy measures, and, crucially, allowing governments to demonstrate toughness against immigrants for electoral gain. It should also be seen within the broader ideological context of imperatives to shift responsibility away from the state onto individuals. According to Geuntner et al. (2012, 6), "the rationale of public welfare has shifted from the founding principle, "from cradle to grave" (Attlee government 1945–1951) to "from welfare to work" under Blair". This has since intensified through the austerity measures of both the Coalition and Conservative majority governments. As immigrants are being positioned as not truly belonging to British society, they are also framed as needing to accept greater responsibility for their own welfare than British citizens. They thus become socially acceptable targets for cuts and privatisation in the context of austerity and stretched public finances. These sorts of measures can be understood in relation to how border controls 'produce the times and spaces of global capitalism' (2013, 4), as Sandro Mezzadra and Brett Neilson argue in *Border as Method*. Contemporary capital, 'characterised by processes of financialisation and the combination of heterogeneous labour and accumulation regimes, negotiates the expansion of its frontiers with much more complex assemblages of power and law' (2013, 5). Therefore, one of the features of contemporary capitalism is the proliferation of borders, which function to select and filter people into hierarchies so that they are included or excluded to varying degrees 'along key lines and geographies of wealth and power' (2013, 7). The measures described earlier should be considered in relation to processes of making access to the welfare state increasingly contingent for certain categories of people, simultaneously undermining the social solidarity underpinning support for the welfare state.

Recent immigration legislation has not only involved restricting access to public services for immigrants but also has involved the outsourcing of immigration controls into public sector organisations, including the institutions of the welfare state. For example, since 2009 universities have been required to monitor the attendance of non-EU students and staff, and inform the Home Office if students have withdrawn from their studies. At the same time, businesses faced a fine of up to £10,000 for employing an irregular immigrant, now increased to £20,000 (UK Government 2014a). The 2014 Immigration Act, in introducing healthcare charges for irregular immigrants, also placed NHS staff in the position of having to check their status. It also required banking staff to check the immigration status of prospective customers and Drivers and Vehicles Licencing Authority staff to check the status of those applying for driving licences (UK Legislation 2014). The 2016 Immigration Act extended this process, requiring landlords to check the immigration status of prospective tenants and creating a new criminal offence of 'illegal working' (Wintour 2015). At the time of writing, a controversial measure has been introduced requiring schools to collect data on the nationality and birth country of children; concerns have been raised that this information will be used for the purposes of immigration enforcement, as there is evidence that this has been done in the past (Gayle 2016). At the 2016 Conservative Party Conference, Home Secretary Amber Rudd proposed requiring businesses to disclose how many non-UK staff they employ – although this was later scrapped (Syal 2016).

These reforms outsource the responsibilities of immigration officials to public sector workers or private individuals (e.g., university administrators, NHS staff or landlords) whose job descriptions do not include immigration control, and for which they are not adequately trained. They are often provided with minimum guidance and complex and confusing regulations. Faced with increasingly stiff penalties, a common response can be to avoid supporting people whose immigration status could *potentially* be a problem and, because of this, discriminating against racialised people, as the Joint Council for the Welfare of Immigrants' study of the piloting of the landlord checks revealed (JCWI 2015). Insidiously, this process normalises immigration controls as *part of the infrastructure of the welfare state*, and as part of the work duties of public and voluntary sector workers – as my interview with an immigration advisor revealed:

> I actually do training for health workers. And the number of people who don't know GPs, their receptionists, whatever, don't know that everyone is entitled to [NHS care] and insists that people need to be able to show passports and stuff like that before they can register and you are telling them no they don't. And actually most times they are really relieved to hear it, they don't want to be doing this hideous gatekeeping routine. (Phil, interview 17 June 2014)

Faced with harsh immigration measures, people can easily assume that rules are stricter than they actually might be. This causes them to be cautious about helping people in need of support, or prioritising those who are obviously British citizens or whose status is in order over those in less certain situations. This conflicts with their duty of care and in some cases the purpose of their organisations. It also requires them to suppress any empathy and concern, instead treating people as suspects and abusers of the system:

> And it is not accidental, there is this whole thing, it is the reason they talked about creating a hostile environment, and . . . that is absolutely what they have managed to do. So to the degree that organisations, individuals, whatever like that will be cautious about offering support to someone even though they can perceive huge injustice and care quite deeply about it. (ibid.)

The perception that immigrants are engaging in deceptive and morally dubious behaviour (the 'bogus asylum seeker') has even been internalised by some public sector workers, as in this account from the immigration advisor about dealing with a mental health worker, who made assumptions about the character of an asylum seeker:

> There was a guy, a very newly arrived Iranian asylum seeker, who had been in jail in Iran and I think he had been tortured and sexually abused and a litany of sheer horror that this guy had gone through. And he was absolutely psychotic. And we were asking for a mental health assessment. And not for the first time I might say we got the response from mental health services saying . . . before they had even met the guy, 'well we will come and do the assessment but we reckon he is probably putting it on to help with his asylum claim' . . . If I think

someone is in mental distress and I am asking for the mental health service, who has responsibility of helping with that to come and do an assessment, I don't expect them to say before even leaving the building 'we will come and see him but he is probably putting it on'. (Phil, interview 17 June 2014)

If this patient were a British rather than Iranian citizen, his distress would be more likely seen as a genuine mental health condition, and he would be seen as in need of treatment and support rather than engaging in dubious activity. The mental health worker's behaviour could also be understood as symptomatic of a wider public mood of suspicion towards immigrants and refugees brought in by both the 'hostile environment' and older prejudices towards them as abusers of the system, so that gatekeeping takes priority over duty of care.

Beyond treating people with suspicion, welfare state institutions can potentially become sites where people are at risk of being handed over to the authorities:

I think that people are very, very worried about approaching organisations for help because they don't know what the consequences for them will be. I was doing some training for some GPs last week and one of the case studies that we used, I don't know if you saw the story, but it was a horrific tale of a woman who, basically, her baby died before she reached term. She was aware that it had stopped moving, but walked around with this dead child inside her for the best part of a month I think simply because she was scared to go to hospital to have the treatment that she needed. Because she was worried she was going to get fined for the treatment, charged for the treatment, which as a matter of fact she was. And she was also worried that she would be reported to the immigration authorities. (ibid.)

For those on the sharp end of the immigration system, hospitals are not places to go for treatment; instead, they become places where one could face financial ruin and potential deportation. The implication is that people such as the woman in the immigration advisor's account become effectively barred from the welfare state, and are made to feel that *their health and welfare do not matter*. But immigration policies designed to create a 'hostile environment' do not only affect those whose papers are not in order. Other categories of people – including those with stable immigration status – are made to feel that their access to public services is contingent. For example, as part of the paperwork for a recent hospital appointment, I was asked to fill out a form in which I stated whether or not I was entitled to free NHS care, and was asked for accompanying identification. Posters in hospitals and clinics were circulated saying that 'The NHS is not for everyone', showing an image of a white, blonde, female patient who patients would, or would not identify, with depending on circumstances (Jones et al. 2017, 44). These posters have three potential audiences: first, the irregular immigrant who, it is hoped, will be discouraged from seeking care or will be made aware he or she may be charged for it; second, the immigrant with stable status, who is reminded of the contingency of his/her access to healthcare. Finally, they reassure British citizens (who are not personally affected by these rules) that the NHS, which is under financial pressure, is being reserved for them and that steps are being taken to discourage those who are not entitled (ibid.).

These practices can be understood as examples of what Nira Yuval-Davis calls 'everyday bordering', which she defines as 'the everyday construction of borders through ideology, cultural mediation, discourses, political institutions, attitudes and everyday forms of transnationalism' (2013, 10). Borders are thus not simply about regulating who can enter or who can leave – *they have become part of everyday life, and have become increasingly integrated with the institutions and practices of the welfare state,* with public sector workers required to play an active role in maintaining them. Although Bruff does not specifically discuss the imbrication of borders into the welfare state in his theorisation of authoritarian neoliberalism (2014), the situation illustrates the impasse he identifies: the difficulty of wholeheartedly defending the institutions of the welfare state when they are used to surveil and deport. It is also important to remember that borders do not only function as a legal mechanism for inclusion or exclusion, they are also *cultural* and *emotional*. As Yuval-Davis (2013) argues:

> In specific border zones, the geographic state border itself becomes embedded in everyday life and in the meanings attached to the local, as well as national, cultural environment, traditions, social habits and emotions. (2013, 15)

As much as they regulate access, borders also are about articulating who belongs to the political community and who does not, and are used to manage public feelings, and thus play a role in consolidating a xenophobic public mood. Therefore, some people are meant to feel fear or unease around the institutions of the welfare state: the unease of being reminded of one's contingent immigration status or, in extreme cases, being afraid to the point of avoiding the hospital or other organisations that could help them. Conversely, British citizens – whose access is not in question – are meant to feel reassured that steps are taken to protect their access.

METAPHORS OF HOME AND THE WELFARE STATE

A central metaphor used to imagine, as well as *feel* the division between insiders and outsiders, is that of the home. The metaphor of the home is not only about the economy as household discussed earlier in this book but also other aspects of governing the state, which William Walters explores in 'Secure Border, Safe Haven: Domopolitics' (2004). Walters defines 'domopolitics' as 'the reconfiguration of relations between citizenship, state and territory', with at its heart 'a fateful conjunction of home, land and security', which is used to justify security measures (2004, 241). As a metaphor, it brings together questions of familiarity and intimacy, property relations and security:

> In a great many of these uses it has power affinities with family, intimacy, place: the home as hearth, a refuge or sanctuary in a heartless world, the home as *our* place, where we belong naturally, and where, by definition, others do not; international order as a space of homes – everyone should have (at least) one; home as a place we must protect. We may invite people into home, but they come at our invitation; they don't stay indefinitely. Others are, by definition, uninvited: illegal migrants and bogus refugees should be returned to 'their homes'. Home as a place to be secured because its contents (our property) are valuable and envied by others. Home as a safe, reassuring place, a place of intimacy, togetherness and even unity, trust and familiarity. (ibid.)

Home, as conceived of within the context of nationalist and anti-immigration politics, is, by definition, the home of those with a clear sense of belonging, and a fixed sense of origins. As Nandita Sharma points out, it is 'a natural home' which guides our emotional, material and physical ties; '[we] couldn't possibly have those feelings for anywhere else' (2015, 80). It is *our* home, rooted in experiences that are familiar to us and associated with the past, possibly even childhood nostalgia, which give us a sense of comfort and familiarity. We can relate to these experiences because we grew up with them: the television shows that we remember the food we ate as children and so forth. Home is thus quite culturally specific. This cultural specificity makes it difficult to imagine how others might associate feelings of home with other experiences which might be unfamiliar to us because they might be located within other cultural contexts. It becomes difficult to conceive of home in a way that encompasses both our own experiences, and unfamiliar experiences. *Our* home, by definition, cannot also be someone else's. This is where home as familiarity and memory connects with ideas of private property: the home which must be protected from outsiders.

Because such a conception of home is rooted in fixed origins, it becomes difficult to imagine that more cosmopolitan conceptions of home might exist. For example, people might feel a sense of familiarity, belonging and comfort in experiences that may not have an identifiable sense of place, or might be based on many different places and cultural concepts at once. Such a conception of home may be more common than we think, as a result of living in globalised, multicultural societies. This is what Paul Gilroy theorises as 'convivial culture': the everyday interactions between races and cultures which take place on a regular basis, not the cosmopolitanism of transnational elites, but something more widely experienced. It means that hearing different languages on the street and the appearance of shops associated with different ethnic communities, for example, may not be interpreted as signs of decline or provoke a melancholic response about losing a sense of place, but might in fact make one feel at home. Such feelings and responses rarely enter official public debates on immigration; as Gilroy notes, such experiences, including any pleasures that might be found there 'are not brought into politics or government' (2004). The possibility of them entering public discourse is even less likely now than at the time when Gilroy was writing. Because such feelings are seen to be at odds with a xenophobic and melancholic public mood, they remain as private and unarticulated.

Anti-immigration policies and rhetoric draw on metaphors and feelings associated with the home as *a culturally specific place* and as a fixed place of origins: that a specific place must remain exactly as it was for us when we grew up, and that any change means decline and loss. In doing so they create a connection with memory and lived experience and the powerful feelings associated with them. They also mobilise fears of immigration as a danger to all that is familiar, which we hold dear. The very act of other people trying to make this place their home by definition threatens our sense of home. Organisations as large and abstract as the welfare state thus become framed as our home and *our property* which must be defended from undeserving outsiders. The lack of evidence of health tourism or other abuses of public services by immigrants as serious problems in need of policy interventions ultimately does not convince, because the appeal to these feelings of home is much stronger.

The metaphor of the home underlies framing of the welfare state as the property of those with a shared cultural identity. One of the ways this has taken place is through the discourse of community. In 'Race, Migration and Neoliberalism', Sally Davison and George Shire explore how this emphasis on 'community' also became used to justify the exclusion of immigrants from the body politic under New Labour and subsequent governments:

> New Labour's communitarianism had been directly conceived of as a repositioning from 'old' Labour ideas (the new clause 4[3] can be understood as replacing the concept of class with that of community). Its policies on cohesion were in the same spirit – and involved not only a disavowal of the need to address structures of inequality, but a shift of responsibility from national government on to individuals or 'communities'. (2015, 89)

According to Davison and Shire, 'community' became increasingly exclusionary and was used to articulate a defensive, inward-looking identity politics – in which the terms of exclusion were primarily cultural rather than economic:

'Community' thus first displaced equality [and, I would add, social class] and then became itself the grounds for exclusion. Indeed, the common-sense concept of community has become increasingly exclusionary as it has become ever more entangled with a politics of us and them that seeks to defend the local against the global. (ibid.)

Within the context of an increasingly exclusionary conception of community, the institutions of the welfare state become perceived within *cultural terms* (e.g., as symbols of Britishness), rather than for their redistributive functions. In part, the intuitive appeal of such ideas may lie in the history of welfare state institutions within post-war nation building. As Michael Bommes has argued, 'the key point of reference for any welfare state has been the 'community of national citizens' (2012 cited in Geuntner et al. 2012, 4). Statements such as by Secretary of State for Health Jeremy Hunt that 'the NHS is not an international health service' in order to justify health charges also appealed to the apparent simplicity of this logic (Travis 2013). It is also important to consider how this intuitive appeal to national symbols and exclusionary discourses of community interacts with neoliberal ideologies which make the universal or redistributive functions of the welfare state harder to conceive. If healthcare and welfare are understood to be individual, rather than social, responsibilities, it becomes more difficult to justify the NHS as providing universal healthcare or the existence of unemployment benefits to prevent people from becoming destitute when they lose their jobs. Instead, it becomes much easier to think of it in terms of 'people taking things' that they do not deserve, and harder to defend paying tax to support people we do not know and may never meet.

It was in the context of New Labour's communitarian turn, The War on Terror, and the expansion of the EU that David Goodhart's 2004 article for *Prospect*, 'The discomfort of strangers' (also published in the *Guardian*), openly claimed that immigration was a threat to the welfare state – a view worth examining as it has since become more socially acceptable. He argues that one of the central dilemmas of political life existed between 'sharing and solidarity' and 'conflict' (Goodhart 2004), which causes:

an especially acute dilemma for progressives who want plenty of both solidarity (high social cohesion and generous welfare paid out of a progressive tax system) and diversity (equal respect for a wide range of peoples, values and ways of life). (ibid.)

These were apparently un-reconcilable polar opposites which Goodhart characterises as 'America vs. Sweden' (ibid.). He claims that 'Scandinavian countries with the biggest welfare states have been the most socially and ethnically homogeneous states in the West' (ibid.), in contrast with the 'fragmentation and individualism' of the United States (ibid.). Notably Goodhart does not make the anti-immigration argument about immigration creating pressure on the finite resources of the welfare state (bearing in mind he was writing in 2004). Instead, his argument is based in the assertion that *cultural difference is incompatible with social solidarity* and that for the public to have confidence in the welfare state, people must assume that their taxes are supporting those who hold the same values and cultural identity, because they could not accept supporting those with different values and different lifestyles. As he argues, 'if values become more diverse, if lifestyles become more differentiated, then it becomes more difficult to sustain the legitimacy of a universal risk-pooling welfare state. People ask: "why should I pay for them when they are doing things that I wouldn't do?"' (ibid.). Crucially, Goodhart conflates the cultural and the economic in the following passage:

> It is important that we feel that most people have made the same effort to be self-supporting and will not take advantage. We need to be reassured that strangers, especially those from other countries, have the same idea of reciprocity as we do. (ibid.)

This equation of being self-supporting or not being a burden on the welfare state and assimilation (not being a 'stranger') serves as another example of the suturing together of contradictory ideas for ideological purposes (Hall 2011). The implication is ultimately that immigrants and ethnic minorities are fundamentally incompatible with British society due to their cultural difference, even if they are financially self-sufficient and pay tax. As Alana Lentin and Gavan Titley note in their critique of the article, the problem of diversity for Goodhart is not a question of ethnicity but a question of values and, ambiguously, 'norms' (2011, 46). But ethnicity is the most obvious and visible sign of different values, and Goodhart also referred to 'changes in the ethnic composition of a city or neighbourhood as reminders of the presence of others' (ibid.). Presenting incompatible difference in terms of values, norms and lifestyles has been used as a way of referring to race without directly mentioning ethnicity or skin colour (Hall 1993). As Lentin and Titley observe:

> emergent articulations of liberalism as nationalism depend on the certainties of a post-racial terrain. Instead, what is identified is the problem of too much culture as a constitutive dimension of just enough culture, or, as [Pathik] Pathak observes, 'he sanctions a sovereign form of community – nationalism – and stigmatises all others'. (2011, 42)

Goodhart's thinking serves as an example of what social policy researchers have called 'welfare chauvinism': a term that was first used to understand how far-right groups politicise access to benefits to draw distinctions between deserving natives and undeserving immigrants, but more recently has been used to understand broader public attitudes towards immigrants' entitlements to benefits (Geuntner et al. 2016, 1). In 'Bordering Practices in the UK Welfare System' (2016), Geuntner et al. interpret the term as 'the ideological construction of an out-group as both threatening and morally inferior so that action to punish, exclude or incapacitate its members is necessary on both moral and existential grounds' (ibid.). It is both a 'public mood' and a policy instrument (Geuntner et al. 2016, 3), involving a 'circular feedback between public attitudes and state action' whereby:

> governments not only respond to chauvinist views, but through laws and administrative practices, also they themselves generate chauvinism, legitimising and rationalising popular anxiety about abuse of a publicly-funded system. The constant invention of new categories of non-citizens gives a basis to chauvinistic practices which are then enmeshed in political and public discourses. (ibid.)

The authors explore the concept in terms of, first, ethnic or nationalist chauvinism which seeks to limit immigrants' access to state welfare provisions (either wholly or partly) and secondly, as class-based welfare chauvinism based in the belief that welfare recipients, regardless of immigration status, are of lower value than those who do not claim benefits (ibid.). Despite the apparent contradictions between these two types of welfare chauvinism, neither group could truly escape their status as despised outsiders:

> Rationalised by public attitudes that are themselves encouraged through political rhetoric and welfare policy, measures imposed on migrants frequently serve as a de facto 'pilot' for sanctions which may in due course also be deployed against the least influential British nationals, who are selected for social bordering. (Geuntner et al. 2016, 16)

The authors give the example of policies on homelessness in the United Kingdom, in which the restrictions and conditions on the right of destitute people to be rehoused were first applied to asylum seekers and were then 'extended to other groups perceived as undeserving' (Geuntner et al. 2016, 12). This is a process which the authors term as the 'bordering-out of national citizens from the welfare state' (ibid.). This process absolves the state of responsibility for the welfare of certain sections of society and simultaneously reduces social solidarity for these groups, justifying further exclusions.

There are also more disturbing aspects of appealing to the specifically *national* character of welfare state institutions underlying welfare chauvinism. As Arjun Appadurai observes in *The Fear of Small Numbers* (2006), the conflation of citizenship with ethnicity is in fact intrinsic to the model of the modern nation state, which is why even supposedly tolerant liberal democracies carry within them the seeds of dangerous nationalist politics:

> no modern nation, however benign its political system and however eloquent its public voices may be about the virtues of tolerance, multiculturalism, and inclusion, is free of the idea that its national sovereignty is built on some sort of ethnic genius. (2006, 2)

The desire for this equivalence forms the basis of what Appadurai calls 'the fear of small numbers', the small numbers being the gap between a statistical ethnic majority and 'the horizon of an unsullied national whole, a pure and untainted national ethnos' (2006, 8), an 'anxiety of incompleteness' (ibid.) which can sometimes erupt into violence against minorities. Similarly, Nandita Sharma argues that 'all nationalisms require a fantasy of a "perfect homeland"' (drawing on Ghassan Hage) and 'because the homeland is not perfect, someone always has to be positioned as the problem' (2015, 79) although "all national societies have had foreigners in them" (2015, 89). When considering immigration and the welfare state, the question of race is never far away, particularly in the light of policies which lead public sector workers to treat those who might 'look foreign' with suspicion, and anti-terror legislation in the aftermath of the War on Terror (e.g., the controversial Prevent[4] strategy).

'TAKING BACK CONTROL'

I have argued in this chapter that bordering practices reinforce neoliberalism through creating categories of citizens with fewer rights, whose status is contingent, and who can be socially acceptable targets for cuts and privatisation. However, it is also important to consider the ways that anti-immigration policies are justified through presenting them as protectionist measures which protect the community against the negative effects of a globalised world by co-opting Left critiques of globalisation. Within this context, appeals are made (e.g., by Goodhart) to community cohesion and stability as an alternative to an isolated *homo economicus* who holds no attachments to any community and is willing to travel to wherever the opportunities are best. In 'The Normalisation of the Right', Mabel Berezin examines how the Front National in France 'won the argument' (despite their limited electoral success to date) through bringing together xenophobic politics conventionally associated with the populist Right with protectionist politics traditionally associated with the Left (Berezin 2013, 251). Although her analysis is based in France, this has particular ramifications for the United Kingdom, where, for example, former UKIP leader Nigel Farage claimed, in response to arguments about how immigrants benefitted the economy, that 'I'd rather Britain was poorer with fewer people' (Chorley 2015).

The claim made by Eurosceptic and anti-immigration politicians is that globalisation has led to a loss of national control to both corporations and transnational governance structures (e.g., the International Monetary Fund or the European Union), as exemplified by Vote Leave's slogan of 'take back control'.[5] As Appadurai notes in *Fear of Small Numbers*, 'globalisation exacerbates uncertainties and produces new incentives for cultural purification as more nations lose the illusion of national economic sovereignty or well-being' (2006, 7). Globalisation appears to unsettle the essential principles and procedures of the nation state: 'the idea of a sovereign and stable territory, the idea of a containable and countable population, the idea of a reliable census, and the idea of stable and transparent categories' – . . . and in particular 'the certainty that distinctive and singular peoples grow out of and control well-defined national territories' (Appadurai 2006, 6). In the face of this uncertainty and loss of control, nationalism and border controls present an immediate and appealing solution: promising to restore the equivalence of population, citizenship and national identity, and also – this is where the co-option of left critiques of globalisation are used – promising to restore the economic and social protections which have been dismantled by globalisation.

However, despite the rhetoric and policies discussed earlier, globalisation has limited the capacity for nation states to significantly reverse population change. As Appadurai argues, it is impossible to eliminate the presence of minorities 'in a world of blurred boundaries, mixed marriages, shared languages, and other deep connectivities' (Appadurai 2006, 11). Borders are navigated all the time by those who seek to travel through them and around them. Welfare state institutions have never been purely national as structures, despite the rhetoric about the NHS not being an 'international health service'. This is demonstrated by the legacy of Commonwealth immigration in building the post-war welfare state, and the 24% of doctors from outside the United Kingdom currently employed by the NHS (FullFact 2015). Public services as staffed by global workforces has become part of everyday experience, even banal. This is an aspect of the everyday, demotic cosmopolitanism which Paul Gilroy theorises, which has become integral to many people's everyday experience. This is the reality of living in a globalised society which anti-immigration policies rhetoric would seek to deny.

The result of the recognition of the inability to reverse population change, for those who are opposed to it, can be anger and frustration at grievances which can never be addressed and unfulfillable desires for cultural homogeneity (Appadurai 2006, 11), and the subtitle of Appadurai's book is 'An Essay on a Geography of Anger'. Appadurai argues that such anger always lies beneath the surface and can erupt into violence, which it did in the former

Yugoslavia in the 1990s (the context for Appadurai's argument). However, his analysis can also be applied to the present moment, although it is much less of an obvious or extreme example as the war in the Balkans. This anger about 'small numbers' can help to understand the pitting of immigrants against another 'population', such as the media construct of the 'white working class', and attempts by politician to displace anger at the effects of neoliberalism and austerity.

The relationship between lack of resources, resentment and immigration as proxy for other concerns (Saggar 2004) was referred to in my interview with the immigration advisor:

> You put people in situations where people are already poor and struggling. And then nothing to provide educational support or anything like that. . . . All you know is there is some kid, again newly arrived in your kid's school, can't speak English, probably will be getting more attention than your child because they need more support, but no additional support put in place. So rather than there being someone there that can actually help that kid to learn, the teacher is having to spend more time, your kids may be coming home saying 'oh this kid can't speak English', but again this kind of resentment building up. (Phil, interview 17 June 2014)

This example illustrates how immigration functions as proxy. Instead of asking why adequate language support is not being put in place, the assumption is to blame pupils whose first language is not English. Within the context of austerity, inadequate resources for schools becomes taken as given, and underfunded schools become normalised as part of everyday lived experience, and, particularly when people feel politically disempowered, it becomes difficult to imagine this changing. Within the context of neoliberal economics and ideologies which are not being publicly critiqued, and within the context of a public mood of resentment and suspicion towards immigrants, it seems immediate and natural to perceive children in competition with each other.

The consequence of all these developments is the normalisation of xenophobic views and the silencing of counter-perspectives, although equality legislation still places limits on how much people can openly discriminate. In my interview, the immigration advisor described a situation where he was delivering training to health workers about immigration:

> I went through a load of case studies around immigration and around the discourse of immigration first off. And this one woman was obviously quite hostile to the exercise and then at the end of it when we were feeding back she said, 'Do you know I know all of that, I know how the press represents immigration, I know X, Y and Z, but whatever I think I leave at home.' And I am thinking

well that is an interesting thing to say because you obviously don't . . . who leaves whatever they think at home?

But afterwards the colleague and I that were delivering the training were kind of feeding back and then he would say, 'What she was basically saying is she is not racist at work.' And that is kind of pretty much what I made out of it as well. But again the fact that she felt able to say 'actually I wish they would all piss off' is what she was really saying but 'I will maintain a professional facade when they come to see me'. And that is quite an extraordinary thing to say. And if I was that woman's line manager I would be extremely concerned. But she felt okay to say that, you know? And again it seems as though it is increasingly acceptable to say things like that. (Phil, interview 17 June 2014)

The situation is one where people feel they must maintain a professional code of conduct at work (including complying with equality legislation), but privately believe that immigrants should not be in the United Kingdom in the first place, a view that is increasingly legitimated by both politicians and the media. Such a split between public and private views also feeds Right populist politics, in which politicians claim to be voicing what people *really think* (as in the 2005 Conservative election campaign slogan, 'are you thinking what we're thinking?') but are unable to say so due to equality legislation and conventions of socially acceptable speech, thereby positioning themselves as courageous anti-establishment outsiders.

As the immigration advisor argued, the larger backdrop to this is the hegemonic view of immigrants as a problem population who should not be in the country in the first place and who should be 'dealt with' in the appropriate manner, to preserve the scarce resources of the welfare state:

It has become unthinkable to consider immigration in any way other than as a problem, that is what immigration is and there is very little opposition to that. You don't hear anything other than that articulated really. And . . . what is the best way, the toughest way, the fairest way, whatever, of dealing with this problem but there isn't ever any question that it is a problem. If someone's presence is inherently a problem then how you deal with the fact of that problem is one thing, but you are already approaching it from the perspective of ideally you wouldn't be here. (Phil, interview 17 June 2014)

If the presence of immigrants is seen to be morally wrong, and if it is a problem, then the most ethical thing to do is to encourage people to leave; or if they cannot be forced to leave, then there is some responsibility to treat people fairly (although begrudgingly) until they finally go. This viewpoint is legitimated through the 'hostile environment', which positions immigrants as a threat and a liability, further normalising the perception that these people should not be there, and can never belong.

CONNECTING ANTI-AUSTERITY AND MIGRANTS' RIGHTS CAMPAIGNS

At the time of writing, a large-scale immigrants' rights movement has not emerged, although it is urgently needed. Important work has been carried out by community organisations in places where there have been histories of grassroots anti-racist organising, such as the 2013 protest by Southall Black Sisters[6] against immigration raids or the Chinatown Shutdown, in which local businesses in London's Chinatown closed for a day in protest against immigration raids (Dhaliwal and Patel 2015). However, beyond such locations, activity has been limited. There seems to have been little interaction or co-ordination between anti-austerity campaigns and migrants' rights campaigns. These have been largely treated as single issues, with austerity cuts framed as having widespread effects on society, and the immigration restrictions as only affecting immigrants. Organisations which have visibly opposed NHS privatisation, such as Keep Our NHS Public, have made little reference to immigration health charges on their website, or, in my experience, in the messaging on banners at protests. The involvement of migrants' rights and anti-racist campaigns within anti-austerity marches, in my experience, has also been quite limited. The converse has been true for protests about the rights of immigrants and refugees, which have been mostly organised by organisations and groups which campaign around human rights, race and civil liberties, but have had limited messaging about austerity. Overall, there has been a sense that fighting cuts to public services and campaigning for the rights of immigrants, for the most part, are two entirely separate issues. Why has this been the case? This may reflect the perception that bringing them together would potentially be complicating the message. It may also be due to the defensive and possibly economistic nature of anti-austerity campaigns and their narrow focus around restoring funding to public services (the limitations of anti-austerity campaigns will be discussed in the next chapter). This narrow focus misses engaging with the transformation of welfare state institutions into sites of surveillance and the resulting danger of destitution or deportation.

There have recently been a few positive signs which suggest the situation may be changing. Recently, some of the large anti-austerity marches have included an 'open borders' block (see figure 4.1).

The most recent of these was the education march which took place in London on 19 November 2016, organised by the UCU and the NUS. Movement for Justice (the campaign group organises protests outside the Yarl's Wood detention centre, see figure 4.2) had many placards about the rights of international students, and the speakers at the end of the march included testimonials from international students who were at risk of deportation due to the Home Office falsely accusing them of cheating on language tests. Unions and

Figure 4.1. Open borders block on education march, London, 2016. *Source:* the author.

Figure 4.2. Demonstration outside Yarl's Wood Detention Centre, Bedfordshire, 2015. *Source:* the author.

other groups representing public sector workers have begun to take official positions opposing the requirement to act as proxy border agents, such as the UCU and NUS in the case of the expectations to monitor student attendance (UCU 2013) and initiatives to restrict the rights of international students (NUS 2016) as well as challenging xenophobic rhetoric (UCU and CLASS 2014). Grassroots organisations such as Students Not Suspects (figure 4.3) and the Black Students' Campaign have also played a key role in raising the migrants' rights and anti-racist activism within student politics.

Figure 4.3.   Students Not Suspects banner protesting discrimination against international students, Manchester, 2015. *Source:* **the author.**

The British Medical Association voted in 2015 to oppose the 2015/2016 Immigration Act, including the introduction of NHS charges. The National Union of Teachers has actively supported the Against Borders for Children campaign.[7] There is a sense that these voices need to be both much louder, and involve many more people, working imaginatively across organisations and communities, in order to challenge rising anti-immigrant populism in the aftermath of the Brexit vote. At the time of writing, a national day of action recently took place entitled 'One Day Without Us', a day in support of the contribution made by immigrants to British society, which included walkouts, protests, public discussions, art exhibitions and so forth.[8]

CONCLUSION: SOLIDARITY AS AN IMAGINATIVE RESPONSE TO XENOPHOBIA

In this chapter I have discussed how debates on immigration, which position certain people as outsiders and undeserving of access to the welfare state, justify austerity cuts and are also premised on the idea that cuts are both unavoidable and inevitable. This draws on neoliberal ideologies and policies (notably predating the financial crisis) which position people as responsible for their own welfare, as well as neo-communitarian discourses, which, as Davison and Shire have argued (2015), first shifted responsibility from the state onto communities, and then define communities within increasingly exclusionary terms. Nostalgic fantasies of the post-war period and the seemingly natural equation of citizenship with ethnic identity are mobilised, as are metaphors of the home to be guarded against outsiders (domopolitics) and the 'fear of small numbers'. Such metaphors relate to everyday experiences and deeply held feelings. These feelings are connected with a fixed sense of origins (a 'natural home'), and associations with our personal histories, such as childhood nostalgia. Anti-immigration rhetoric mobilises fears around the home being under threat from unwanted others, and anger and a melancholic sense of loss as appropriate responses to social and cultural change. Other ways of feeling about home, which may be more at ease with change, remain as private feelings and do not cohere into a *public mood*. The powerful appeal of these feelings can override rational arguments about the economic benefits of immigration, as statistics can do little to challenge strong feelings about nostalgia and loss.

However, such feelings are also challenged by the reality of globalisation, in which significant population change cannot be practically reversed, and it is impossible to turn back the clock to a time before mass immigration. As Appadurai argues, the recognition of this fact is central to a vicious cycle whereby public anger and resentment must be appeased with tough policies, which then are inevitably ineffective as they cannot meaningfully reduce numbers or reverse demographic change, creating yet more anger and resentment and progressively undermining migrants' rights in the process. As my interview with the immigration advisor has demonstrated, this then becomes internalised by some public sector workers, who may not necessarily openly discriminate against immigrants (due to professional codes and equality legislation) but might begrudge their presence.

In response to this situation, it is now an urgent task to imagine forms of social solidarity which cross ethnic and racial lines, and which cannot be reduced to simply identifying with people who are culturally similar to us, as Goodhart would imagine it – in other words, people who might share the same understanding of *home* in terms of shared origins and cultural references, and with whom we would unite against outsiders. Solidarity is fundamentally an *imaginative* process as much as it is about material conditions, institutions and group interests. Solidarity means finding, and more importantly *feeling* something in common with other people, even if we might have different cultural backgrounds and might be acting in different contexts. It is thus about being able to see beyond a tribal identification with those who share the same histories, cultural references and cultural habits (which often gets mistaken for solidarity, particularly by neo-communitarian commentators such as Goodhart). It also goes beyond empathy for those who are suffering. The imaginative aspect of solidarity is about being able to recognise what might seem like separate individual struggles as shared. Solidarity thus enables us to go beyond the limitations of single-issue campaigns, as it is about creating imaginative links between struggles. The scale of the challenge posed by anti-immigration politics means that this imaginative work has now become urgent.

NOTES

1. An immigration advisor is licensed by the Office of the Immigration Services Commissioner to offer legal advice to immigrants and conduct training sessions for public sector workers on the immigration system and supporting immigrants.

2. 'Benefits tourism' was a term coined to characterise fears that large numbers of immigrants, particularly from the countries which joined the European Union in 2004, would come to the United Kingdom to specifically rely on what was seen as the country's generous social welfare system.

3. Clause 4 was the section of the Labour Party Constitution which outlined the party's values. It was originally drafted in 1918 and included a commitment to 'common ownership of the means of production' – or nationalisation. Tony Blair proposed removing reference to nationalisation as a break with the party's past; this change was adopted at the Labour Party conference in 1995.

4. The Prevent Strategy is a UK government strategy to prevent people being involved in terrorism, as part of the Counter Terrorism and Security Act. It has been controversial due to its targeting of ethnic minority and Muslim communities.

5. 'Take back control' was the slogan used by the Vote Leave campaign during the referendum on the United Kingdom's membership of the European Union.

6. Southall Black Sisters is an anti-racist, women's rights organisation based in the South Asian community in Southall, West London. http://www.southallblacksisters.org.uk/.

7. The Against Borders for Children campaign is a parent-led campaign to oppose the collection of data from school pupils on nationality and country of origin, out of concern that such data will be used for immigration enforcement purposes and encourage discrimination. See https://www.schoolsabc.net/.

8. See http://www.1daywithoutus.org/.

Chapter 5

Austere Creativity, Community and Impasses around the Welfare State

I ended the previous chapter by calling for a linking of anti-austerity campaigns and migrants' rights campaigns, as well as an imaginative leap that would enable us to think of the two together. This chapter will focus more closely on anti-austerity campaigns, based on my experiences in a campaign to save five local libraries from closure in Lewisham, South London, in 2011. I will examine how concepts of 'community' and 'creativity' were mobilised by local authorities to turn the libraries over to charities (with volunteers replacing qualified librarians), and how these ideas were reflected in the reaction of local campaigners. Faced with cuts to public services, local citizens were expected to be resourceful and ingenious in adapting to them; for example, through managing and staffing libraries for free, services which were once funded by the state. The expectation for citizens to volunteer to run their own public services was also framed in terms of how it could restore a perceived lost sense of community, and appealed to the belief that austerity provided the opportunity to restore this lost community by forcing citizens to rely on each other rather than on the state. However, some of the campaigners did, at least initially, also believe that the transfer of the libraries allowed for radical possibilities to re-envision both public services and local community. The case reflects the impasses intrinsic to anti-austerity campaigns, in which one is often faced with a defence of existing public service provision which does not ultimately satisfy desires for an alternative. These impasses make it easy to claim, as will be seen, that the conversion would foster both a sense of community and creativity not possible under council[1] ownership.

I will begin by examining the instrumentalisation of the concept of 'creativity' within neoliberal policy discourses before the financial crisis, and will consider its application within the austerity context. I will then discuss the case of the 2010–2011 campaign to save the libraries in Lewisham. The analysis will be based on three in-depth, semi-structured interviews with key activists involved in the libraries campaign (who have been given pseud-onyms), as well as reflections on my own involvement as an activist. Grey literature on the outsourcing of public services and a promotional video about the volunteer-run library will also be examined.

NEOLIBERAL CREATIVITY

Here I will offer a brief genealogy of the discourse of 'creativity' as it has been used within neoliberal policy discourse. This will first be discussed within a global framework, and then will focus on the United Kingdom, particularly within the context of austerity. As with previous chapters, this represents an attempt to map connections between phases of neoliberal-ism. From the late 1990s until the financial crisis, utopian rhetoric which informed cultural, urban and employment policy promised that creative work and creativity itself could lift people out of poverty, fix economies and provide work satisfaction: a certain 'magic bullet solution' (Pratt and Jefcutt 2009, 1). These promises were central to a 'creativity' discourse developed by policymakers, media commentators, academics, think tanks and others, which increasingly defined creativity within the framework of technology and business, and more fundamentally, competition.[2] Central to the creativity discourse was the claim that 'creativity' exemplified innovation, flexibility and the willingness to embrace change, and was thus a resource to be mobil-ised by business (Howkins 2007). In connection with this, conditions which have been common practice within cultural work (e.g., project-working and self-employment) were heralded as being at the forefront of economic, social and technological change. By contrast, other forms of employment (e.g., work in industry or in public sector professions) were seen to be rigid, inflexible and ultimately residual, within the context of post-industrialism. According to Justin O'Connor, such perspectives rested on the assumption that the destruction of manufacturing and the welfare state in industrialised countries were inevitable historical developments rather than the product of specific political actions and decisions (2015, 385). These perspectives also were premised on the distancing of the entrepreneurial 'creative class' from the traditional Left, which was perceived to be anachronistic and irrelevant (O'Connor 2015, 382). This discourse of creativity also accompanied the rhetoric around New Public Management under the New Labour adminis-tration that the state stifled the 'creativity, dynamism and competitiveness', which were seen to be intrinsic qualities of the free market (see Clarke and Newman 1997; Du Gay 2000).

While the discourse around creativity was initially applied to cultural labour, what is relevant here is its wider generalisation, and the expectation for *citizens* to be creative, including those not engaged in cultural labour. A key example of this was the increasing popularity of 'social innovation' as a fashionable policy term. 'Social innovation', coined by Geoff Mulgan, CEO of the Young Foundation, is commonly defined as 'new ideas (products, services and models) that simultaneously meet social needs and create new social relationships or collaborations' (Grisiola and Ferragina 2015). According to Sebastian Olma, the term 'innovation', as it is often conceived, does not mean any new idea, but carries strong associations of business and technology, and so new ideas become, by definition, entrepreneurial ideas (2014). Olma warns of the tendencies within the idea of social innovation towards what Evgeny Mozorov terms 'solutionism', or approaching complex social problems as simple technological problems (Mozorov cited in Olma 2014.). Other critiques of 'social innovation' include its mobilisation of the ingenuity of ordinary citizens as a *resource* that can be used to shift responsibility from the welfare state onto individuals and the private sector, who are then encouraged to 'make do with less' (Grisiola and Ferragina 2015). This particular expectation for the creativity of citizens to substitute for public investment has had particular consequences under austerity. As will be discussed, it is used to justify the outsourcing of public services to charities, mutuals and citizens' voluntary labour. As discussed earlier in this book, challenges to austerity have to date been relatively modest, both in terms of alternative arguments and in terms of social movements, beyond short-term single-issue campaigns. More recently, inequality has entered public debate through the publication of books such as *The Spirit Level* by Richard Wilkinson and Kate Pickett in 2010 and *Capital in the Twenty-First Century* by Thomas Piketty in 2014. In the United States, the Occupy movement mobilised around the slogan of 'we are the 99%'. However, these developments have yet to transform into large-scale social movements and it is unclear how much they have significantly shifted the public mood.

One of the challenges faced by resistance to austerity is the Conservatives' successful co-option of libertarian critiques of the welfare state. For example, the Coalition Government's 2010 election campaign drew on libertarian imagery, as illustrated by a billboard which read: 'social revolution not state control'. As discussed in chapter 1, the concept of the 'Big Society' and Phillip Blond's book *Red Tory* combines such libertarian concepts with neo-communitarian arguments about how the state had become too distant from people's lives, and proposed the involvement of citizens in the running of public services. This represents a continuation of the legacy of New Labour's communitarian approach, in terms of the expectation for civil society to compensate for free market failures. While thinkers such as Blond have been largely sidelined in the current Conservative majority administration, and the 'Big Society' dismissed as a policy fad, the outsourcing of public services continues.

Since the onset of the financial crisis and the election of the Coalition government, there has been much public debate around the purpose of public services, due both to reductions in public spending and their characterisation as top-down, technocratic and unresponsive to public needs. Within this context, austerity has come to be seen as an opportunity both to foster creativity and to restore a missing citizen engagement. I want to examine this through an analysis of grey literature from the Nesta[3] think tank, which was central to the creative industries discourse under New Labour (Oakley et al. 2014). After the change in government, Nesta became involved with a series of initiatives on public service reform. The think tank commissioned a project in 2011 entitled *People Powered Public Services*, which was based on the principle that the public should play a greater role in the running of public services (Colligan 2014); they also administered a £14 million 'innovation fund' in connection with the Cabinet Office for Social Action, which was about integrating volunteers into the running of public services (Nesta, n.d.). The *People Powered Public Services* blog by Nesta Chief Executive Philip Colligan spelled out the project philosophy:

> Our narrative around public services reform starts with the need to move from a paternalistic model of public services where they are 'done to' people, to a more collaborative approach where people are involved in the design and delivery of the services that they rely on. *This isn't about austerity, although that accelerates the need for change* (my emphasis). What it's really about is a recognition that the public services bequeathed to us by our great grandparents aren't up to the challenges of the 21st Century. (Colligan 2014)

Colligan called for greater public involvement 'in the design and delivery' of public services (notably, without explaining how people will find the time, or if they will be compensated for their efforts). Nesta's recommendations from their Creative Councils project, entitled *A Call for Action: Ten Lessons for Local Authority Innovators* by Sophia Parker and Charles Leadbeater (the latter has a long history with Nesta),[4] stated that 'the challenges of austerity and rising demands, combined with the potential of new technologies, have spurred a new wave of civic entrepreneurialism' (Parker and Leadbeater 2013, 5). The authors also characterised a 'creative council' as a 'resilient council', displaying the very same qualities as a resilient individual: adaptable, capable of withstanding disruption and, more importantly, making do with less.

Creativity, within the austerity context, thus combines entrepreneurial self-reliance with neo-communitarian politics. As I have pointed out, neo-communitarianism has been central to austerity's intuitive appeal. Austerity has promised to counter the excesses of the boom period, by taking us 'back to basics', particularly the simpler, more frugal lives and imagined close-knit communities of previous generations, which are also perceived as more resilient. It is not only about living within our means, but also about responding to anxieties about the complexities and uncertainties of globalisation. My previous chapter mostly focused on the nation state within the context of anti-immigration politics, and examined moves to restrict access to welfare state institutions to those deemed to be deserving citizens. This chapter will focus on the local as another site for neo-communitarian politics, in terms of both local campaigns and the expectation for citizens to run their own local services as volunteers. In *No Local* (2012), Greg Sharzer critically examines the appeal of the local in terms of the perception that the problems of capitalism are largely those of scale, and that problems can thus be solved by scaling down to the city, town or neighbourhood (2012, 8). Interactions with local shopkeepers, knowing your neighbours, buying local and so forth can humanise capitalism and restore a lost sense of immediacy (Sharzer 2012, 20). This is similar to the dynamics of community as characterised by Miranda Joseph in *Against the Romance of Community*, in which community is positioned as opposite or other to capitalism, but also as having the capacity to balance and humanise capitalism (Joseph 2002, 3). Because 'community' is seen as an 'other' to capitalism, but also is deeply imbricated within it, it has a particular insatiable dynamic of loss, as efforts to restore a missing sense of community will always fall short. It appeals to the logic of an unfulfillable desire, making it very easy for corporations and politicians to exploit. The narrative of lost community is ultimately a disempowering one, leaving little room for agency. Any attempt to restore community will always fall short, contemporary experience will always disappoint when measured against an imagined past. Similarly, as Sharzer argues, localism is premised on the impossibility of larger-scale social change (2012, 3), and thus is ultimately pessimistic. Although it is not synonymous with the view that reversing cuts is impossible and it is better to creatively adapt to them, there are strong parallels.

However, it would be problematic to entirely dismiss these desires for community as sentimentality and reactionary politics as they point to a sense of collective agency which has been lost, particularly in relation to the ending of the social democratic settlement. Angela McRobbie observes that the decline of social democracy and the debates around the politics of social welfare is 'strangely unmarked and hence unmourned' (2013, 126). Janet Newman and John Clarke also argue that the state can no longer embody a unified form of public interest or a singular public, and that 'the social and political settlements on which earlier forms of the state rested have now unravelled' (2015,

7). Although the financial crisis has led to a renewed focus on the need for stability in the face of economic uncertainty, there is also now widespread disenchantment with the state, reflecting 'the experience of the kind of state we currently have to live with' which has been 'commodified, marketised and managerialised, and seems to ignore the human relationships at stake in its encounters with citizens' (2015, 1). I would add that this disenchantment is also driven by increased state surveillance, and the outsourcing of immigration controls. The search for new forms of political and social engagement which mark new social movements (Clarke and Newman give the example of the Indignados[5] in Spain) does not see the state as a worthwhile site for political imagination or struggle. This means that the role of the welfare state is rarely addressed in relation to these discussions of community or its loss. The erosion of the conditions which enable collective organisation, combined with the loss of interest in the welfare state as a political project, thus cannot be entirely dismissed as nostalgia for an idealised past. This might explain why it might be so easy and intuitive to agree that cuts cannot be reversed and that services which close cannot be restored, and why other responses, such as volunteers taking on responsibility for running public services, seem more viable.

This also shows how 'community' is invoked in various, often contradictory, ways, for different political purposes, which do not map easily onto the political spectrum. In some cases, this might be about romanticising a lost golden era but in other cases mourning a genuine loss of sociality – one which may have previously functioned as a resource for alternative values and may enable mobilisation against neoliberalism. It is not always easy to determine what motivates the claim that sense of community has been lost: a real sense of loss, or an inability to recognize current forms of sociality and community which do not fit our preconceptions. Equally, the linking of community to place (a common-sense connection which is taken for granted) can also serve different political purposes. Community as place can counter the homogenising tendencies of globalisation, but can also be used to assert parochial and exclusionary conceptions of belonging and cultural identity.

In the aftermath of the financial crisis, there is a sense of only two bad choices being available: neoliberal individualism, or conservative conceptions of community, reflecting the extent to which the current conjuncture is also a political crisis. Other alternatives seem much more difficult to imagine, for the reasons discussed earlier, although some of these will be addressed in the chapters that follow. All this suggests the importance of considering what is at stake when the need to restore a lost sense of community is invoked, and the importance of finding ways to reconsider the role of the welfare state in relation to such appeals, or at least of being reflexive about its absence in the discussion. The following section will explore these questions in relation to the case of the libraries in Lewisham.

ANTI-AUSTERITY CAMPAIGNS IN LEWISHAM

In the rest of this chapter, I will examine how the dynamics I have explored earlier played out in a campaign to save five libraries in Lewisham[6] in 2010–2011, and how 'creativity' and 'community' were mobilised within the campaign. I will focus on the response of campaigners to the takeover of three of the libraries by Eco-Computers (a social enterprise), and one by the Age UK charity. The takeover of New Cross library by a charity, Bold Vision, will also be explored. I was involved in these campaigns as an activist within the Lewisham Anti-Cuts Alliance (LACA), and worked with some of the key campaigners. I will first reflect on the role of LACA and my involvement. I will then discuss the campaign developments chronologically, including the takeover of New Cross Library by Bold Vision, and its rebranding as New Cross Learning, in order to examine how 'creativity' and 'community' were articulated. The case study is based on interviews with three key activists in the campaign, auto-ethnographic reflections on my involvement as an activist, as well as an analysis of Social Enterprise London's pamphlet on social enterprise–run libraries and New Cross Learning's promotional video.

Many local anti-cuts campaigns were quickly established in the immediate aftermath of the election of the Coalition Government. From the autumn of 2010 to the summer of 2011, I became involved in the LACA because I was concerned about how cuts would affect my local area. LACA organised local campaigns together with People Before Profit (a local campaign group and political party which stands in council elections on an anti-privatisation platform), Keep our NHS Public and other local groups in the area. According to one of the activists interviewed, LACA was able to bring people together in a way that was relatively non-sectarian and open-minded, some of whom worked together on further campaigns (Miguel, interview 20 February 2015).

However, the LACA meetings were also often fraught – symptomatic, in retrospect, of many of the impasses of the Left, and of how the public mood has affected the Left, leading to an attitude of resignation and acceptance of the idea that they could have little influence. Consequently, energies became directed towards argumentative meetings rather than practical organising work. Arguments often centred around a clash between two activist cultures. Some of the activists were interested in creative tactics, and a more horizontal structure. Others, mostly members of Trotskyist political parties, held quite rigid ideas of organisational tactics: stalls, marches and support for strikes were favoured, while direct action tactics and the use of social media were viewed with suspicion. Such arguments took up considerable time and energy, meaning that some of the basic practical tasks (e.g., the maintenance of the blog and the email list) were neglected. There was also some confusion and conflict about which campaigns should be supported. In retrospect, this may have been based on conceptions of the industrial working class as privileged revolutionary subject, problematic given both Lewisham's economy, in which a significant percentage of the population are employed by the council (Lewisham Strategic Partnership, n.d.), and the relative lack of union activity at the time, particularly from UNISON,[7] who represented many of the council employees. Those who attended the meetings had known each other for a long time and tended to be white and middle-aged or older, and therefore rather unrepresentative of the population of a borough in which two out of five local residents are from a black or minority ethnic background (Lewisham Joint Strategic Needs Assessment, c. 2012). I frequently found myself to be the only person in the room who wasn't white, which made me slightly uncomfortable at times. The meetings were largely made up of a core of experienced activists; others occasionally attended but did not become actively involved.

The Labour Party in Lewisham were contradictory in the way they responded to the cuts, which affected LACA's activities. They held a majority in the local council and at the time of writing hold fifty-three out of fifty-four council seats (London Councils 2014). According to one of the activists interviewed, many local residents voted for the Labour Party as insurance against the cuts, which were perceived as being a wholly Conservative policy (Jonathan, interview 13 February 2015). These conditions produced a situation where the council did not have to be accountable to their own constituents and seemed unused to being challenged by them. One of the activists interviewed saw the cuts as 'essentially an issue of failed democracy' (Joe, interview 13 February 2015). However, the local Labour Party also treated local anti-cuts activism as a potential threat to their credibility in the borough as the *only* voice of social justice, and thus their electoral prospects. This placed them in the contradictory situation of *both* implementing the cuts, and *simultaneously* campaigning against them, leading local activists to suspect they were using their involvement in local campaigns to manage dissent.

A 'BIG SOCIETY' SOLUTION FOR LIBRARIES

In the summer of 2010, Lewisham Council announced that they were going to close five of the libraries in the borough.[8] Prior to 2010, the borough had thirteen libraries. The announcement to close the libraries represented the first round of cuts after the 2010 election (News Shopper 2010). A large and high-spirited campaign to save the libraries developed quickly in response (figure 5.1). It drew 'people who had never been involved in political things before' (Jonathan, interview 13 February 2015).

Figure 5.1. New Cross Library with posters protesting its closure, 2010. *Source:* the author.

The campaign consisted of marches, protests at council meetings, a petition that attracted thousands of signatures and demonstrations outside the Department for Culture, Media and Sport (the relevant UK government department, based in central London). There was support from national campaigns, such as Voices for The Library. Billed as a 'carnival', a march to the council chambers in October 2010 drew hundreds of demonstrators.

Despite this opposition, in May 2011 the council made the decision to stop operating the libraries and transfer them to charities and social enterprises with volunteers replacing librarians, and the library at New Cross still set to close altogether (Lewisham Council 2011). This decision was very contentious at LACA. Some argued for the importance of defending publicly funded services and that closure would be preferable to the spread or normalisation of volunteer-run public services. Others believed, pragmatically, that transfer was better than closure. One activist summarised the second approach:

I think it's better to keep a facility open even with volunteers than for it to close, because it's much harder to reopen it again later. . . . There were people

who didn't think it was right for the libraries to be run by volunteers and I think
you can be too purist. I think . . . it's worth trying to keep something open
so you can get it back into public financing later on. (Jonathan, interview 13
February 2015)

This reflects the difficult choices facing many campaigners: between closure
and keeping the libraries open under compromised circumstances. In practice,
according to one of the activists interviewed, the libraries turned over to Eco-
Computers functioned only partly as libraries: one became a café, with another
being used primarily for recycling computers with some space for library services. The branding of the social enterprise was quite prominent (ibid.).

This model has since become more widespread, as figures suggest there
are now close to 250 volunteer-run libraries in the United Kingdom (Public
Libraries News, n.d.). Unsurprisingly, such developments are heralded as
largely positive by Social Enterprise London (SEL), an agency for supporting
social enterprise (since incorporated into Social Enterprise UK). SEL published a report entitled 'Libraries in Transition: Are There Creative Alternatives?' presenting social enterprise as the solution for underfunded libraries.
Crucially, SEL asserts that unlike those run by social enterprises, libraries
operated by local authorities are '*in* communities but not *of* communities'
(Social Enterprise London 2011, 2). This claim is not substantiated by any
evidence (the accompanying descriptions of social enterprises simply outlined their mission statements and described their activities, but did not discuss results). The report articulates several key claims: that this approach is
creative ('a creative new alternative') (ibid.) and has an organic relationship
to communities – that libraries will become 'much more central to the lives
and needs of local people' (ibid.) – and that it is good for society because it
provides voluntary and employment experience and skills training (2011, 5).
SEL argues that furthermore, because social enterprises have expertise delivering in these areas, they are 'well placed to succeed' in a climate of 'reduced
public spending' (2011, 7). The claims for such an approach to public service
as both more creative and more conducive to community engagement (the
assumptions behind *Libraries in Transition* as well as the Nesta proposals
discussed earlier) suggest deeper ideologies about creativity being opposed to
the rigidity of the welfare state and simultaneously taps into the public mood
which is nostalgic for lost community, asserting that a sense of community
is lacking and in need of restoration. It may also reflect the ubiquity of community economic development as a dominant model for public service provision, particularly within Canada, the United States and the United Kingdom,
which, according to James De Filippis et al., has 'been accompanied (and
accomplished) by a focus on *the community* in-and-of itself' and has been
mirrored by a 'diminished set of critical political perspectives' (2007, 38).

On a practical level, questions have also been raised about the effectiveness of public services operated by charities. Concerns about leisure trusts[9] were raised by the European Services Strategy Unit (ESSU) charity in a report entitled *The Case Against Leisure Trusts*. Drawing on data from the Audit Commission, ESSU pointed out that the quality of services provided by trusts was 6–10% lower than those delivered by local authorities (ESSU 2008, 3). ESSU also questioned the financial stability of trusts as they lack the surpluses and the economies of scale of local authorities (2008, 4), while, at the same time, the local authorities still shoulder the risks. Workforces employed by leisure trusts experience the casualisation and lack of trade union recognition endemic to the private sector (2008, 5). ESSU also questioned the claims that are made about reinvigorating local democracy. Using the example of sports clubs as the first large-scale instance of where local public services were transferred to charities, ESSU cited lack of consultation with users (2008, 6). Due to the transfer of the service out of local authority hands, councils had limited control over the quality of services, leading to a loss of accountability (2008, 6). Similar concerns have been expressed about the viability of social enterprise–run services. A report by Social Enterprise UK also pointed out that social enterprises lack the resources to compete against large for-profit companies such as Serco or G4S, which are treated by government as 'too big to fail' (Social Enterprise UK 2013, 3). The most contentious aspect of social enterprise–run public services has been the replacing of paid staff with volunteers, and the difficulty this poses for deprived neighbourhoods where people have little free time, and cannot reasonably be expected to provide the same level of expertise and reliability as trained librarians.

AUSTERE CREATIVITY AND THE FATE OF NEW CROSS LIBRARY

In early 2011, New Cross Library was still under threat of closure; in response, an occupation took place at the library on 5 February 2011 for one night, in which many local campaigners, including myself, participated (figure 5.2). The occupation coincided with Save Our Libraries Day, a national day of action in defence of libraries, which included eighty 'Read-In' events by authors (Smale 2011). The occupation began with a series of public readings in New Cross Library, after which we then refused to leave the building and held the library door open. The occupation led to the national campaign receiving significant media attention.

A compromise was eventually struck in which the library was turned over to volunteers, who would run it unpaid, but who would also be responsible for the rent and utilities; the library was renamed 'New Cross People's Library'.

Figure 5.2.   Occupation in New Cross Library, 2011. *Source:* **Peter Conlin.**

During the brief transitional period when the library was not run by any established organisation, some activists felt that this could provide an opportunity
to envision the library as a radical space (rather like an activist social centre),
rather than as a library in the conventional sense, arguing that it had been a
rather depressing space when it was run by the council. However, these possibilities never materialised because New Cross People's Library was turned
over to Bold Vision and rebranded 'New Cross Learning'(figure 5.3), which,
according to one of the activists interviewed, was because Bold Vision had
credibility as an organisation and an established reputation in the area (Jonathan, interview 13 February 2015).

    However, another activist I interviewed was more cynical about the role
of Bold Vision, characterising them as 'a bit of a middle-class charity, they
want to do stuff down in the rough bit' (Joe, interview 13 February 2015).
The council eventually decided to charge peppercorn rent, but according to
another activist (who was now involved with the running of the library), the
space was being subsidised by the council as a matter of principle:

> It's subsidised and supported by the council and the councillors, but not only
> that, they love it, they like to talk about it, you know, they like to talk about how
> they helped [out] the library. (ibid.)

Similar to private finance initiatives,[10] the conversion could potentially end up
costing the local authority more, but because of the ideological commitment

Figure 5.3.   New Cross Learning, 2015. *Source:* **Peter Conlin.**

to the principle of transfer, it will likely be perceived as both an innovation and a success regardless of any risks or failings. The claims of SEL provide a framework for how the library conversion could be construed as successful, despite the fact that it is potentially both costly and carries significant risks.

The claims made in New Cross Learning's promotional video were consistent with those made by SEL: being embedded in the community and providing skills training. The documentary was filmed entirely inside the library, with no shots of the neighbourhood. The organisation's two chairs were interviewed in the library (with library activities taking place in the background). They claimed that New Cross Learning was serving the community, using phrases such as that the community 'came together' and 'we live here so we know people by their first names'. They presented the library as the 'glue which glues our community together' (New Cross Learning 2013). There were several testimonials from people who had found jobs after volunteering at the library. There were also shots of school pupils (mostly black and Asian, in contrast to the two co-chairs). The two co-chairs described how 'volunteers with no confidence come into a situation and find their feet . . . feeling they can participate in society again' (ibid.). In the background were many shots of craft workshops: knitting classes, *papier-mâché* workshops, singing, 'baby bounce' classes; notably, nothing challenging or oppositional. These activities also embodied what Nick Mahony and John Clarke have termed (drawing on Jacques Rancière's theorisation of spectatorship) as 'communitarian immediacy', whereby people come together and communicate in an unmediated way, which is then seen to embody authentic experience (2013, 946). According to one of the activists who became involved in New Cross Learning, 'they [Bold Vision] do good things for the community but it's what they *think* the community needs' (Joe, interview 13 February 2015, my emphasis). This respondent also raised concerns about the lack of formal processes for involving the community in decision making.

The question of who speaks for the community and what the community needs is an important one (Joe, interview 13 February 2015). In the video, one of the chairs of New Cross Learning says that 'Some people would like the council to run the library and get a qualified librarian. [But] the people who actually use the library would prefer it as it is', adding that 'we see these people every day and they trust us' (New Cross Learning 2013). The other chair said that 'We're never going to go back to a small local library run by a librarian' (ibid.). According to one of the activists interviewed:

> [The chair of New Cross Learning] says, and I don't dispute it, that the library is much better than when the council ran it, so she doesn't want it to go back to being a council library, whereas our [campaign group's] policy is, well it's great that it's still open and it's run by volunteers but long-term we want it to be back in part of the library service and with paid staff. (Jonathan, interview 13 February 2015)

What does it mean to say that the 'library is better'? There were admittedly more cultural activities taking place at New Cross Learning than when it was run by the council, but could this compensate for its uncertain funding situation? Another activist interviewed felt that such arguments were dangerous because it showed that running a library without paid staff was a sustainable option for cash-strapped local authorities (Miguel, interview 20 February 2015).

This raises questions about what sort of community space or creativity was being fostered. Does this depend on the avoidance of controversy, conflict and debate? New Cross Learning were committed to fostering (non-challenging) forms of creativity, and to excluding conflict and direct political expression. For example, those interviewed described an incident where people were not allowed to hand out leaflets for Lewisham People Before Profit outside the library (the reason given was that the council would not approve, ironic given the council was no longer running it), and said that events which were seen to be 'too political' were shunned. They also mentioned that the key volunteers involved in running New Cross Learning were members of the Labour Party, and highlighted the contradictions of setting up a volunteer-run library in response to cuts imposed by the Labour-run council. This can be seen as an example of what Kate Oakley calls the 'mainstreaming' of creativity, 'stressing its pro-social elements . . . excluding creative expression that is marginal, radical, counter-cultural or in some way deemed to be anti-social' (2009, 405). It can also be interpreted as symptomatic of a particular depoliticised model of community development, which De Filippis has characterised as 'neoliberal neo-communitarianism', based on the assumption of a conflict-free society where power relations do not exist. De Filippis traces its origins to the split between community development and community organising that occurred in the 1960s, when community development organisations became sponsored by the United States national government, leading them to become disconnected from radical politics (2004, 56). Within the austerity context, communities mobilise their creativity and resourcefulness to adapt to public service cuts, but do not have the space to ask why they are being made, let alone mobilise creativity towards the exploration of meaningful alternatives. This may reflect a wider public mood in which people have resigned themselves to the idea that they cannot change the decisions made by policymakers and should instead focus on managing the situation. In a wider sense this reflects what Jeremy Gilbert sees as the difficulty under neoliberalism of putting creativity to work 'in a collective, political, democratic fashion' – more difficult and counter-intuitive than mobilising it for individual, consumerist purposes (2014, 212).

The situation also raises larger questions about the role of the voluntary sector in public service provision within the austerity context. A succession of governments positioned the voluntary sector as an alternative provider of public services within a mixed economy, with consequences for its independence.[11] Recent changes to funding arrangements (e.g., the replacement of grant aid with project-based contracts and 'payment by results') have made financing more precarious (National Coalition for Independent Action 2015). Recent legislation such as the Lobbying Bill (UK Government 2014b) has limited the ability of charities to publicly criticize government policy. This positions charities as the upholders of social cohesion, civic responsibility and the defence of dominant social and moral norms, but makes it more difficult for them to undertake advocacy work or encourage meaningful democratic engagement. This places the voluntary and social enterprise sectors in an awkward position: they have to provide services, often on reduced budgets, possibly on a transitional basis (as they may ultimately be outsourced to for-profit corporations), with limited resources to engage citizens, or address the root causes (e.g., poverty, inequality) of the need for their services.

CONCLUSION: CREATIVITY AGAINST AUSTERITY?

There are some difficult, but important, questions to be asked about why such models of outsourced public service provision develop and have at least some limited appeal within the austerity context. The campaign to save the Lewisham libraries was a defensive campaign, and was about preserving the status quo (functioning but severely underfunded libraries), and was marked by an underlying perception, according to my conversations with other campaigners, that a win was unlikely because the council would not listen, so protest could only ever be symbolic. This may be due to wider public acceptance of the need for cuts, and a public mood of fatalism and resignation. When leafleting for the library campaign, I frequently encountered people who had accepted that cuts must be made, or who argued that the internet had rendered libraries obsolete, or that if libraries were saved, then something else must be cut.

There are also difficult questions about why the LACA meetings were so counterproductive. In retrospect, they were often fractious, involved rigid dogmatism and were more concerned with grandstanding and point-scoring than doing practical organising work. This could be understood as an example of what Wendy Brown has termed 'left melancholy' in her classic essay drawing on Walter Benjamin's theorisation of the concept. She characterises this as:

> a Left that has become more attached to its impossibility than to its potential fruitfulness, a Left that is most at home dwelling not in hopefulness but in its own marginality and failure, a Left that is thus caught in a structure of melancholic attachment to a certain strain of its own dead past, whose spirit is ghostly, whose structure of desire is backward looking and punishing. (Brown 1999, 26)

How else to interpret the infighting and sectarian manoeuvring that took place at these meetings? Beyond clichés about boring meetings and the worst habits of the orthodox Left, the campaign participants' conduct may also reflect a public mood in which citizens have become resigned to the lack of agency in the face of decisions that have already been made and politicians who take their constituents for granted. This public mood of resignation and defeatism also marked the wider library campaign, possibly limiting its scope for success (because nobody believed they really would win). Although initially hopeful and high-spirited, it did not sufficiently catalyse energy and creativity around a publicly funded alternative (particularly faced with the impasses around imagining the welfare state as flagged up by Newman and Clarke). Nor did it communicate such alternatives convincingly to the public. This impasse may also be symptomatic of the defensive, single-issue orientation of anti-cuts campaigns, which, according to one of the activists, are difficult to transform into prefigurative experiments in democratic engagement (Joe, interview 13 February 2015). The campaign did not mobilise around libraries as what Jeremy Gilbert terms 'sites of collective joy' or as a 'commons' (2014, 201). The exceptions to this were the more imaginative and vibrant protest actions, such as the march to the town hall with its lively spirit and broad range of creative expression which included many homemade placards and banners, and a funeral for local libraries as well as the occupation of New Cross Library. Such actions offered a fleeting glimpse of the possibilities of a politicised creativity which could shift austerity as a public mood. This might be characterised as creativity as the opening of political space. This sort of creativity would enable invention and experimentation with alternatives, which would ultimately go beyond a simple defence of public services, and which would not be afraid of making demands on the state without accepting that cuts are inevitable.

In the face of the melancholia and sectarianism of anti-austerity campaigns, projects such as New Cross Learning can appear as a creative model of community building (along the lines of that envisaged by SEL, Nesta and other organisations). This model is, however, one that *accepts the principles of austerity and in fact sees austerity as an opportunity*. It is precisely this form of creativity – in which the ingenuity of citizens becomes a resource to exploit in the absence of state funding, but they are not given the autonomy to challenge the state's directives – that becomes central to the cultural politics of austerity, and entrenches a public mood in which citizens are resigned to their disempowerment. As the Lewisham case demonstrates, austerity promotes a particular form of creativity which is about resourcefulness and restoring what is seen to be a lost sense of community and taking on activities which were once seen to be the responsibility of the state, but has little space for anything challenging or oppositional. It is reflective of a wider depoliticising dynamic in which problem-solving by individuals, charities and the private sector replaces political struggle or larger contestations; impulses towards self-organisation, instead of challenging the state, become mobilised to absolve it of responsibility.

However, one of the activists I interviewed saw the situation differently, characterising it as 'quite a painful process of the Left falling to bits and people who'd been in the Left for a long time coming to terms with that' (Miguel, interview 20 February 2015), 'the Left' in this case referring to the dogmatism and tactical conservatism which have been the legacy of traditional Left organisations. The relationships that had been developed and the experience that had been gained through the library campaign and LACA played an important role in the campaign to stop the Lewisham Hospital Accident and Emergency ward from being downgraded, with a much wider range of the public involved and a successful legal challenge against Health Secretary Jeremy Hunt (ibid.). These relationships also enabled the successful campaign to stop Lewisham council from selling off properties. This involved squatting as a protest action, and created links with the Focus E15 campaign in Newham (which will be discussed in chapter 7). Both involved imaginative tactics and a more open approach to organising. This can be understood as a more hopeful conception of creativity, one which is not afraid of being oppositional or challenging, and which prefigures alternative futures.

As a point of comparison, it is worth considering the role of volunteer-run services in Greece (where austerity measures have been much more severe), which Owen Jones described in his article on the 2015 election:

> Outside one polling station, I speak to Georgia, who works at a hospital clinic manned by volunteers which caters for the impoverished. For unemployed Greeks denied access to the public healthcare system, such clinics are lifelines. Georgia has one clear ambition – that after a year or two of a Syriza-led government, her clinic will no longer be needed and will close. (Jones 2015)

At the time of writing, the fate of Syriza has since become more uncertain. However, the significance of the clinic is that the provision of volunteer-run services and mutual aid systems is specifically intended as a temporary stopgap. Unlike with New Cross Learning, the goal is not to permanently institutionalize volunteer-run services. Instead, the volunteer-run clinic can be temporary precisely because it is part of a larger social movement which will hopefully create better healthcare provision, making volunteer-run clinics unnecessary in the future. This could be seen as an example of how the Big Society could be interpreted, through a utopian lens, as containing the seeds of 'another potential society' (Levitas 2012, 336). Such utopian thinking envisages a significant role for the welfare state, but also takes into consideration the critiques of post-war Keynesianism and engages with the questions around material conditions ignored by Nesta, SEL and others, particularly around who has time and energy to engage in volunteering. Rather than writing off the welfare state or public service provision as a worthless site for political imagination or struggle, it is to engage in what Janet Newman and John Clarke call 'imaginaries of the state' (2014, 158): trying to re-imagine the function and purpose of the state, and its role in the making of publics. Beyond official dialogues about the relationship between state and citizens, or political parties, Newman and Clarke note that rather than imposing a hegemonic vision of a singular public (as in public relations 'listening exercises') this process needs to engage with a wide range of publics and foster the emergence of new ones (2014, 16), and to engage with both desires for collectivity and security in the face of uncertainty and emergent desires for a better life. Creative politics would engage in this sort of re-imagining process and the fostering of new publics, and would imaginatively consider and enact what alternatives might look like.

NOTES

1. The council is the elected municipal legislature for a borough or county.

2. This has now been extensively critiqued; see Garnham 2005; Peck 2005; Lovink and Rossiter 2007; and Hewison 2014, among others.

3. The National Endowment for Science, Technology and the Arts (Nesta) is a foundation and think tank in the United Kingdom for promoting innovation. It was closely associated with the New Labour administration. See http://www.nesta.org.uk/.

4. Leadbeater has written publications for Nesta since 2006 and is currently a Fellow of the organisation.

5. The Indignados, also known as the 15-M Movement, was a movement which occupied squares in Spanish cities and protested both austerity and the failures of the electoral politics.

6. The libraries were Blackheath Library, Crofton Park Library, Grove Park Library, New Cross Library and Sydenham Library.

7. UNISON is a trade union representing public sector employees, including many who are employed by local authorities.

8. The borough of Lewisham measures 35.15 km² (an average size in comparison to other inner London boroughs) and has a population of 275, 885 according to the 2011 census (Lewisham Council 2012); Lewisham is the 31st most deprived local authority out of the 351 local authorities in England (Lewisham Joint Strategic Needs Assessment, c. 2010).

9. A leisure trust is a particular type of charity which was set up to manage leisure centres and other sports facilities, and which were created as part of a process of outsourcing municipally provided services.

10. Private finance initiatives (PFI) involve funding public infrastructure projects and public services with private capital, and are used as part of a programme of privatisation. They have been controversial in terms of lack of transparency and perverse incentives.

11. See Jane Lewis, 'New Labour's Approach to the Voluntary Sector: Independence and the Meaning of Partnership', *Social Policy and Society*, 4 (2005), pp. 121–131. See also National Coalition for Independent Action, *Fight or Fright: Voluntary Services in 2015,* 2015, http://www.independentaction.net/wp-content/uploads/2015/02/NCIA-Inquiry-summary-report-final.pdf.

Chapter 6

Trade Union Activism after the 2010 Student Protests

This chapter will be based on my own involvement and experience of trade union activism within the austerity context. It will also explore the experiences of trade union activists I have encountered who have brought fresh perspectives to campaigning and organising, and have developed some important campaigns. I came to trade union activism out of an involvement with social centres[1] in London and the student movement of 2009–2010 (figure 6.1). This was at the tail end of the boom period and the New Labour settlement, just before the Conservative–Liberal Democrat Coalition government came into power. Some of the activities around this time which social centres supported included the Climate Camp[2] and Plane Stupid[3] actions against the expansion of the fossil fuel economy, and a housing march at the Bank of England[4] to coincide with a G8 meeting. There were numerous benefit concerts to support various grassroots organisations. The social centres supported free schools, art exhibitions, reading groups and other cultural activities which were more about prefiguring alternatives than about protest as conventionally defined. They enabled space for creative expression not possible in a city where space had become pressurised,[5] especially for those without independent means (to be discussed in greater detail in the following chapter).

The re-politicisation of higher education began with protests and occupations to oppose course closures at Middlesex University and the London College of Communication in 2009. Following plans to increase the cap on university tuition fees to £9,000/year, a joint demonstration organised by University and College Union (UCU)[6] and the National Union of Students (NUS) in November 2010 culminated with the occupation at Conservative Party Headquarters at Millbank in London. Protests were organised to coincide with each reading of the bill in Parliament which authorised the tuition fee increase. Although the vote in the House of Commons was lost, it was very

Figure 6.1. rampART Social Centre, interior. *Source:* Debra Benita Shaw.

Figure 6.2. Anti Cuts Space (occupied building in Bloomsbury, London). *Source:* the author.

Figure 6.3.   Sign outside Anti Cuts Space. *Source:* **the author.**

close at 323–302 (United Kingdom 2010). A wave of university occupations also took place during 2010–2011 (see figures 6.2 and 6.3).

The UK university system has followed a model of 'wide access, but fee for service' (Bousquet and Terranova 2004 cited in Dyer-Witheford 2005). In 1998, tuition fees were introduced in England[7] in response to the Dearing Report (Rustin 2016, 151) with income-contingent loans of £1,000 replacing grants.[8] A series of legislative reforms drove through the marketisation of the sector, and the introduction of the £9,000 tuition fees should be understood within this context. Institutions were expected to compete with each other for students, funding and league table rankings. The number of students attending university aged eighteen years and older has increased from 5% to 50% in fifty years (Rustin 2016, 160). This process can be understood as what Nick Dyer-Witheford terms 'student biopower' (2005, 80), arguing that 'neoliberal apologists point smugly to increasing participation rates in post-secondary institutions, while ignoring the stress and sacrifice this involves' (ibid.). It was this marketised model of education which was specifically questioned within the many discussions and teach-ins which took place during the student protests. Radical alternatives were also being put forward: free education, alternative university structures and so forth. Some of these built on experiments which had first developed within the social centres.

The student movement declined in the aftermath of the vote in favour of increasing tuition fees. However, the energy and creativity of this movement had influenced trade unionism. My involvement began through a part-time administrative job in a UCU branch. Being employed part-time as a visiting lecturer, I was also a member of the union. The branch was very active and dynamic, and did concentrate not only on bread-and-butter workplace issues but also on wider political debates around the nature of education. The creativity and energy of ordinary members were encouraged. It was this conception of trade union activism that stayed with me, as I became involved as rep and activist at other institutions where I worked following the completion of my PhD. I came to realise that this initial experience was the exception rather than the norm. Instead, a staid and conservative organisational approach dominated by the servicing model[9] was prevalent, and new campaigning and organising tactics were viewed with suspicion. There was also reluctance to involve new or junior members of staff, particularly those on temporary contracts.

My first permanent job was at an institution where the branch had been moribund for twenty-five years. As a result, staff morale and membership were low, and active engagement seemed unfamiliar and counter-intuitive. I became involved as Branch Secretary because I felt it was important for staff to have a voice. Over the next few years, I and a few others – slowly and persistently, and with the support of the regional officials – rebuilt the branch. At the time of writing there is now an active branch committee and a network of school reps, and membership has increased. Gender equality became a particularly important campaigning issue within what seemed like a predominantly male-dominated institution. We did this through encouraging new staff, many of whom had come from workplaces where an active union presence was a norm, to join and be actively involved. Unfortunately, this was where I also encountered organisational conservatism. For example, I was told by other reps that union activity was pointless and that I would be targeted, and was also told by colleagues that unions were obsolete in the twenty-first century. On an intuitive level, I felt I was going against a public mood in which individualised responses to problems at work seemed much more immediate than collective ones. What I was doing felt odd and even anachronistic: *someone like me should not be doing this*. I did not fit the stereotype: I was female, an ethnic minority, a foreigner and a new member of staff. Also, my previous involvement in direct action and social centre politics set me apart from those who had habituated to traditional Left politics, and made me an outsider to those traditions. Consequently, what seemed as self-evident and common sense to me seemed counter-intuitive to others.

UCU currently has a national executive, and there are regional committees; there are also self-organised equality groups. It was through involvement through these structures that I came into contact with activists who were doing significant work, including those interviewed for this chapter. This work brought imaginative approaches to trade unionism which included national days of action on particular issues, investigative journalism, producing films and the use of social media. Like myself their involvement was rather unlikely, but this enabled us to engage with workplace activism in imaginative ways. I do not claim they are representative of trade union activism, particularly in the face of the organisational conservatism which threatens its future viability. In addition to my own personal reflections, this chapter will be based on interviews with these leading activists, two of whom been given pseudonyms (Louise and Robert). I will begin the chapter by considering some of the dominant narratives around the decline of unions, and outline the dangers of the folding of such narratives into the melancholic and nostalgic conceptions around work and community critiqued in previous chapters.

ACCOUNTS OF THE DECLINE OF UNIONS AND THE NEED FOR ANOTHER APPROACH

There is not sufficient space in this chapter to undertake a comprehensive evaluation of the changing role of unions. However, it is important to briefly consider analyses of union decline, which has been experienced as a loss of membership, density and influence. Union membership has declined from 12m in 1980 to 6.4m in 2005 and 5.8m in 2015 (Gall 2016). The number of strike days is now at the lowest point since records were taken (Office of National Statistics 2016) – and with the provisions brought in by the Trade Union Act – which place stringent restrictions on the right to strike – this number looks set to decrease further (UK Government 2016). Union decline has been interpreted as symptomatic of the loss of relevance of twentieth-century mass organisations in the context of the decline of collective identities in general – and social class in particular – as mobilising principles.[10] Post-Fordist developments which have undermined the bases of work-based identities have posed significant challenges to unions (Piore and Sabel 1984; Lash and Urry 1987; see Kelly 1998 for a critique). In *Farewell to the Working Class* (1987), Andre Gorz argues that the industrial worker has been overcome by such developments:

> The majority of the population now belong to the post-industrial neo-proletariat which, with no job security or definite class identity, fills the area of probationary, contracted, casual, temporary and part-time employment. . . . Any employment seems to be accidental and provisional, every type of work purely

contingent. It cannot feel any involvement with 'its' work or identification with 'its' job. Work no longer signifies an activity or even a major occupation; it is merely a blank interval on the margins of life, to be endured in order to earn a little money. (1987, 69–70)

Gorz characterises a situation where norms of the job-for-life and stable work identities are becoming less hegemonic, and less achievable. This poses particular challenges for unions, particularly if the commitment of activists depends on such stable work identities and relationships; how union activism continues in the face of these challenges will be discussed later in the chapter.

Gorz's comments can be interpreted as both an analysis of social change and as a critique of the relative inability of trade unions to meaningfully respond to new social movements and the 1960s counterculture. Critiques which drew attention to the limitations of unions were made by those within the Post-Operaismo[11] tradition. Through the concept of the 'social factory' (Tronti 1962), capitalism was theorised as encompassing many aspects of everyday life (society had become a factory), and the definition of labour was expanded to include many activities outside of the workplace to include those who were not in paid employment (e.g., the unemployed and those engaged in unpaid domestic work) and who were traditionally outside of union representation (Federici 2012; Federici and Cox 2012; Negri 1989). The refusal of work was also proposed as a radical rejection of the social discipline of the workplace (Tronti 1966). More recently, Nick Srnicek and Alex Williams have proposed a politics of post-work (2015) which embraces 'a fully automated economy' (2015, 109). They envision a future in which automation liberates humanity from both drudgery and scarcity (ibid.) and propose a universal basic income so that unemployment does not mean poverty, and to 'make work voluntary rather than coerced' (2015, 120). Srnicek and Williams also develop some incisive critiques of the work ethic, arguing that it structures our lives around competitive self-realisation and that people 'must prove their worthiness before the eyes of capital' (2015, 126). They also caution against the Left embracing rhetoric about work as the only means to escape poverty, and as a mechanism for social integration (2015, 124). At the same time, they critique the work ethic as based around the idea that only a life with suffering is a meaningful life. This has some resonances with what I have argued in this book in relation to austerity. However, where I part company with Srnicek and Williams, and where they also part company with the Post-Operaismo thinkers, is their dismissal of horizontal organising practices as an ineffectual and unthinking 'folk politics' (2015, 13). This, in my view, is wrong. Such practices have much to offer, as my next chapter will demonstrate. They also dismiss the politics of emotion (which they term 'a broader trend that has come to privilege the affective as the site of real politics' as symptomatic of 'folk politics' and the absence of a coherent political pro-gramme (2015, 7); they argue that this emphasis on emotion stymies abstract analysis (2015, 8). Throughout this book, I have demonstrated the centrality, and furthermore the unavoidability of emotions in both entrenching consent for austerity and in challenging it.

In *Nice Work If You Can Get It,* Andrew Ross highlights a 'longstanding debate within the labour movement about the moral virtues of hard work' which has yet to be resolved (2009, 113). The moralising discourses around work flagged up by the critiques discussed earlier underpin the current divi-sive public mood of harsh judgements of the unemployed, as I have pointed out. This is ironic at a time when employment has become more insecure,[12] and there is not only a greater risk of losing one's, but due to developments such as zero-hour contracts,[13] work does not necessarily pay. In a more general sense, the moral virtue attached to work reinforces the conservative emphasis on employment as social discipline and as a marker of normality and respectability, regardless of the experience, quality or career prospects of the job. In *The Problem with Work* (2011), Kathi Weeks notes that the moral virtues of work are 'routinely espoused in managerial discourse, defended in the popular media, and enshrined in public policies' which present employ-ment and employability as the only solution for economic and social security (2011, 10–11). In a discussion with Jo Littler and the members of the Precari-ous Workers' Brigade campaign group, Nina Power points out that:

> we have a massive increase in very low paid work, expanding hours, zero- hours contracts, unpaid internships, exploited grey-market labour and prison labour' but there is simultaneously a framing of work as an individual moral respon-sibility: 'improving your attitude, cutting your hair, trying harder, believing in yourself. (Littler et al. 2014)

This moralising around work produces a sense of guilt and shame – that if one is unemployed or in insecure employment, it is one's own fault – because 'normal people' are in proper full-time, permanent jobs. Job insecurity or problems at work become treated as individual private matters which cannot be discussed with others (for fear of appearing not normal or respectable), let alone serve as the impetus for collective action – particularly if there is little union presence in the workplace. This is where a public mood of harsh moral judgements and guilt associated with hardship can be understood as the result of declining union membership and activity. Such a public mood also makes collective action more implausible and unimaginable. This public mood also makes it easier to feel guilty about union activity or afraid that it will lead to being branded as a troublemaker. The appropriate course of action, according to the logic of this public mood, would be to keep one's head down and not complain, and keep things to ourselves.

Other critiques of the relevance of unions have historically been related to the challenges of coming to grips with other social struggles around gender, race or sexual equality in the 1960s and 1970s (Touraine et al. 1987). The myth of the 'family wage' or the male wage which could support a family framed women's employment as a threat to men's earning capacity. Because this myth was embraced by the trade union movement for many years, it proved to be a significant barrier in supporting gender equality (Coote and Campbell 1987, 63–64). Notably, the 'family wage' myth was also connected to normative conceptions of work: the 'proper job' that 'lasted for at least eight hours a day; it might spill over evenings and weekends; and its most demanding phase tended to be the first twenty years' (Coote and Campbell 1987, 68). These still-persistent conceptions of the 'proper job' also inform the moral judgements which I have critiqued throughout this book. Jo Littler has also pointed to 'an implicit nostalgia for Fordist culture' on the Left – which is problematic 'given the place of women in the mid twentieth century' (Littler et al. 2014). Populist demands for a return to Fordist industries also imply a return to the 'family wage' and gendered divisions of labour (Coote and Campbell 1987, 256).

Historically, struggles for gender equality within the trade union movement have not been taken sufficiently seriously. At best, trade union leaders have been ambivalent towards equal pay campaigns. (Boston 2015; Coote and Campbell 1987). Consequently, women and ethnic minorities have been systematically under-represented in leadership roles. Despite the election of Frances O'Grady as General Secretary of the Trades Union Congress umbrella organisation, and female leadership in four of the major unions, this under-representation persists today (Kirton and Healey 2012). The development of self-organised groups for women workers and the influence of feminism on the trade union movement have also led to the greater involvement of women, as have positive action strategies (for an analysis of such initiatives see Colgan and Ledwith 2000, and Kirton and Greene 2002). At the time of writing, union membership is currently higher among female workers than it is among male workers (BIS 2016). This change in membership suggests that unions are now different organisations, although greater progress has yet to be made in terms of a leadership that is genuinely representative of membership.

Similarly, Satnam Virdee's *Race, Class and the Racialised Outsider* (2014) studies union resistance to the presence of black and migrant workers, including support for the 'colour bar' in the United Kingdom during the 1950s and 1960s[14] (Virdee 2014, 101). However, Virdee also examines unions themselves as a site of struggle for race and gender equality particularly as a result of shifting attitudes following the social movements of the 1960s and 1970s, which became 'a durable current' (2014, 165). For example, black and Asian local authority workers successfully established self-organised groups within unions in the 1970s and 1980s (ibid.). This has now become common practice.

At stake within the acknowledgement of such struggles is the continued relevance and future of unions. To relegate unions to the past is to incorporate them into reactionary narratives. A melancholic and neo-communitarian tone has marked some popular accounts of the decline of unions, particularly when positioned within a broader narrative of post-industrial decline. The decline of unions is perceived as symptomatic of the loss of gendered work-based identities and codes of social discipline. This may also reflect sociological realities in terms of how these losses are narrated and mourned by post-industrial communities. For example, participants in Valerie Walkerdine's study of a town in South Wales which had recently lost its steel industry expressed nostalgia for the gendered division of labour and how this created 'shared spaces, shared activities' as well as strict rules about what one could say at work or at home (2010, 99). The service-industry jobs on offer were perceived by Walkerdine's respondents as a feminised and debased form of labour, in contrast with the dignified and manly jobs of the steel industry (Walkerdine and Jimenez 2012). As has been discussed in previous chapters, nostalgia for authentic jobs carries powerful emotional appeal, meaning that disentangling it from the need for decent pay and conditions becomes an urgent task.

More disturbing than these mourning processes have been the charac-terisations of the labour movement as defending shared norms of working-class respectability. This includes those associated with the Blue Labour tendency I have discussed earlier or, more recently, in the aftermath of the EU referendum, those who have argued that the Labour Party must speak for those who voted to leave the EU, particularly in post-industrial com-munities (e.g., Matthew Goodwin or John Harris). The *Spirit of '45* film (see chapter 1) also represents this sort of nostalgic tendency. Race may not be explicitly mentioned but can be implied in terms of the shared cultural references, histories and insularity of close-knit communities. These are the very norms which I have challenged throughout this book, and they are also those which Stuart Hall critiques in his theorisation of traditionalism, argu-ing 'this is where and why sexism and racism lurk' 1988f, 194). While it is perhaps impossible to unburden unions of the weight of history, there is some urgency in challenging their framing within nostalgic and melancholic narratives.

TRADE UNIONISM IN THE AFTERMATH OF
THE STUDENT MOVEMENT

In order to counter such nostalgia, I am focusing on trade union activism in the current moment, and on the present-day experiences of activists. The rest of this chapter will be based on interviews with activists who have

played a leading role in campaigns, primarily around the rights and conditions of staff on temporary contracts. Job insecurity is very prevalent within
higher education. According to figures by the UCU, 54% of academic staff
and 49% of teaching staff in UK universities (UCU 2016, 1) are employed
precariously. Many contracts are only one year and, in many cases, are
hourly paid (UCU 2016, 2). It is a condition that has affected many early
career academics as many of these posts are in the early to mid-career level,
below Senior Lecturer/Senior Researcher[15] (UCU 2016, 6). I have spent
several years on these contracts myself and it is also a condition which has
affected the activists I have interviewed. The experiences of working life
they have discussed are quite widespread, and may be familiar to many
readers of this book.

These are also the activists who have brought imaginative responses to campaigns, including teach-ins and national days of action which have included a
range of campaign tactics and public debates about important issues in education. Louise is on the UCU's national executive and other national committees,
and Jamie and Robert are both branch committee members. Jamie and Robert
are currently on part-time contracts as teaching staff, and Louise is currently
on a full-time contract as an administrator, having left the academic field after
too many years spent on insecure contracts. As none of them with the exception of Louise are on full-time permanent contracts, their union activism takes
place within the context of job insecurity, in either their present employment
conditions or immediate history. They also became involved in trade union
activism out of other activist histories, including the 2010 student protests.

Both Jamie and Robert were postgraduate students at the time of the 2010
student protests and, although the fee increase would not affect them personally, they were drawn into campus activism and saw union activism as following on from this:[16]

> I suppose it dates back to 2010–2011 and the protests against the student fees.
> I fell into campus activism around the issue, and specifically the occupation here
> [at my university] and subsequent to that I was really looking for somewhere
> to continue that campaign. As a member of staff, UCU seemed like the natural
> option. (Jamie Melrose, interview 15 May 2016)
>
> Through the student movement I was radicalised and I was looking [for]
> somewhere to put that energy. (Robert, interview 1 June 2016)

In the face of waning student activism after the tuition fee vote, they were
looking to find another place for their energies, particularly as they had
become employed at the same universities where they had been studying.
For Robert, the union did not seem apparent at first as a site for this, and he
noted that many casualised staff were not unionised, but he was also struck

by the unfairness of being paid less than full-time permanent staff for the same work:

> I'm doing the same job as someone else, this person's my friend, we go to the pub together, and they're earning £35,000 a year and I'm earning £10,000 at best. And so I thought, this is something that really needs to change, innit? (Robert, interview 1 June 2016)

A similar recognition of injustice motivated Louise to be involved in the union, when she realised that she routinely was not being offered contracts as a visiting tutor due to nepotistic recruiting practices. Louise noticed that teaching work was being allocated through informal networks and mostly to male colleagues, 'if they . . . were a boy and maybe went to the pub with the right people and stuff like that' (Louise, May 2016). Her initial response was to internalise this as a judgement on her teaching ability: 'feeling really shit about myself, and, like, wondering if it was because I was a bad teacher and . . . doubting myself' (ibid.). However, a positive teaching observation in another department served as 'one of those turning point moments' where she realised that her lack of teaching opportunities was not due to a lack of ability, but were the result of sexism (ibid.):

> One of the most empowering things I think has ever happened to me is realis-ing . . . that something really wasn't my fault . . . actually a lot of what was going on was unjust and unfair employment practice and that it wasn't like this for everyone and that it was that kind of intersection of the equality issues like gender. (Louise, interview 23 May 2016)

Inspired by social movement theory, industrial relations academic John Kelly has identified the importance of private grievances being transformed into collective ones, thus becoming the object of collective action (1998, 24–26). This has been the case for Louise, as the recognition of gender inequal-ity enabled to her to see the situation as 'unjust and unfair employment practice' (Louise, May 2016), and to end the individualised self-blaming which, as I have suggested, is a manifestation of the way that public mood is internalised.

As was the case with Robert, for Louise, joining the union and becoming actively involved was not obviously apparent. Because she was on a tempo-rary contract she was reluctant to pay for subscription fees, and she did not think the union could help with her situation. But what ultimately encouraged her to become involved was speaking with another activist (Jane), who said her voice needed to be heard or otherwise it would not be taken seriously. In retrospect, the concern showed by Jane towards people who were not

her immediate colleagues was important to Louise in joining the union and
becoming involved:

> But I just have this really lasting impression of Jane and her commitment and
> caring. [She] wasn't a postgraduate; she teaches in a different capacity . . . you
> know, caring about what was happening to people that she didn't work directly
> with was really what stuck out. (Louise, May 2016)

Significantly, Louise uses the term 'caring'. This term has particular
emotional resonances. In this context, it describes feeling cared for by
someone with whom one does not have immediate contact, and who has
nothing to gain in terms of self-interest. Drawing on the work of the Spanish feminist group *Precarias a la Deriva*, Isabell Lorey has explored the
concept of the 'care community', in which vulnerabilities are acknowledged rather than shamefully hidden, and people care for each other (2015,
79). For *Precarias a la Deriva*, a care community is specifically about
redressing the undervaluing and depoliticising of feminised reproductive
labour, particularly that involving care for children, the ill and the elderly.
As Anna Coote and Beatrix Campbell have pointed out, the myth of the
'family wage' was in fact based on the devaluation of reproductive, caring labour (1987, 259). However, I would argue for a broader politics of
care, beyond the family and domestic labour, which would encompass
the interactions between Jane and Louise. Care, in this case, would be
combined with the recognition of injustice and the importance of taking
collective action to oppose it. Although Jane did not work in the same area
or capacity as Louise, she saw precarious contracts as a wider condition
that was common to both, and which required collective action (standing
up for each other). Care as feminist solidarity also has precedents within
the labour movement, such as the support for the Ford sewing machinists'
1968 strike for equal pay – which, according to Coote and Campbell, was
a key moment of politicisation for many women at the time (1987, 10).
Within feminist science studies, caring practices have been theorised as the
basis of a relational understanding of the body and society, and a 'rationality of responsibility for others' (Rose 1994, 49) in which emotion and care
become seen as intrinsic to work, including knowledge work, rather than a
function only of domestic labour. Care also recalls the concept of solidarity
as in an imaginative act which involves the recognition of shared conditions
and shared struggles (see chapter 4).

In her interview, Louise described her experience of being at a national
meeting. The space created by the meeting for people to speak about experiences of discrimination without fear of judgement was significant for her.
The creation of such spaces within social movements will be discussed in the

following chapter in greater detail, but it is also worth noting their presence within the trade union context:

> talking to people who were disabled and felt like they were being discriminated against because of various issues there, or there is a particular woman who was on a mobility scooter at the meeting that I met . . . and she was talking about her experiences. And like I think it was something about being in a space, being in a room where it was safe to talk about experiences. (Louise, May 2016)

Being able to speak solely about everyday experiences of discrimination and to acknowledge it as a structural condition were important for Louise. Such moments also have precedents within feminist history, particularly the tactic of consciousness-raising in the late 1960s. Consciousness-raising groups involved the discussion of personal issues within a political context. As Anna Coote and Beatrix Campbell describe it:

> Small groups of women began to get together. They began to talk to each other in a way they had not done before. They discussed their day-to-day experiences, and their feelings about themselves, their jobs, their husbands, their children and their parents. Of course, women had been doing this since language was invented – but what was new was that they were now drawing political conclusions from their personal experiences. (1987, 5)

Although the term 'consciousness-raising' may no longer be commonly used to describe such processes, Coote and Campbell also recognise 'the process whereby personal experience – explored among women in a supportive context' and using this as a basis for strategy has an important legacy (1987, 256). Louise's description of the meeting could be understood as an example of this legacy. Louise contrasted her experiences explored here with meetings of her local union branch, which she described as rather conservative and for the most part unsympathetic towards the plight of staff on temporary contracts and new members of staff. This reflects the organisational conservatism I have described and is an indication of how rare such moments still are within the trade union movement. However, the fact that they did occur at all reflects the impact of practices developed through feminist struggles on contemporary organising, although their effects remain marginal.

ORGANISERS INSTEAD OF HEROES

Louise, Robert and Jamie also brought an approach to organisation and working with others that, to an extent, presents a way out of the impasses discussed in the previous chapter. They all felt that what trade unions ultimately had to offer was their capacity for communication and co-ordination and bringing people together:

> I have a lot of energy and I'm good at organising and so the more I got involved the more I was structuring things . . . I think [Branch] Secretary was an obvious . . . I didn't see anyone in the branch who would be good at secretary and I thought John is a really good chair, and Asif is a really good chair, and there are a couple of people who have special interests, but there was nothing bringing people together and I thought I could do that job really well. So it's not the most glamorous role but I think nobody else could have done it (Robert, interview 1 June 2016)
>
> I definitely saw a need for organisation: someone who wouldn't be overwhelmed by the task of coordinating, someone who wouldn't be overwhelmed by sorting the really boring stuff out. I'm an activist but I'm also quite good at organising things. (Robert, interview 1 June 2016)

Robert acknowledged that organisation was boring and unglamorous behind-the-scenes work, but it was nonetheless necessary in 'bringing people together' and the active functioning of the branch. Jamie made similar comments about the importance of organisation:

> Devoting yourself to organisation is important because it's a function that doesn't take place on its own accord. So that's what I really learnt about organisation, you have to put a lot of effort into trying to co-ordinate people to try to get them together, to try to build networks of solidarity, try to make sure that people not only propose policy, but come up with means of effecting that policy, if you see what I mean. (Jamie Melrose, interview May 2016)

What is significant is that both Jamie and Robert see themselves as *organisers* and saw their role primarily as enabling others: building structures, interactions and dense social networks which will enable collective action (Kelly 1998, 37). This is very different from the heroic, masculinist conceptions of the charismatic trade union leader romanticised in some media representations, or the grandstanding speeches with no practical follow-up critiqued in the previous chapter. This may represent a reaction against the historical dominance of charismatic models of leadership on the Left (for a debate about this see Mouffe and Erejon 2016), or may simply reflect their backgrounds in horizontal organising practices which have been sceptical of charismatic leaders. Jamie noted the irony of being involved in a rigid vertical structure after the spontaneous approaches he encountered in the student movement. He also admitted, rather ruefully, that some of the best organising work he had ever done was his involvement in the student occupation:

> It's counter-intuitive because those occupations were supposed to be horizontal and spontaneous to some degree, and open, and very much trying to prefigure

an alternative university, whereas you could argue that trade unions, and specifically the UCU are the opposite of that. They're vertical, part of the official university negotiating mechanism. (Jamie Melrose, interview 15 May 2016)

However, later on, he pointed out that he felt that despite some of these misgivings, what trade unions do have to offer is infrastructure and capacity for organisation, beyond the spontaneous moments such as the student occupations:

> A trade union in and of itself doesn't need to be vertical, it doesn't need to be a management tool, a shadow HR problem solving lobby group, it can be whatever its members want it to be, I went into UCU very much from that point of view. Organisation was key, I needed to work with other members of staff, other university participants in a common cause, and the union allows that to happen, as much as any organisation can. (Jamie Melrose, interview 15 May 2016)

For Robert, because 2010 student protests were a formative moment, he tried to bring the creative tactics directly into union organising. This included organising a teach-in to coincide with a strike day. It included a range of speakers, including those who spoke on the key issues of the strike (pay, casualisation and the gender pay gap) but also addressed broader questions about the nature of education and the effects of neoliberalism on education and society. Although such creative tactics around the use of the strike as a platform for debate are yet to be taken up on a broader scale, it was a particularly successful and imaginative model that offered brief glimpse of how unions could function as platforms for such discussions.

Louise characterised her involvement in a national committee within similar terms, seeing it as a *collective* organisation and a space for generating creative ideas rather than where individuals claimed ownership; she also saw her role primarily as a facilitator or co-ordinator rather than as charismatic leader, and in terms of collectively taking credit, rather than claiming to own particular ideas:

> I don't think anyone on the committee would ever try and take credit for a particular idea, like it's very collective, that focus is really there . . . I feel genuinely proud to be involved in something that is set up that way. I'm the chair, brilliant, you know, great but like I don't do weird executive chair's decisions unless I can actually not avoid it. (Louise, interview, 23 May 2016)

By saying 'it's very collective', Louise is referring to an approach to organising in which members are actively engaged and take collective responsibility, rather than defer to a leader who speaks on their behalf. Collective identity is not something which can be assumed, either based on workplace identities or a rooted and stable relationship to place and community. Instead, it must be actively created, in the present, through the process of campaigning and organising together.

As Louise made clear, this requires being attentive to the micro-politics of interpersonal relationships:

> So I think that, yeah, we are creative and actually we have really good discussions and we certainly don't always agree with each other on the best way to do things. We try and maintain that kind of respect I guess on the committee, like it's not as confrontational as some might be. I think to be honest we've all been so much crapped upon in our working lives that we try and be a space where we don't crap upon each other within the committee. (Louise, interview 23 May 2016)

She characterises this in terms of 'maintaining respect' and being careful not to 'crap upon each other' even though people may not always agree, although she acknowledged more confrontational politics exist elsewhere. This presented a different approach than the bitter factionalism I have discussed in the previous chapter, or elsewhere in the labour movement – in which there seemed to be a blindness around interpersonal relations so long as someone was seen to have the 'right politics'.

To pay attention to interpersonal relationships and the micro-politics of meetings, to do organisational work behind the scenes rather than playing the role of the charismatic leader is to take on board some of the lessons of horizontal movements, in terms of the attention to meeting facilitation and conduct, and the importance of engaging with others rather than talking at them. The confrontational scenarios described in the previous chapter have contributed to sectarian power struggles in which the meetings become spaces of judgement, and where very little listening takes place. This can be alienating for those new to the labour movement, potentially contributing to union decline. The tactics that I have described engage directly with and acknowledge the public mood of individualised self-blame and how it can affect the dynamics of collective action. The legacy of the feminist movement is important here because the notion of care as a strategy for forming collectives directly confronts the more divisive emotions mobilised by austerity and its effects in the workplace.

DEMOCRATIC RITUALS AND MIS-RECOGNITIONS OF CLASS

As with other unions, policy within the UCU is made through rather complex democratic structures. Decisions on policy are made at the annual conference.

There is also a national equality conference which then feeds into the main conference, and motions passed become official union policy. Conference usually takes place over three to four days in a convention centre big enough to host hundreds of people. Motions are presented in two- to three-minute speeches by delegates from a branch, or a regional or national committee; they typically include a statement about a particular concern followed by a list of action points, which commit the union to a particular policy and/or involve spending the union's resources. Louise saw the annual conference as a place for some important concrete action which is based on members' experiences:

> I think that Congress is a really important part of the story because obviously there are representatives from all these branches and regions and what have you there, and it's an opportunity if you bring a really good motion that's kind of comprised of stuff that [has] come through from the grass roots, it speaks to people because it's based on real experiences, not just something that someone has pulled out of their bum. (Louise, interview 23 May 2016)

Louise saw annual meetings for equality groups as places to flag up areas of collective concern, and as the impetus for campaigns. She saw the democratic process as a conduit for taking actions on concerns which 'come through the grassroots' and were 'based on real experiences', enabling them to become official policy – and more importantly leading to action (ibid.).

However, the annual conference can also be rather alienating as an activist; I did not find it particularly welcoming at first, due to its hierarchical and bureaucratic character. In many ways it replicated some of the problems discussed in the previous chapter. The debating of motions could be rather ritualistic and theatrical. For example, there were shouty, long-winded speeches with rather simulacral language about the working class – ironic given this was a union representing white-collar professionals. This perhaps reflected unresolved issues around reconciling trade union activism with knowledge work, and possibly reflected the difficulties in imagining trade unionism for the post-Fordist context. There were also factional power games around positions on the national executive, for which few members voted.[17] This recourse to nostalgic conceptions of trade unionism could be interpreted perhaps as a reaction to the prevalence of the servicing model, as discussed earlier. In my experience, this servicing model manifested itself through attempts to limit democratic decision-making forums, and the use of political marketing techniques which addressed members as a silent majority. The mishandling of national industrial disputes (where concerted action would then dissipate, often leading to a stalemate) was also symptomatic of this situation, and may have also reflect a wider public mood in which people accept that unions are in decline and can never become a truly effective force. The legitimacy of the annual conference was also undermined by a lack of new blood (possibly due in part to the resistance to involving new people), meaning the same individuals would come as delegates every year, making it seem like a rather closed social club.

Louise also described feeling unfamiliar with the union's democratic structures and processes. For her, this was connected to coming from a 'very apolitical home' where she 'just didn't grow up with that sort of atmosphere' in her family (Louise, May 2016):

> I certainly didn't have even the most basic idea, do you know what, when I joined the union I didn't know anything much about the history of trade unions, I think I vaguely knew something about the miners' strike . . . I didn't know anything about the history of it, I probably picked up what I did know from bits of films and some stuff I occasionally heard from my mum, do you know what I mean? (ibid.)

How accessible are union processes and structures to those unfamiliar with the history of trade unionism, or the history of the British Left? What happens when such a background or familiarity is expected or assumed? Louise's mention of upbringing and family suggests tacit knowledge or *habitus* must be transmitted from one generation to another, or through belonging to a community with strong links to labour history. Because Louise lacked this tacit knowledge she had to learn about these structures and processes on her own. However, her unfamiliarity with these traditions and histories meant she did not take this tacit knowledge for granted:

> And so now when I'm talking to people who are not really sure about how the union works or whatever, I try really hard not to accidentally sound condescending and I try really hard not to assume that people know stuff about how it works because I literally had no idea. (Louise, interview 23 May 2016)

Louise also connected her lack of familiarity with union processes and structures with an ambiguous class identity, saying that 'although I'm not from an underprivileged background, my mum's from a very working class background' and also mentioned that 'nobody else in my family before me, apart from my dad, had been to university', but she also did not have a strong regional accent (ibid.) which would mark her out as obviously working class. This, in combination with 'being not very politically literate', meant she belonged neither to a traditional working class, nor a left-wing intelligentsia. This led others to project assumptions about her background and motivations. For example, Louise mentioned another union activist saying to her that 'I thought when I first met you that you were like some kind of corporate

Labour [Party] shill but now I realise that you're actually a nice person' (ibid.). When asked about the source of these projections, her response was 'from my accent apparently' (Louise, May 2016). Class, in this case, must be connected to an identifiable marker of place, within a national (British) context. More generally, this reflects the specifically British habit of identifying class with accent. This can be understood as a residual practice which dates to a period in history before mass immigration; however, consistent with these dynamics discussed throughout this book, it continues to carry cultural authority; those who do not fit then are judged harshly. I was subject to this myself due to my North American accent, being perceived immediately as either from a wealthy background – which I am not – or somehow outside the class system, reflecting an inability to conceive of those who have immigrated to the United Kingdom within the context of social class, or assuming foreignness marks one as belonging to an elite.

This demonstrates the narrowness and cultural specificity of such expectations, and the framing of class within primarily cultural, rather than economic, terms. Again, this is ironic in a union representing white-collar professionals. It may also reflect broader impasses around class whereby our vocabulary for thinking about and imagining social class and class politics has become very limited, beyond the cruel 'chav'[18] stereotypes that were mobilised on the Twitter reactions to *Benefits Street* in relation to bad habits, reckless lifestyles, poor parenting and so forth. The prevalent conceptions of class may be bound up with an earlier period in history and forms of employment which are now less common; only 8% of the workforce was employed in manufacturing in 2015 (Rhodes 2015, 6). It does not account for the precarisation and proletarianisation of white-collar professional work. It was these impasses which the EuroMayDay[19] movement attempted to address in the period between 2000 and 2010 through a global protest which took place on the 1st of May, the traditional workers' holiday, by drawing attention to the conditions of those workers who had been historically unrepresented by the trade union movement, including low-paid service industry workers and immigrant workers. The phenomenon which EuroMayDay was addressing has been exacerbated by the casualisation of the workforce (particularly through app-based self-employment with companies such as Deliveroo and Uber). Louise's experience also reflects class as imagined in terms of markers of place-based identities and communities (e.g., an identifiable regional accent). It does not account for those who move between different regions (e.g., Louise), let alone the globalisation of the workforce. Louise's experience also indicates that the labour movement may not be open and welcoming enough to those who do not conform to such rigid conceptions of class, possibly reflecting a public mood among the labour movement of retrenchment into these sorts of class identities. Within this context, class becomes treated as a marker of authenticity, particularly when it is framed in terms of an identifiable relation-ship to place, as signified by accent. At worst, one's credibility within the labour movement is judged not by one's actions (possibly reflecting a climate where victories are rare) but instead by the legitimacy of claims to authentic-ity. It also means that entire range of experiences – including those of the many people who do not belong to the traditional working class or a left-wing intelligentsia – are seen to be outside of class terms: as *déclassé*. It also means that signifiers for class, as they become disconnected from everyday lived experience, become abstracted and even simulacral (see chapter 3). Instead of solidarity – let alone class struggle – class becomes instead about classifying and judging individuals in relation to authentic experience.

Such conceptions of class also do not account for the hardship Louise describes, which is becoming increasingly common due to the casualisation of the teaching profession:

> I mean I still have a mountain, like I mean, beyond a mountain of debt from basically having to pay household bills and food and stuff on my credit cards, like multiple credit cards and huge amounts of debt. And also my passport expired in 2008 and I haven't been able to afford to renew it. . . . For so long I was just like, well there's no point having a passport because I can't afford to travel anywhere. (Louise, interview 23 May 2016)

Louise is not describing the hard graft of manual labour jobs, or the depriva-tion which characterised historical experiences of poverty, although it should also be acknowledged that there are many in much more difficult circum-stances than Louise. Instead, her story is about credit card debt, a condition that will be discussed in greater detail in the following chapter. It is tempting to assume that this is a temporary condition – similar to student poverty – with a stable and comfortable future assured. However, Louise does not rule out such experiences in the future. Although she now has the possibility of a permanent contract, she still feels that her job is insecure, given the current tendency to outsource support staff posts; she says, 'I am still terrified that I'm going to lose my job' (ibid.).

PRECARISATION AND POLITICISATION

Even if it does not address the broader questions around class, the theori-sation of precarity (particularly Lorey 2015) enables us to understand the expansion of insecure work. In *State of Insecurity: Government of the Pre-carious* (2015, 11), Isabell Lorey theorises precarity as the normalisation of insecurity throughout the population, and its role in population management as 'governing through insecurity' and thus entrenching hierarchies of inequality, with particular sections of the population treated as expendable. Louise describes a situation where no job is really secure:

> How safe do you really think those kind of permanent positions are when more and more people are kind of being taken on in these [temporary] contracts? And you only have to look at the job adverts to see that, you know, so many of them are fixed term. Say you're made redundant, well what are you going to do next? If you get another job it's most likely to be fixed term, maybe even hourly paid, and I think that reality bites, doesn't it? (Louise, interview 23 May 2016)

Robert described a similar recognition of the widespread nature of precarious work when dealing with a drastic restructure, in which everyone below senior management in his institution was at risk, and how the recognition that *nobody was safe*, instead of perpetuating a mood of individualised fatalism, led to a degree of politicisation and involvement with the union:

> The fact that middle management were part of that restructuring. Up to the top tier, everyone was effectively. . . . Deans lost their jobs, Heads of Schools, Heads of Departments, it was mad. Even if you try to reproduce that at another institution, it might have the same effect, but it had this . . . completely new, new committee. New attitude, no-one's safe. It's very interesting. It's not explainable, really. (Robert, interview 1 June 2016)

In Robert's institution, the recognition of their own insecurity pushed his colleagues towards collective action. This situation demonstrates the possibility of mobilising in conditions where stable work identities and relationships are not guaranteed. However, in my experience – within a context where there had been little history of collective action – individualised responses seemed so much more immediate, and I encountered them frequently – reflecting how much a mood of individualised fatalism had become entrenched. For example, I saw people commonly accept voluntary severance packages, even without another job lined up elsewhere. Another common response was to keep one's head down and simply manage difficult situations rather than speaking out, or to go on long-term sick leave. Some individuals believed they could be self-sufficient and face the situation on their own, perceiving support from the union as an acknowledgement of weakness.

When asked about these responses, Robert acknowledged that all this did happen at his institution, but it caused his colleagues to question the status quo:

> And I'm not saying that now it's a militant university, you've got a lot of apathy . . . with the recent strike, who knows who struck. But the people you do

speak to, they have a different view of the union. They have a more realistic view of their material conditions. They may not be activists but they turn to the union for a kind of honest [account of their situation] . . . they don't turn to management for support. (Robert, interview 1 June 2016)

Such victories are limited, but it is worth considering what would have happened were the union not there to respond to concerns. Would the individualised responses I have described, which seemed to fit in with the prevailing public mood, become even more common as the appropriate response to such situations? Would there be a greater acceptance of the pitting of employees against each other, and the entrenching of value hierarchies?

WORKPLACE POLITICS VERSUS THE MORALISATION OF WORK

I have discussed the responses of the activists I have interviewed in relation to precarious work, and the recognition of precarity as a broader, shared condition, beyond those employed on temporary contracts. But how does precarity relate to the broader themes of this book, particularly the moralisation of work? As discussed in previous chapters, the persistence of full-time, permanent employment as a social norm can be used to stigmatise the unemployed. Furthermore, it encourages those employed on precarious contracts to either blame themselves, interpreting their situation as a result of individual failure, or to perceive it as a temporary hardship before a stable and secure future. Louise flagged up similar moralising discourses which framed temporary contracts as 'just like a phase, a fact of life, a rite of passage . . . you're only going to end up on successive rubbish contracts if you're not quite good enough, if you don't make the grade' (Louise, May 2016). The guilt and shame can make it all the more difficult to share experiences with others and act collectively. Unions could potentially play a greater role in countering these norms and showing – as was the case for Louise – that precarious employment is a collective and structural condition rather than a question of individual ability within an essentially meritocratic system – and one which operates through hierarchies of gender, race and class.

However, it is worth questioning whether the hardship which Louise has described can simply be addressed through greater job security (as implied by the UCU's campaign slogan 'security for all'). Simply calling for greater job security does not address the institutionalised sexism, nepotism or power hierarchies raised by Louise earlier in the chapter. To challenge these power hierarchies means considering how the security of some might depend on the precarity of others, and how this might be socially stratified. Does this foreclose on radical possibilities that have come out of social movements, including the student movement, such as calls for free education, or the radical re-envisioning of education or work? Although there is not enough space to discuss this here, it is worth considering that this situation calls for a re-envisioning and re-imagining of security: one that does not reproduce socio-economic hierarchies or moralising discourses of respectability.

CONCLUSION: SHIFTING THE PUBLIC MOOD IN THE WORKPLACE?

I began the chapter by discussing my experiences within the trade union movement. Following this, I examined the ways in which union decline has been narrated. I considered post-Fordist economic developments which led to changes to the nature of work, as well as new social movements which unions did not meaningfully engage with, and the decline of density, activity and collective bargaining. I also discussed the dangers of particular decline narratives, usually around the losses experienced by post-industrial communities. Such narratives have positioned unions, within socially conservative and neo-communitarian terms, as the upholders of social norms about gender, work and place. They are dangerous because they perpetuate some of the problems identified earlier in this book which produce moralising narratives about work and community and exclude many experiences.

In order to counter such decline narratives, I have examined the experiences of activists who have become involved in trade unionism out of other backgrounds and other trajectories (in two of the three cases, the 2010 student protests). Although they cannot be taken as representative, I have interviewed them because of how they show, in a limited way, potential ways out of the impasses identified both in relation to union decline and the factional politics discussed in the previous chapter. They became involved in trade unionism not through multigenerational cultural memories or involvement in work-based communities, but through their experience in the 2010 student protest movement (in the case of Robert and Jamie) – in the case of Louise, a developing feminist politics through recognition of gender inequality. Because all three activists are outsiders to the more entrenched histories, traditions and campaign tactics of the Left, it has made them – and Louise in particular – aware of how some of the processes and structures within unions may alienate or exclude those who are not habituated into the structures of trade union activism or traditional conceptions of class identity. This has led them to take different approaches to organising, eschewing charismatic conceptions of leadership for behind-the-scenes organising work and becoming attentive to the micro-politics of interpersonal relations.

I ended the chapter by considering conditions of precarious work, and the role played by moralising discourses about work in justifying precarity and individualising a sense of blame. Unions potentially have a role to play in challenging this and creating spaces for sharing experience, but could be doing much more. As discussed before, these experiences are not typical and the wider context, particularly at the national level as well as in many local branches, is still marked and even shaped by an entrenched culture of factionalism, defeatism, resignation and fatalism, reflecting a wider public mood in which union decline and ineffectiveness are assumed and individualised responses seem the most immediate. However, through their openness, their inventiveness, their attentiveness to interpersonal relations and their collective approach, the organisational strategies which Louise, Robert and Jamie's experiences elaborate represent a way forward.

NOTES

1. A social centre is an autonomously run cultural and political centre; it is similar to a community centre but normally does not receive state or corporate funding, and decisions are made by members.

2. The Camp for Climate Action, otherwise known as Climate Camp, were a series of protest camps near major producers of carbon dioxide. The camps were intended to prefigure a zero-carbon society and were frequently organised according to anarchist principles.

3. Plane Stupid is an environmentalist organisation which takes non-violent direct action tactics against the expansion of the aviation industry due to carbon emissions. See http://www.planestupid.com/.

4. The Bank of England is the United Kingdom's central bank and is responsible for setting monetary policy. It is located in an iconic building in central London.

5. For an extensive study, see Lucy Finchett-Maddock 2016.

6. The UCU represents staff in post-16 education in the United Kingdom, including higher, further and adult education. At the time of writing it has around 110,000 members. These members comprise of academic staff, and professional services staff including librarians, IT technicians and administrators. Unlike some of the unions in the United Kingdom, it has no political party affiliation.

7. Prior to 1997, students in the United Kingdom did not pay tuition fees for university education.

8. Different arrangements exist in Northern Ireland, Scotland and Wales.

9. The 'servicing model' is whereby unions function as insurance for individuals in need but not for collective action. For more information, see Heery et al. (2000).

10. See Gorz 1987; Hall 1992; Ebbinghaus 1995; and Castells 2007. See also Beck 2000, and Beck and Beck-Gernsheim 2002, on individualisation.

11. Post-Operaismo, or Post-Workerism, are a set of radical Left theories and social movements in Italy which challenged the traditional Left's emphasis on workplace politics and the industrial worker.

12. According to the Trades Union Congress, one in every ten workers is on an insecure contract (TUC 2016).

13. Zero-hour contracts are a type of contract in which the number of hours is not guaranteed.

14. The colour bar was a rule which prevented ethnic minorities from taking on particular jobs, and did not afford them the same rights and freedoms as white workers.

15. Senior Lecturer and Senior Researcher are equivalent to the Associate Professor in other academic contexts.

16. For a detailed account of the 2010 student protests, see *Springtime: The New Student Rebellions* ed. Claire Solomon and Tania Palmieri (Verso, 2011).

17. See Scrutineer's Reports on the UCU National Executive Committee at https://www.ucu.org.uk/article/8270/Officer-and-national-executive-committee-elections-2016#Scrutineer%27s%20reports.

18. The 'chav' is a stereotype of a young, working-class person. For more detail see *Chavs: The Demonization of the Working Class* (Verso, 2017) by Owen Jones.

19. https://twitter.com/euromayday.

Chapter 7

Spaces of Solidarity

The previous chapter discussed how people come to perceive their individual situations in the workplace in terms of shared conditions and structural inequalities, and were motivated to take collective action. I also discussed how horizontal organising practices have offered insights, approaches and ways of relating to each other, which the activists I interviewed applied within the vertical structures of trade unions. In this final chapter, I will discuss anti-austerity social movements which have gone much further in experimenting with these approaches. These campaigns have focused on housing and debt and include Debt Collective (formerly Strike Debt) in the United States, *Plataforma de Afectados por la Hipoteca* (PAH) in Spain (the Platform for People Affected by Mortgages in Spain) and Focus E15 in the United Kingdom. I will be taking a different approach than in previous chapters, in that I will not be focusing only on examples of social movements within the United Kingdom, but will be discussing examples in the United States and Spain. I am doing so in order to highlight shared conditions of hardship across geographical contexts, but also to explore the forms and processes of experimentation that have taken place elsewhere.

In this chapter, I will also be focusing on debt and housing as central to the dynamics of austerity in terms of the privatisation of hardship (as individuals compensate for policy failings), but also in terms of the moralising discourses I have discussed throughout this book. As suggested in Louise's account of credit card debt in chapter 6, indebtedness has become a prevalent feature of everyday life under austerity. It has had significant effects in the three countries discussed in this chapter. According to a report produced for the Foundation for Credit Counselling, 2.6 million people in the United Kingdom are in 'severe problem debt', with 8.8 million in moderate financial difficulty (De Santos 2015, 2). Debt is often the only resource available to get through difficult times, with civil society often 'filling the policy void' (Montgomerie and Stanley 2015, 6). In Spain, there is no official definition of over-indebtedness; however, a report for the European Commission found that over-indebtedness was closely linked to income fluctuations and, in particular, job losses as well as cuts to healthcare and education connected with austerity policies (Gumy 2013, 41–462). In Spain (as is the case in the United Kingdom), debt is used to manage difficult situations, particularly informal loans from friends and family (Gumy 2013, 463). The demographics of those most likely to be over-indebted are also similar in both countries: young families headed by one wage-earner who is in low-paid employment (Gumy 2013, 460). In the United States, household debt is at $12.25 trillion at the time of writing (Lieseman 2016), mostly driven by the rising costs of education and healthcare (Ross 2014, 38). Debt is socially stratified, with women, ethnic minorities and the urban poor on the least favourable repayment terms, and at the greatest risk from predatory lenders (Ross 2014, 42–43).

The financialisation of housing has also played an important role within the austerity context. The period immediately before the financial crisis of 2008–2009 was marked by a property boom, particularly in countries such as those I am focusing on in this chapter, where policymakers have been reluctant to regulate. Unemployment and precarious work during the financial crisis then placed many mortgage holders at risk of default, particularly in Spain. More generally, property also has played a central role in driving wealth inequality, as returns on capital, including financial investments and property, have become significantly more profitable than wage income – benefitting those already in possession of assets (Piketty 2014). Stagnating wages and insecure employment, in combination with an increasingly lucrative property market, have thus led many to see property as the only option for a decent retirement; in the United Kingdom, this was even suggested by Andy Haldane, a Bank of England economist, in a *Guardian* editorial (2016).

In addition to their effects on households and livelihoods, debt and home ownership are central to many of the social norms and moralising discourses examined throughout this book, drawing on and perpetuating the politics of respectability. In *Creditocracy* (2014, 83), Andrew Ross uses the term 'payback morality' to characterise the honouring of debtors who keep their promises, regardless of the personal costs, as virtuous, and the shaming of defaulters as irresponsible and feckless. Ross compares this to the nineteenth-century Protestant work ethic and judgements about the 'shiftless of the factory era' (ibid.). Similarly, home ownership serves as a marker of responsible adulthood and personal success; those who do not own property are commonly seen to be failures. As I have discussed in relation to Berlant's concept of 'cruel optimism', the unachievability of these norms within the context of austerity and precarity can lead to harsh judgements towards others and towards one's self.

Self-judgement is connected to a sense that experiences must be kept private because they are shameful. In *The Cultural Politics of Emotion,* Sara Ahmed theorises shame as 'a feeling of negation, which is taken on by the subject as a sign of its own failure, which [is] experienced before another' (2004, 103). Shame thus involves a sense of being over-exposed and vulnerable; 'an ashamed person can hardly endure to meet the gaze of those present (Epstein 1984 cited in Ahmed 2004, 103). Shame thus 'involves an attempt to hide, a hiding that requires the subject turn away from the other and towards itself' (Ahmed 2004, 103). But this introspection and turning inward does not provide reassurance – as to feel ashamed is to 'feel myself to be bad, and hence to expel the badness, I have to expel myself from myself' (Ahmed 2004 104). Shame is isolating, damaging and disempowering; prolonged experiences of shame can even bring the subject close to suicide (ibid.). Shame can be experienced through snide comments and judgements from others, including the cruelty of online abuse but also, crucially, self-judgement and criticism. Throughout this book, I have explored a public mood where moral judgements towards those experiencing poverty and hardship have become normalised; individualised shame is another aspect of this public mood. It is thus crucial for social movements to find ways of countering shame, particularly ways which do not have the consequence of deflecting it towards others. The movements I am describing in this chapter were connected to the large-scale occupations of public spaces: in the United States, the Occupy Wall Street protests and in Spain, the 15-M movement.[1] While Focus E15 was not specifically connected to Occupy, their occupation of public buildings had similar effects in terms of the appropriation of space in ways that temporarily shifted social relations.

AFTER THE SQUARE

The Occupy Wall Street camp in Zuccotti Park, New York City, served as a space for sharing testimonials about the destruction of lives and futures by the financial crisis and neoliberalism more generally, breaking taboos around what was seen as appropriate to discuss in public. In *Unspeakable Things* (2014), journalist Laurie Penny describes the importance of storytelling and personal testimonial for the protests of 2011:

> Across the world, storytelling was an enormous part of the uprisings of 2011. Against the single story of an individual striving towards, inevitably, prosperity

that has dominated the past thirty years of political inheritance in the West, people offered their own stories, hard, raw stories of debt and disease and disappointment. (2014, 85)

Penny witnessed this 'storytelling-as-protest' two days after the eviction of the Occupy Wall Street camp. As the demonstrators were about to be arrested, 'suddenly they began to step forward one by one and give impromptu speeches about how the American Dream had failed them' (ibid.). These stories included:

> a schoolteacher who barely made her rent; another was a disabled parent struggling with no health insurance; a blue-collar worker whose home had been foreclosed; a young student facing lifelong education debts. (ibid.)

These stories of 'ordinary suffering and everyday rage' (ibid.) would not normally receive an airing in public. Penny sees the sharing of such experiences as 'a queer activity in every sense, particularly for men, when it is forbidden unless you're in a war movie . . . it allows us to reimagine the present' (ibid.). The liminal space (Turner 1967) created by the protest camp, its role as a 'temporary autonomous zone' (Bey 1991), enables the temporary suspension of the codes of behaviour which would prevent the telling of such stories. As these people shared these testimonials (quickly because they were about to be arrested), 'there was a sense of elation, a relief in finally being able to be open about the truth of their lives' (Penny 2014, 85). The space created by these stories can be understood as embodying what Judith Butler and Athena Athanasiou term a politics of vulnerability and interdependency – which is about 'the abiding and vital potentiality of being affected and of owing ourselves to others' (2013, 158) – it is an admission that one is not self-made and self-sufficient. This storytelling took place not only within the protest camps, but also on a blog, which also enabled those who were not able to physically participate in the protest camp to share their stories. During the time of the Occupy protests, a Tumblr blog entitled *We Are the 99%*[2] hosted images in which people photographed themselves with testimonials written on sheets of paper, held up to the camera. These stories were simultaneously mundane and disturbing: accounts of low-paid, precarious work; unemployment; ill health; family strife and spiralling student loan debt. Stories about difficulties accessing healthcare, welfare benefits and disability support were also common. Claims to be 'one of the lucky ones' were frequently followed by descriptions of grinding in-work poverty.

The Occupy Wall Street protest camp attracted many who were frustrated at the loss of their future. As Ruth Milkman points out in her demographic study of camp participants, many were young, university-educated and employed in low-paid service industry work (2014, 55). Milkman notes that 66% of this generation had voted for Barack Obama in 2008; many had actively mobilised around his campaign (ibid.). Penny also draws attention to yet another category of participants who were absent from mainstream media accounts and were not mentioned in Milkman's study: the homeless teenagers who 'didn't fit any of the neat stories about dirty hippies or passionate anti-capitalist revolutionaries' which characterised many mainstream media accounts of the Occupy camps (Penny 2014, 83). According to Penny, many of the homeless teenagers were gay or transgender, and had fled homophobic families and communities; they were drawn to the Occupy camp as a space where, at least temporarily, they did not have to conform to gender and sexual norms. She noticed many of them bore signs of self-harm or abuse: 'scars on arms and shoulders, the marks of knives and cigarettes on tender skin, some of them self-inflicted, some I was told, anything but' (ibid.). Penny remarks on their sense of excitement at 'finding something to belong to . . . finding love and acceptance after years of frustration and rejection' (2014, 84). For Penny, the Occupy movement 'with its parades, its crazy costumes and its proud declarations of solidarity, was like a great big coming-out party' (ibid.).

As Athena Athanasiou and Judith Butler argue in *Dispossession*, the experience of staying in one space, which they called 'the practice of stasis', 'creates both a space of reflection and a space for revolt, but also an affective comportment of standing and standpoint' (2013, 150). This 'derails, if only temporarily, normative presuppositions about what may come into being as publicly intelligible and sensible in existing polities' (ibid.). David Graeber saw Occupy and other similar movements as 'opening up space for radical imagination' (2015, 8) which enabled thinking beyond how to stop the cuts (as exemplified by the defensive slogans on the posters in figure 7.1).

Figure 7.1.   Anti-cuts protest, London, 2015. The messaging on these posters illustrates the limits of defensive campaigning: 'anti-austerity', 'Tories out'. *Source:* the author.

As Penny notes, the space created by the Occupy camps also included different ways of interpersonal relating, as well as a questioning of those norms and expectations for respectability which currently function as a form of social discipline. As Butler and Athanasiou argue, the experience of inhabiting the protest camps and negotiating relationships to other camp inhabitants also potentially challenged distinctions between insiders and outsiders:

> the heterogeneity of precarious bodies, actions, frameworks, and affective states invites and requires the continuous political work of engagement, translation, and alliance, work that veers away from essentialised understandings of identity and representation, and, of course, that effectively opposes nationalist discourses and practices. (2013, 154)

Such spaces are not entirely harmonious or free of existing socio-economic hierarchies. In 'Why Does Occupy Matter?', Jenny Pickerill and John Krinsky point out that 'despite often being physically close to different ethnic communities (such as Chinatown in New York), or in cities where the majority of residents were non-white (such as Oakland, California) there were accusations of racism and exclusion within Occupy' (2012, 4). There were also some disturbing accounts of sexual harassment and assault in the Occupy camps (Lomax 2011; Jender 2013). 'Safe spaces' were created within the camps where harassment was not tolerated and where women felt free to communicate their experiences of marginalisation. However, such spaces were ultimately an inadequate response to lack of gender equality in the movement (Pickerill and Krinsky 2012, 4). Butler and Athanasiou also note the challenge for such movements to 'engage in an intersectional political reconceptualisation of class, race, gender, sexuality, and ability' (2013, 154). In retrospect, the extent to which they have meaningfully met this challenge is unclear.

My involvement with the Occupy protests in London was mostly through participating in reading groups at Tent City University and the Bank of Ideas, which took place at a squatted Union Bank of Switzerland branch not far from the Occupy camp at St Paul's Cathedral. This later spawned Occupy Research.[3] Like the Zuccotti Park camp, the London Occupy protests demonstrated the potential to shift social relations. The Bank of Ideas and Tent City University brought discussion of ideas and theory outside of universities and into the public arena and, in doing so, replicated the success of similar actions in Athens and elsewhere in providing a space for lively debate across intersectional boundaries. However, a part of me worried that there was a tendency to replicate some of the impasses that emerged in connection with the management of the libraries in Lewisham (chapter 5) particularly around volunteer service provision of public services. Mutual aid systems are a practical necessity within protest camps and other occupations, but, as Pickerill and Krinsky point out, they raise other questions and contradictions:

> The camps began to take on elements of service provision for all involved which extended beyond mere food provision to dealing with mental health issues, temporary housing and in some cases alternative employment in return for a share of the food. While such organisation is a credit to the importance of voluntarism and the possibility of alternative ways of living, it created further dilemmas for participants. There was concern by some that they were in effect replacing (or creating anew) resources that the state should be providing, especially for the homeless or those with mental health or drug use issues. (Pickerill and Krinsky 2012, 5)

It is also important to ask whether the uncritical, automatic turn to mutual aid systems as a solution is inevitable in situations in which the state is perceived as primarily coercive, with all supportive structures stripped away, making it difficult to think of the state in supportive terms.

What is the legacy of such moments? There have been a number of debates about the effectiveness of the Occupy movement. It has been criticised widely in the mainstream media for its lack of concrete demands (see David Graeber 2011a for a challenge), lack of political strategy, its fetishisation of organisational form (Harvey 2012) and its lack of staying power (Dean 2016). However, these questions should equally be asked of more established and better resourced organisations (Gilbert 2013, 179). As my previous chapters have illustrated, these would benefit from self-reflexive questioning. However, to judge the Occupy movement on the basis of its legacy is to assume that it must continue with a recognisable identity and durable organisational structure, rather than as a kind of catalyst for other movements and organisations. Other organisations which developed out of the protests and took on the 'Occupy' name include Occupy Sandy, which set up mutual aid responses to Hurricane Sandy;[4] the Occupy Our Homes anti-eviction movement[5] and, as will be discussed, the Debt Collective. Butler and Athanasiou also critique the dismissal of the Occupy movement by elite commentators as immature and overly emotional in contrast with a more technocratic approach (2013, 177). They argue that such as emphasis on political strategy is 'premised upon the normative and normalising reduction of the political to juridical reason' (2013, ibid.) which politically devalues passion 'in all its assigned connotations of irrational sentimental femininity, uncivilised primitiveness and an inarticulate working class' (ibid.). They point out that public gatherings like Occupy, Syntagma Square and the 15-M movement bring 'a politics that involves and mobilises affective dispositions, such as apprehension, outrage, despair and occasionally hope, but is not thereby sentimental' (ibid.), thus challenging the stereotyping of participants in the camps as unthinking and governed by emotions. As I have emphasised throughout this book, consent for austerity is mobilised on the level of feeling as much as rational argumentation, and in some cases rational argumentation may be ignored or dismissed if it does not fit with the public mood. Resistance, therefore, must also work on an emotional level. It is worth also asking how much political strategy, which we take to be rational, may be in fact driven by emotion (e.g., nostalgia in campaigns to restore Keynesianism). There are also pitfalls in not paying attention to emotion within the context of interpersonal dynamics. In chapters 5 and 6, I have criticised organisations which prioritise political strategy such as unions, anti-cuts groups and far-left organisations for their lack of attention to group dynamics and interpersonal relations, potentially alienating those without a background/history of involvement in such organisations. The rest of this chapter will explore how movements which have developed out of, or in connection to, public space occupations mobilised on an affective level, and particularly through the sharing of stories and making private issues public.

YOU ARE NOT A LOAN: THE DEBT COLLECTIVE

Strike Debt developed out of the Occupy Wall Street protests in New York, during which household debt repeatedly came up as a widely experienced condition, including student loan debt, credit card debt, mortgage debt and healthcare debt.[6] As suggested earlier, one of the goals of the Occupy movement was to challenge taboos around debt as a shameful sign of personal failure, which can be interpreted as an attempt to shift the public mood in which individualised shame is normalised. The Debt Collective developed out of the recognition of debt as a collective grievance, and the result of the privatised nature of public goods such as education, housing and healthcare (ibid.). Strike Debt spread to other US cities (Strike Debt, n.d.), using the slogan 'you are not a loan'.[7] Strike Debt organised the 'Rolling Jubilee' (Rolling Jubilee 2013), which used funds raised to purchase bad debt, and in doing so revealed the secretive process through which individual debtor accounts are bundled together and sold by banks to debt buyers, who are often linked to debt collectors. After the debt was purchased, it was immediately cancelled (ibid.). The Rolling Jubilee was intended as a symbolic gesture and educational project to draw attention to the financialisation of household debt (ibid.). As it was not meant to be a long-term solution, it ended in 2013, after cancelling $13 million of student debt for 9,438 people and $14 million of medical debt (ibid.). After the end of this process, Strike Debt continued its activities as the Debt Collective, focusing on specific campaigns around debt.

Drawing on the storytelling processes developed through the Occupy camps, Debt Collective developed the Debt Assemblies. Debt Assemblies are public gatherings in which people share their experience of debt (Debt Collective, n.d.). They are publicised via word of mouth and social media, and are facilitated using the techniques developed through the Occupy protests such as the 'human mic'[8] for large gatherings (ibid.) – so as to avoid shouty speeches and grandstanding. 'The Debt Resistor's Organising Kit' notes that 'the very act of gathering and speaking together about our struggle to survive the debt system was itself a crucial first step in the process' (Strike Debt 2012a, 6). The authors observe that the debt economy 'relies on our thinking about indebtedness as a moral failing on the part of individuals – something to be ashamed of and hidden away' (ibid.). Therefore, 'breaking the silence through public testimony and storytelling help[s] to dispel the shame and create a safe community space for people' (ibid.). They also encourage people to 'reach out by using your own experience as a debtor, and remember how difficult it can be to speak openly about one's own debt' (ibid.). They acknowledge that such an approach poses particular challenges:

> On the face of it, the speak-out assembly format is simple; it just requires bringing people together in a circle to tell their stories. But getting the right crowd entails some initial one-on-one conversations, spreading the word through contacts and networks, and then finding a space that will be accessible and welcoming. (ibid.)

A video shared via personal correspondence with the Debt Collective demonstrated an example of a debt assembly, which took place in Washington Square in New York City (2012b). People shared stories of their experiences with debt. This included a woman who sold her house to return to university to change career, and a man who had amassed so much credit card debt that he had accumulated 'shopping bags full of unopened envelopes' containing unpaid bills. Some spoke about how debt had affected their life choices, forcing them to stay in jobs they hated in order to pay off debts, including a man who resigned from a well-paid job he found personally meaningless, after realising he was doing it only to pay off student loan debt (ibid.). This reflects what Joe Deville and Gregory Siegworth theorise as the temporality of debt (2014), forcing people to live in the present and blocking them from planning for the future. As demonstrated by the accounts of working at meaningless jobs, debt also affects the choice of career and other significant life decisions. There are also resonances with the discussion of precarity and the lack of time and energy to be actively engaged as citizens, which has consequences for social movements. In other words, it is not only that people are unable to plan for their own individual futures, but they also lack the time and energy to imagine a better future society and to put their thoughts into action. The role of debt in deepening social inequality was acknowledged by the participants in the debt assembly. Two speakers mentioned that the City University of New York, as well as the State University of New York, at one point in time, had free or very low tuition fees for local residents; another pointed out that higher education was still free elsewhere in the world. Participants in their forties and fifties said they remembered a time when 'all you had to do is work hard', and one woman expressed frustration that 'doing the right thing' (saving money for her children to attend college) required so much debt. These conversations exposed the contradictions between the norms of the good life and the ideals of meritocracy ('all you had to do is work hard'), and the recognition that for many people, conforming to these ideals requires taking on considerable personal debt. Such conversations open up discussion around the nature of the good life, the need to reclaim the good life for everyone, and not just the privileged few, as well as the extent that the norms which govern the idea of the good life may actually limit the political imagination.

According to the Debt Collective, the fact that these discussions took place in public enabled passers-by to 'stop, listen, hear something they hadn't heard before, and make the connections' (personal correspondence 2016). The main challenge of such gatherings, according to the Debt Collective, was 'too-long soapboxing' (ibid.), which, as observed in previous chapters, is an ongoing problem within activist circles. They felt this could be handled with 'careful, empathic facilitation' (ibid.), reflecting the attention to interpersonal relations which is part of the legacy of horizontal approaches. Debt Collective pointed out that the purpose of such gatherings was to challenge perceptions of debt as a problem of individual personal responsibility. By creating spaces for sharing debt stories, the Debt Collective is encouraging people to find common ground over seemingly very different debt situations:

> There are people with, say, student debt, who shares a home or a community with people who have, say, mortgage debt, or credit card debt, or medical debt, and they don't usually see themselves as having a common situation in that regard; this is part of the individualization of debt – you 'took' this debt (notice the agency), it is your 'responsibility'. (ibid.)

This functions as an example of 'frame bridging' (Snow et al. 1986, 467) whereby individuals share common grievances, but may lack the organisational base for expressing these discontents and acting collectively (ibid.). What is common between these different debt situations is that for many people, it is the only way of making ends meet: 'one is forced into a need, be it medical, educational, housing, incarceration, or simply poverty or paycheque-to-paycheque living, and that need is filled by debt' (personal correspondence 2016). They also noted that much of the debt in the United States was 'held by the same small number of corporations' (ibid.) which traded in bad debt on the financial markets. This is thus about rearticulating disparate debt situations as a shared grievance which demands collective action.

Debt Collective was also involved in campaigns around specific debt issues. As an example, they mentioned mobilising around predatory student loans from Corinthian College, a for-profit private college chain specialising in vocational courses targeted at low-income, mature students and which, at the time of writing, has gone into administration. The Debt Collective's role was to support the students to 'find community' and to 'learn to build and make demands together; to see that they have collective power via this debt' (ibid.). Two hundred students carried out a 'debt strike' and refused to pay their student loans (Debt Collective, n.d.). Notably, 'community' is being invoked in a different way than the nostalgic conceptions I have critiqued earlier in this book, which is about a stable relationship to place and identity which has been lost and must be restored. Instead, community is something which is created through identifying shared experiences of debt and common grievances.

Debt Collective saw the role of debt assemblies and other organising work as '[encouraging] many other types of debtors to find community, both within their narrow silos of medical or tuition debt and, then, perhaps, more broadly, *a class*' (personal correspondence 2016, my emphasis). It is significant how the term 'class' is being invoked in order to interpret and politicise debt as a shared condition of inequality: as comprising those who must go into debt because of precarious work, low pay and lack of investment in public services. The focus on this condition of indebtedness, like the mobilisations around 'we are the 99%', can be understood as attempts to find a 'new syntax' for understanding inequality, 'more so than old-fashioned partisan politics' (Harcourt 2013, 58). Debt both reflects and entrenches social inequality as it becomes increasingly used to supplement low wages and precarious employment and pays for education and services that do not receive adequate public funding, including (in the United States in particular) healthcare. As discussed earlier, debt repayment terms also perpetuate socio-economic hierarchies. The politicisation of debt thus represents an attempt to move beyond the nostalgic and identitarian conceptions of class. It is also another example of solidarity as an imaginative act, as it is about recognising indebtedness as a shared condition, encompassing many different types of debt, and thus has the potential to connect people in many different places and circumstances.

COUNTERING ISOLATION AND SHAME: THE CASE OF THE *PLATAFORMA DE AFECTADOS POR LA HIPOTECA (PAH)*

Similar tactics to Debt Collective are used by *Plataforma de Afectados por la Hipoteca* (PAH) to counter the shame, isolation and hardship caused by mortgage default and eviction. And, like Debt Collective, PAH also uses the sharing and politicisation of personal experiences as part of their organising processes. While the Debt Collective emerged out of the Occupy movement in the United States, the PAH worked closely with similar social movements in Spain, including Real Democracy Now and the 15-M movement (Colau and Alemany 2015, 17), offering mutual support (Colau and Alemany 2015, 122). In discussing the work of PAH, I will be drawing on the book *Mortgaged Lives* written by two founders of PAH, Ada Colau (at the time of writing, mayor of Barcelona) and Adrià Alemany, as well as the film *Si Se Puede! Seven Days at PAH Barcelona* (Faus 2015), in order to explore PAH's organising process.

As noted in a recent report, *The Over-Indebtedness of European Households*, Spain is unique within the European context in that mortgage holders are more likely to be over-indebted than tenants; in most other countries, the reverse is true (CPEC 2013, 77). This has historical roots, dating back to the later part of the Franco era when property ownership was seen by the government as the primary solution to homelessness (Colau and Alemany 2015, 38). During this period, in 1957, the First Housing Minister made a famous speech in which he said that 'we want a country of property owners, not a country of workers', with 'workers' used to refer to a politicised class identity, rather than literally meaning people who are in work. This underlines the role of the property market in managing social conflict (ibid.). Most social housing had been demolished as a legacy of the authoritarian Franco regime (Colau and Alemany 2015, 52) and, as Spain's economy globalised, policies were implemented which facilitated mass housebuilding and easy access to credit (Colau and Alemany 2015, 39). Simultaneously, legislation was passed restricting tenants' rights (Colau and Alemany 2015, 56). This was justified by rhetoric linking property ownership with respectability and responsible adulthood, with renting stigmatised as 'a symptom of failure and inferiority' (Colau and Alemany 2015, 46). As Colau and Alemany characterise the situation:

> For almost a decade, the Spanish population was subjected to, by land, sea and air, an avalanche of messages that reinforced one idea: if you were not a property owner, you were nobody. In every place and at all times one heard the same song over and over again: that the housing bubble didn't exist, that the prices of houses would never go down, that the purchase of a house was the best option for retirement, that for the price of renting you could be a property owner and that, when comparing prices, it was better to buy. (Colau and Alemany 2015, 43)

Everyone was encouraged to get a mortgage regardless of economic circumstances. The result was that in 2007, 87% of the Spanish population became homeowners, as compared to the European average of 60% (Colau and Alemany 2015, 37). According to Colau and Alemany, this functions as a form of social discipline as people become forced to accept any work available, even if it is low-paid and insecure (2015, 38). Mass unemployment (22%) resulting from the financial crisis placed many at risk of mortgage default (Colau and Alemany 2015, 33). Eviction made it difficult to rent another place, open a bank account, obtain a telephone contract or even receive public assistance (Colau and Alemany 2015, 35). As relatives were asked to sign as guarantors for mortgage holders for people in financially unstable circumstances, mortgage default would also put extended families at risk (ibid.). This situation caused the narratives around respectability and property ownership to lose credibility (Colau and Alemany 2015, 88).

The PAH originally developed out of a 2006 campaign called *V for Vivienda* (or, in English, 'H for Housing'), a tenants' rights campaign highlighting the concerns of young people who were dealing with the combination of precarious, low-paid employment and unaffordable housing (Colau and Alemany 2015, 85). This can be understood as a parallel to the EuroMayDay movement in terms of the constituency that it mobilised (the young, precariously employed people who were often ignored by the media and mainstream political organisations) and the tactics used, including playful imagery and provocative slogans such as 'you will not have a f*cking house in your life' (Colau and Alemany 2015, 86). It did not attract widespread public support at the time because these conditions did not yet affect the majority of people; however, in retrospect, the campaign had the capacity to 'anticipate the future' of the housing crisis and identify the housing crisis as a public issue (Colau and Alemany 2015, 87).

The PAH was established in Barcelona in 2009 (Colau and Alemany 2015, 85); then, between 2009 and 2012 it developed a network of over seventy 'nodes' based in cities across Spain. These nodes adopted a set of agreed principles but had autonomy for developing local strategies (Colau and Alemany 2015, 101). The PAH nodes offer collective advice to people who default on their mortgages; help them negotiate with banks and the government, and resist evictions by mobilising a group of people to stand outside the door so that bailiffs cannot enter. They also help people who have lost their homes through showing them how to squat empty buildings and organise protest actions which name and shame banks who have profited from predatory lending to low-income people. PAH also campaigns for changes to housing legislation (2015, 91–101). As shown in the film *Si Se Puede* (Faus 2015), the induction sessions for new PAH members begin by the facilitator telling them that 'you are not alone, and you will never end up on the street' (Faus 2015). Their work thus combines practical mutual aid with political campaigns which make demands on the state and banks. This is a notably different approach from the Lewisham library case, where volunteering was expected to replace public services such as library provision on a permanent basis.

After the failure of the campaign to save the libraries as council-owned public services, it was assumed that demands on the state could not be made, and that, instead, communities had to creatively adapt and run the public services themselves. In contrast, PAH channels this creativity towards protest actions.

One unique aspect of PAH's organisational process is their collective advice sessions in which people who have defaulted on their mortgages offer each other guidance and support. PAH emphasises collective advice rather than individual counselling in order to create trust and practical solidarity between those affected. The collective advice sessions are primarily intended to help people develop the knowledge and skills to better negotiate with banks (Alemany and Colau 2015, 96). According to an interview with Ada Colau in the film, this is based on the idea that 'people are their own best advocate' in negotiations, but also can pass the knowledge on to others (Faus 2015). This approach, significantly, challenges the idea of the servicing model discussed in chapter 6 in relation to trade unions, but which is also quite common in the voluntary sector, whereby professionals speak and act on behalf of people who are treated as helpless and passive. It is based on the principle that through building knowledge and skills, people who have received advice will be eventually able to advise others – and thus build the PAH movement (ibid.), and more generally an active and informed citizenry (ibid.).

Writing about the emotional challenges associated with mortgage default, Colau and Alemany draw attention to the 'difficulty that we victims have in speaking publicly about the reality we are experiencing as a personal failure, in a society that rewards people for their successes' (2015, 120) and to the importance of overcoming 'shame, stigma and fear' (ibid.). According to Colau and Alemany, responses to mortgage default are often gendered due to the persistence of the male breadwinner ideal. This means that mortgage default becomes a threat to identity and thus an additional source of anxiety, at worst leading to domestic violence (2015, 95).

In response to this, the PAH organised specific meetings to discuss emotional concerns and share experiences. According to Colau and Alemany, the importance of these meetings is both to combat shame and isolation, and to create a space for people to talk about their situation in a confidential environment, away from the family – therefore mitigating the risks of family conflict and breakdown (ibid.). *Si Se Puede!* includes an interview with Mari, an elderly woman whose daughter's mortgage went into default leading to her being subsequently affected as a guarantor. This meant that Mari had to go into debt and that her daughter had to move in with her. Mari felt she could not tell anyone about her situation for fear of judgement; she mentioned that she knew her neighbours only 'superficially' (Faus 2015). She said the stress of the situation caused her to take anti-depressants. But the PAH meetings allowed her to share her feelings and feel less isolated; she said, 'I feel the warmth and support of everyone', and was grateful for 'the way they speak and care for you' (ibid.). PAH is significant in terms of their development of these spaces of support; due to their extensive network, they have developed many such spaces. Crucially, these spaces for sharing experience are also combined with practical support and the planning of a range of protest actions, some of which address immediate concerns; others make demands on the state and banks. In the following section I will discuss another housing campaign, Focus E15. It has not existed as long as PAH, nor has it developed as extensive a network, but it also makes use of a range of imaginative tactics, and similarly challenges stigma and shame, working to shift the public mood.

SOCIAL HOUSING, NOT SOCIAL CLEANSING: FOCUS E15

A London-based housing campaign, Focus E15, began in 2013 when Newham Council[9] ended funding to the Focus E15 Hostel for homeless young people, serving the young mothers living there with eviction notices. The council was unwilling to rehouse them and informed them they would have to move to private rented accommodation as far away as Manchester (Focus E15 2014). In an interview with journalist Kate Belgrave, Focus E15 organiser Jasmin Stone said they were frightened about the disruption this would cause, as they would be forced to move away from the friends and family who helped them with childcare; they also found many landlords were unwilling to rent to them because they were on benefits (Belgrave 2014). In 2012, Newham Council had decided to prioritise people who were in paid employment or in the armed services for access to social housing (Newham Council 2012). In a press release, the council claimed that 'Newham is leading the country in progressive housing policy' by 'prioritising those who have seen active service in defence of our nation' (ibid.). This, they claimed, would 'drive aspiration and form a stable community' (ibid.). This decision and the rhetoric supporting it mobilises the conceptions of work and community discussed throughout this book in determining who deserves access to the scarce resources of the welfare state, thus tapping into a nostalgic and socially conservative public mood. Patriotism, respectability and economic contribution are used as criteria for excluding those seen as less worthy of belonging to their 'stable community'. This appeal to a public mood also justified Newham Council's 'resilience strategy' which also involved cutting translation services as mentioned in chapter 1.

The wider context of such decisions was the financialisation of housing discussed earlier in this chapter. In London, this has been particularly marked. According to the Office of National Statistics, the average house price in 2016 was £474,000, over double its value in 2004 which was £219,000 (Office of National Statistics 2016), and currently double the average house price in the rest of the country which was £233,000 in 2016 (ibid.). At the time of writing, private sector rents in London are double the national average (GLA 2016). In Newham, house prices increased by 22% between 2014 and 2015 (BBC 2015c). The 2011 Localism Act discharged local authorities of their duty of care for homeless residents, exacerbating the housing crisis (United Kingdom 2011). Newham also has the highest number of residents in temporary accommodation and overcrowded housing in London, as well as one of the highest rates of homelessness (Aldridge et al. 2015). It is also one of the local authorities most likely to shift homeless people out of the capital (Spurr 2015 cited in Hardy and Gillespie 2016).

Focus E15 launched a campaign for the mothers to be rehoused, which began with approaching their elected officials. In an interview, Saskia O'Hara, one of the Focus E15 organisers, noted that 'the first thing that you're told to do in this society when there's a problem, in your life, or with housing or with anything like that, you're told, go and speak with your councillor, go and speak to your MP, go and speak with your Mayor' (Saskia O'Hara, interview 14 January 2017). However, the response was unsympathetic, and even threatening:

> So we went down to the Council, we went down to the Mayor and the first thing Robin Wales said to the mothers, like Jas and some of the other mums, was, 'I know who you are and I know what you're doing and I think it's disgusting'. That's the words that came out of his mouth. (ibid.)

As I pointed out in chapter 3, calling others 'disgusting' is a performative speech act which is simultaneously about othering, and the positioning of the speaker as belonging to the decent and normal. Wales also reacted in a similar way when Focus E15 held a protest at the Newham Mayor's Show in 2014. A video documenting the protest showed Wales shouting aggressively at the Focus E15 mothers to leave, for which he later had to publicly apologise (Saskia O'Hara, interviewed 14 January 2017). As Wales told them to leave, he yelled at them that 'this is a family event' (Focus E15 2014a), missing the irony that 'many families would have loved to have attended but have been evicted and moved out of London as a result of his policies' (ibid.). Wales suggested that single mothers with children are not legitimately 'families', revealing particular prejudices about what might constitute a proper family. 'Family event' in this context was code for keeping politics out and maintaining a depoliticised community space free of debate and dissensus. This recalls the New Cross Learning video in which creative activities took place as long as politics, and particularly those challenging the Labour Party or the council were kept out. Such reactions are consistent with the politics of respectability underpinning Newham's 'Community Resilience' plan and the tactics discussed in this chapter, reflecting the public mood of nostalgia, and desires to return to an imagined past of stable employment and unproblematised conceptions of the nation state (as represented by the prioritisation of those who have acted in 'defence of the nation'). People in work and members of the armed forces are welcome in the neighbourhood, but homeless single mothers are not. Kate Belgrave argues that the council's response could be easily interpreted as 'a lack of sympathy for young, impoverished mothers' (Belgrave 2014). She also observes that 'nobody wanted to make an argument for the rights of young single mothers in the anti-welfare era', not even the Labour Party (ibid.), although, as I have pointed out, such anti-welfare sentiment has existed within the Labour Party for a long time. It is significant that the campaign slogan of Focus E15 is 'social housing, not social cleansing', challenging this imperative to remove the undesirables.

O'Hara acknowledges the challenges of countering these attitudes. She refers to a 'common narrative that's really peddled, as though it's completely mainstream that society doesn't really value these people, doesn't really like these people'; she points out that Robin Wales was 'very happy to push that' to discredit the mothers' campaign (Saskia O'Hara, interviewed 14 January 2017). According to O'Hara, this narrative was also present in the negative responses to the videos they posted online (ibid.). For example, a YouTube video documenting one of their protests includes below-the-line comments which are very similar to those made about White Dee in *Benefits Street* (e.g., campaign organiser Jasmin Stone is called a 'fat fuck'). It also rehearses familiar stereotypes about poor women having too many children, as well as Malthusian sentiments about overpopulation. Notably, the women are pitted against 'decent working-class people'.

> These poor destitute women should not be bringing children into the world if they can't support them themselves. The world is overpopulated enough, it's very selfish behaviour to pop babies like that and expect others to pay for them and then cry if they won't. (nkomp18)
>
> I see the fat fuck in the video was not short of money for her chips and cider though! (Chris66able)
>
> Fuck these women, why have the rest of us got to work to house these fuckers. These are the ones who get preggo to get homes & claim. These are the type of people who are professional claimants. Decent working class people loose [*sic*] their jobs, then get told theres [*sic*] fuck all for them, but these little skanks get everything ! (Chris66able) (PressTV 2013)

Belgrave also mentioned snide below-the-line comments about birth control and generous benefits for single mothers on news articles about the campaign (2014). This reflects how easily the space of online commenting lends itself to the perpetuating of these stereotypes, particularly when anonymous: that unemployed people are lazy scroungers, that working-class women are overweight and that lone parents only have children to get more benefits. As has been discussed in relation to *Benefits Street*, vilifying people in this way affirms the normality and respectability of the commenter. However, O'Hara pointed out that local residents – who she sees as the audience for the mothers' actions – were more sympathetic because 'they know that that's the reality, because they've been in that situation themselves', making it harder for them to distance themselves sufficiently to make pejorative judgements (Saskia O'Hara, interviewed 14 January 2017). It is worth noting that the campaign did receive considerable mainstream media attention, with sympathetic, and, in some cases, extensive, coverage in the *Guardian*, *Independent*, the *Mirror* and the *Evening Standard* newspapers.

According to O'Hara, the council and the Mayor also reacted negatively to the Focus E15 campaign because it threatened to expose their role in housing politics (ibid.). There are similarities here with the position of Lewisham Council with respect to library closures (chapter 5). Like Lewisham, Newham is a Labour-dominated council and, at the time of writing, all councillors are currently members of the Labour Party (Newham Council 2014). The Newham councillors are also in a contradictory position in relation to austerity cuts, where they would often find themselves responsible for voting through cuts budgets and would claim they could do nothing to change the situation. Yet, as Labour councillors, they wanted to distinguish themselves from the Conservatives. Focus E15 thus threatened to draw attention to this contradiction. According to O'Hara, Newham Council had been involved in some dubious financial arrangements, which the campaign could potentially expose (Saskia O'Hara, 14 January 2017). For example, she said that 80p of every pound paid in council tax was going towards paying the interest on loans, and instead of being invested in local services was going to banks such as HSBC and RBS (ibid.). She also mentioned a scheme for homeless people which she called 'Robin Wales's loans', consisting of 'a couple of hundred pound loans so they could buy their way into a homeless shelter', effectively forcing homeless people to go into debt (ibid.). They also threatened to make visible what was ultimately a democratic deficit, again like Lewisham Council, in which the councillors had come to take their own constituents for granted, had little democratic accountability and were threatened by active citizenship.

Faced with such unsympathetic responses, Focus E15 turned to more radical tactics. This included occupying a showroom flat in the East Thames building (a housing association which also sells luxury flats) and then

Newham Council's housing offices. Kate Belgrave described the experience of occupying the showroom flat:

> You could hear the collective intake of breath as the women strode into the building and pushed their prams into the flat showroom. Once inside the showroom, they set out cakes, balloons and fruit juice for their party. Their little kids began to eat the cake and to dance. 'It's the party that we couldn't have at New Year and Christmas, because we had nowhere to go,' Jasmin [one of the mothers] said as music played. 'We didn't have any space there, but there's space here'. (Belgrave 2014)

After receiving a noncommittal response from the East Thames Housing manager to their demand for rehousing, they walked to Newham Council's housing office and occupied that as well. The council was hostile and called the police, but the local residents in the waiting room were supportive. According to Kate Belgrave's account:

> A real solidarity quickly built in the waiting room between the young mothers and the many people who were queuing to meet with officers about their own housing problems. People cheered and clapped as the women rolled out their protest banners. Some came over to talk with the women. One woman even began to cry as she spoke. She said that she was homeless and was hoping to find temporary accommodation and that she did not know what to do. Another woman with a baby said she'd been told she'd be sent to live in Birmingham, miles away from anyone she knew. (Belgrave 2014)

Similar to the Debt Assemblies and the PAH meetings, the protests encouraged the residents to share their stories. With the goal of raising awareness about housing in good condition being left empty, Focus E15 subsequently occupied a disued block of flats on the Carpenters' Estate, another estate owned and administered by Newham Council. Furniture was brought in to make the flats liveable, and there was a series of events, including workshops, poetry and comedy events; after the occupation, which lasted for two weeks, the council agreed to rehouse forty of the residents there as temporary accommodation (Focus E15 2014b). After three years, the mothers were rehoused long term (Focus E15 2016). Since then they have supported other housing activists in the United Kingdom and elsewhere, continue to hold a street stall and have an office space in Newham town to host Focus E15's operations and hold meetings. One of the organisations they are in contact with is PAH, and, according to O'Hara, they are looking to one day adopt their model of large-scale housing occupation and eviction defence (Saskia O'Hara, interviewed 14 January 2017).

Through the occupation of offices and buildings, Focus E15 thus found imaginative and creative ways to shift social relations – at least temporarily.

Housing problems could be shared publicly, and furthermore could be treated as an explicitly political issue rather than a shameful private problem. More generally, the appropriation of space by those who *do not belong* has the potential to subvert what has long been a common-sense viewpoint underpinning the London property market, and which was also present in Newham Council's rhetoric: that London, like other major urban centres, is reserved only for those who conform to neoliberal norms of 'aspiration' and socially conservative norms of respectability. Anyone else, and particularly those who are struggling, has no right to be there. In mounting these actions, Focus E15 have opened debate about who has the right to housing, and whose voices are heard within local democracy.

CONCLUSION: TOWARDS A POLITICS OF INTERDEPENDENCY AND CARE

In this chapter, I have discussed three social movements within different geographical contexts, which have focused on housing and debt. These conjoined issues are significant in terms of the hardship experienced by many people within the context of austerity, but also in terms of how they refer to the social norms and moral discourses around personal success or failure. The Occupy movement and the campaigns I have described have been instrumental in countering the shame and moral judgements associated with indebtedness, homelessness and mortgage default. They have created platforms for sharing experiences and feelings so that people no longer feel isolated and ashamed, and have also enabled people to act in solidarity with each other, to care for each other. In doing so, they have challenged the social norms and moralising discourses which position financial difficulties as individual failures. The liminal spaces created by public square occupations or, in the case of Focus E15, the occupation of government offices and empty buildings offer the potential to shift social relations. They hold the promise of creating alternatives to the value systems that would lead us to see vulnerability and dependency on others as shameful, and which make gendered distinctions between the hard and the soft, the strong and the weak, or which judge contemporary experience by the norms and expectations of the past; a mythologised past to which the present can never live up, as we have supposedly 'gone soft'. Although they do not spell this out as a specific political programme, the movements I have described prefigure this through their organising practices. Through the practice of sharing stories of debt and hardship which are meant to remain private, they challenge norms around respectability, divisions of public and private, and feelings of shame – and, in doing so, work to shift a public mood in which we keep such experiences and feelings to ourselves and judge, rather than act in solidarity. They are experimenting with new ways of being, and feeling together, and creating spaces where recognition of precarity and interdependency can form the beginning of a future politics.

NOTES

1. The 15-M movement was a series of demonstrations which took place in Spanish cities and, in particular, Madrid's Puerta Del Sol square during 2011, organised by the Real Democracy movement – which demanded radical change but which did not identify with any political party.

2. See http://wearethe99percent.tumblr.com/.

3. http://occupyresearch.net/.

4. http://occupysandy.net/.

5. http://occupyourhomes.org/.

6. There is no comprehensive public healthcare in the United States.

7. The slogan suggests both that people cannot be reduced to their financial circumstances and that they are not alone.

8. The 'human microphone' is a technique for amplifying speakers' voices without the use of a sound system, and developed in response to the banning of public address systems. It involves a group of people repeating every few words a speaker says en masse so that everyone at a protest can here.

9. Newham Council is a local authority in East London. In 2016, the population was estimated at 338, 600.

Conclusion

From Austerity to Brexit and Trump, and the Politics of the 'Ordinary'

In this book, I have explored the links between austerity and social conservatism on the level of emotions, particularly involving feelings such as guilt, shame, nostalgia and resentment, or pleasure at the misfortune of others (schadenfreude). In order to appeal to such emotions, austerity discourses exploit the gap between contemporary experiences and the social and cultural norms associated with previous periods in history. In such comparisons, contemporary experience is always lacking: we do not work at 'real jobs', live in 'real communities' and contemporary experiences of poverty and hardship lack the *gravitas* of those of the past. Austerity discourses also draw on long-standing memories, habits and prejudices, which is why there are historical continuities between the tendencies I have described within the austerity context and earlier periods of history. Divisions between the deserving and undeserving poor have existed at least since the nineteenth century. Immigrants and unemployed people have long been blamed for a variety of social ills, as revealed by Stuart Hall's analysis of authoritarian populism and traditionalism. However, what is specific to austerity politics is that they ultimately define who deserves the scarce and dwindling resources of the welfare state. As I have discussed throughout this book, socially conservative values provide a convenient and immediate set of criteria to deny access to public services to particular sections of society, while deflecting blame away from those responsible for making the decisions to cut these services. Such values have an intuitive appeal due to their long history and familiarity. They 'feel right'; they fit in with a 'public mood' marked by nostalgia, judgement and resentment towards others, and individualised shame.

Austerity policies undermine material security for many people, exacerbating precarity and inequality. Simultaneously, austerity discourses offer certainty on the level of values and moral judgements. Politicians and commentators have appealed to nostalgic conceptions of the close-knit community, which in some cases is seen to be incompatible with a globalised, multicultural society. They have also appealed to norms of work which are at odds with the actual experiences of working life for many people. These refer to full-time permanent employment and the 'real jobs' associated with the Fordist era. The gap between these norms and experiences is then mobilised to judge those deemed less deserving because they are unemployed or precariously employed. This is evidenced in representations of the 'undeserving poor' on reality television programmes, provoking judgemental responses on social media. In some cases, these acts of judgement are pleasurable: schadenfreude towards those who are worse off while simultaneously affirming our own respectability.

In *Towards a Performative Theory of Assembly*, Judith Butler describes even crueller examples of this dynamic. She discusses a Tea Party[1] meeting in which Republican Congressman Ron Paul suggested that 'those who have serious illness and cannot pay for health insurance, or 'choose' not to pay as he put it, would simply have to die' (2015, 11), which caused 'a shout of joy' to 'ripple through the crowd' (ibid.). Butler asks, rhetorically, why the statement – which effectively condemned the poor and the unemployed to suffering and death – could have provoked such cruel and sadistic joy (2015, 12). She suggests that one aspect of this joy is the affirmation of the principle that we are only responsible for our own welfare, freeing us from responsibility towards others (ibid.). I would also add that such statements affirm both the self-sufficient neoliberal subject and traditional social norms connected to work: specifically, that only those in stable and in employment well paid enough to qualify them for private health insurance are worthwhile as human beings. The pleasure in such moments is thus also about the identification with status quo values.

RIGHT POPULISM AND 'ORDINARY PEOPLE'

The tendency which Butler describes prefigures the disturbing moment which shapes the end of this book, where Right populist politics appear to be on the rise. Within this environment, constructions of 'ordinary people' or 'the people' are regularly mobilised to exclude certain sections of society from the body politic. On the 23rd of June 2016, the United Kingdom voted by 52% to leave the European Union after a campaign marked by xenophobic bile, including a controversial billboard headlined 'breaking point' and showing a group of supposed Syrian refugees marching towards the viewer. The billboard worked on a chain of associations: European Union=Syrian refugees=Islam=terrorism. The refugees also appeared as a threatening mass or horde, who, the billboard implied, could overwhelm the country with their foreignness. The poster was produced by Leave.EU, the UKIP-backed campaign to leave the EU. The image of the crowd also had resonances with other posters produced during previous periods in history, including the First World War propaganda intended to shame those not 'doing their part'. The image of the crowd was used again during the 1979 General Election; the Conservative Party's adverts, produced by the agency Saatchi and Saatchi, showed the image of a long queue to the unemployment office with the slogan reading 'Labour isn't working'.

On 16 June, shortly before the referendum, Jo Cox, the Labour MP for Batley and Spen, was murdered by a man shouting 'Put Britain First!'. An increase in xenophobic attacks on the street and on public transport followed the Brexit vote, with the Institute for Race Relations finding that Eastern Europeans and racialised people, including those who are British citizens, were most likely to be the targets (Komaromi et al. 2016). Homophobic attacks also increased by 147% in the three months after the referendum vote (Townsend 2016). I have discussed in chapter 2 how UK Independence Party leader Nigel Farage claimed that the EU referendum result was a victory for 'ordinary people' and 'decent people'. In doing so, he was positioning the 48% of eligible voters who opted to remain in the European Union, as well as the European citizens who did not have the right to vote in the referendum, as indecent and as unordinary – as simultaneously a privileged metropolitan elite and as undesirables, whose experience was not ordinary and thus not relatable.

What does the term 'ordinary' mean for far-right politicians such as Farage and their fellow travellers within mainstream political parties? In 1958, Raymond Williams wrote that 'culture is ordinary', and in doing so opened up the question of how culture was defined. It is now the understanding of ordinariness that must be similarly opened up to question. What types of experience do we think of as ordinary? Who do we think of as an ordinary person? It is assumed that ordinariness can exist only within national borders: the ordinariness of everyday experience within another culture has become impossible to imagine; it is by definition strange and exotic. Ordinariness from this perspective is thus an insular position, uneasy with social and cultural change, defined within the context of a public mood in which ordinariness has becomes code for those who feel anxious about globalisation and challenges to socially conservative values. This highlights the power relations which operate through the naming of people or experiences as ordinary or, conversely, as unordinary. For example, at the time of writing, there have been a series of strikes at post offices, on trains and in the airline industry, which reveal the contested nature of these definitions. Invoking the silent majority, Prime Minister Theresa May accused the strikers of having 'contempt for ordinary people', which journalist Paul Mason challenged by arguing that the strikers are in fact ordinary people, and that it may not be so difficult to relate to their experiences:

> Everybody knows a BA cabin steward, a train guard, a baggage handler or a Post Office counter worker. What's more, because so much of our work has become modular, low-paid and deskilled, many people know, or can guess, exactly what they are going through. (Mason 2016)

Mason also points out that 'we seem to love the working class as long as it is a) white and b) passive', in contrast to the multi-ethnic workforce taking strike action (ibid.). This situation demonstrates specifically what is at stake in the invocation of 'ordinary people' – suggesting that the 'ordinary' and who can be an 'ordinary' person has become a site of struggle.

The term 'people' is also invoked here, to similarly create divisions between insiders and outsiders. Several months after the vote to leave the European Union, the investment manager and philanthropist Gina Miller launched a court case against the government on the basis that Article 50 (the legislation which begins the Brexit negotiations) needed parliamentary approval rather than royal prerogative, meaning it would require parliamentary debate and legislation.[2] The case was successful, but Miller received death threats and misogynistic and racist online abuse (Blair 2016). The three judges ruling on the case were also attacked as 'enemies of *the people*' by the *Daily Mail* newspaper (my emphasis), with photographs of their faces presented on the front page as a kind of 'naming and shaming'. The sexual orientation and former career of one of the judges were explicitly mentioned in early coverage in the newspaper, describing him as a 'openly gay ex-Olympic fencer' (Law Gazette 2016) – presumably to highlight his lack of ordinariness. The inflammatory, authoritarian tone of this language was openly criticised by the judiciary, politicians and others; it was pointed out on Twitter that 'Enemies of the People' was in fact the title of a 2009 film about the Cambodian dictator Pol Pot; the layout also echoed a 1933 Nazi newspaper showing head shots of people whose citizenship had been revoked, with a headline reading 'Traitors of the People' (FullFact 2016). However, the government's response was slow and rather half-hearted. There was a sense that the government was reluctant to be seen on as on the wrong side of an increasingly populist public mood in which judges were seen to represent the elite, and the 52% who voted to leave the EU were taken as representative of all public opinion.

This situation suggests that the concept of authoritarian populism still has resonance. In this case, the government is trying to keep the Brexit negotiations secret from public and parliamentary scrutiny – which is the sort of concentration of executive power theorised by Poulantzas. The attacks on the judges as enemies of the people demonstrate how the tactics described by

Hall are being used to divide the public between the loyal and the disloyal. Notably, the term 'authoritarian populism' has recently re-entered circulation in the mainstream press, as a way of explaining this phenomenon. For example, writing in the *Independent*, Lizzie Dearden discusses how recent polling demonstrates that voters with 'authoritarian populist' views are driving the growth of the far right across Europe and in the United States. Authoritarian populist voters, according to Dearden, are united by opposition to immigration, hawkish views on defence and cynicism over human rights (ibid.). However, typical of such polling-based commentary, there is little discussion of the construction of authoritarian populist views and the role played by politicians and the media. It is important to consider here the emotions being mobilised against Miller and the three judges – in this case, intense rage and desire for retribution, coupled with a renewed confidence that this rage *genuinely represents the public mood and the public will, which could now be set free because it has official legitimation.* Against such strength of feeling, it is easy to feel that the defence of the independence of the judiciary or the rule of law would only amount to limp defences of the status quo. However, I cannot dismiss the wider criticism that neither the campaign to remain in the European Union nor the Hillary Clinton campaign for president of the United States offered anything more than the lesser of two evils. They did not present a meaningful alternative to continued austerity or economic decline that could have given people something to hope for, or to feel passionate about. Nor – particularly in the context of the EU referendum – was the challenge to deep-seated anti-immigrant prejudices bold enough, nor did it come soon enough to have undone the damage of years of continual xenophobic and Eurosceptic public discourse which consolidated the public mood. As the political commentator Stephen Bush noted, the Brexit vote had been years in the making (Bush 2016).

A parallel development took place in the United States not long after the Brexit vote. Donald Trump was elected president of the United States on 9 November 2016 due to winning the Electoral College, although he lost the popular vote to contender Hillary Clinton. This followed a toxic campaign in which he called Mexicans rapists and promised to build a wall to keep them out, which the Mexican government would supposedly pay for. He also called for Muslims to be banned from the United States and insulted the parents of a dead Muslim soldier. He bragged about sexually assaulting women, exemplified by the circulation of a leaked recording in which he claimed that as a celebrity he could grab women 'by the pussy',[3] and claimed he would throw Democratic Party candidate Hillary Clinton in jail as soon as he was elected. Trump was endorsed by the Ku Klux Klan, and only denounced this hesitantly (England 2016). His campaign slogan was 'Make America great again' This echoes both the decline narrative and nostalgia for past eras. Greatness, as invoked by the slogan, conjures up a past era of prosperity before globalisation. The changes which have destroyed this prosperity, it is implied, are mass immigration and post-industrialism. Trump's economic policies were based in trade protectionism and promised a return to the industries of a previous era, including promises to reopen the coal mines (Davenport 2016) and return outsourced American jobs through a confrontational approach to trade (Trump 2016). Such inflammatory statements or impossible promises did not damage his electoral prospects. Instead, they tapped into a sense of frustration and rage, which likely has many, possibly contradictory, sources, including the devastation of post-industrial communities; precarity; declining social mobility and loss of hope for the future; misogyny and the loss of white privilege (the irony of Trump's victory following the first African-American US president cannot be missed). Since entering office, Trump has implemented a series of executive orders, including (at the time of writing) an order banning citizens of six Muslim majority countries from the United States for ninety days, including those who were born in those countries but who have subsequently taken up citizenship elsewhere, suspending the refugee programme for 120 days and banning the intake of Syrian refugees indefinitely (McCarthy 2017).

In the aftermath of both Trump's election and the Brexit vote, numerous polls have been conducted about the demographics, attitudes and cultural preferences of those who supported both; there were also endless attempts to find the one answer that would explain it all. The most common narrative centred around a disenfranchised 'white working class', also frequently characterised as the 'left behind', who had been abandoned by mainstream political parties, their concerns dismissed as racist and ignorant, and who have now 'had enough'. This narrative continues to be remarkably persistent and potent, despite data estimating, for instance, the average annual income of Trump supporters at $72,000 – higher than for Democrat supporters (Silver 2016). For example, in a recent article, *Guardian* columnist John Harris claims that both Trump's election and the Brexit vote were due to the public's inability to deal with complexity – meaning the complexity of globalisation and contemporary life in general – and that 'the contemporary zeitgeist' (Harris's term for the public mood) is to opt for the simple answers provided by Trump and the Brexit campaign, which must now be heeded (Harris 2016). JD Vance, author of *Hillbilly Elegy* (a book widely claimed to provide insight into Trump supporters), argues that despite his privileged background, 'in style and tone, Trump reminds blue-collar workers of themselves' and that he was 'the candidate of a patriotic people who feel an almost apocalyptic apprehension about the future' (Vance 2016). Related to this is the blaming of the liberal Left for caring too much about fashionable 'identity politics' such as campaigns for racial, sexual or gender equality. The argument is that, in doing so, they had played a role in the abandoning of the 'white working class' and thus had unwittingly played into Trump's victory (ignoring the specifically identitarian nature of the construct of the 'white working class'). Writing in *The New York Times* immediately after the election result, political scientist and journalist Mark Lilla claimed that Clinton had made a 'strategic mistake' in 'calling out explicitly to African-American, Latino, LGBT and women voters at every stop' – which then excluded 'the white working class and those with strong religious convictions' (Lilla 2016). He also accused liberals and progressives of being 'narcissistically unaware of conditions outside their self-defined group' (ibid.), and, worse, getting involved in obscure campus battles (notably around the rights of transgender people) which were supposedly incomprehensible to the 'average voter' (ibid.).

Such narratives frequently involve emotion. The year 2016 was characterised as the year of 'post-truth politics', where emotions won out over facts, and large numbers of people voted against their interests because it felt right, and because people like Trump or Nigel Farage spoke to their anger, fear and hopelessness. Notably, it is only certain people who are seen to be emotional: the white working class, the 'left behind' who became so angry that they ignored all statistics. Their feelings are seen to be volatile, on the verge of transforming into despair and hatred, and so they must be pandered to through stricter controls on immigration or harsh rules on benefits, despite the lack of evidence that either is a serious enough problem to warrant policy intervention. Notably, the feelings of other groups in society are not seen to be as volatile or dangerous, including those who have suffered the effects of austerity but who do not display Right populist voting tendencies. This includes the ethnic minority working-class people who experience higher unemployment rates than their white counterparts, the young people who have much bleaker prospects than the previous generations and the European citizens in the United Kingdom who were not allowed to vote in the referendum and are now worried about their status, as well as those dealing with the sharp end of the immigration system. This also includes the Muslim communities who have been targeted with clumsy and discriminatory counter-terrorist legislation. The feelings of these groups in society, in fact, are barely discussed at all, and they are not seen to really matter. They are not seen to represent the public mood. It could be argued that the categories of people I have just described deserve the label of 'left behind' more than those with Right populist sympathies. However, the fact that they are not characterised as such is revealing: it reveals that nobody owes them anything, beginning with the government. To call someone 'left behind' suggests both abandonment and a continuing moral obligation. This characterisation recalls Stuart Hall's moral authority attributed to the lumpen bourgeoisie, as discussed in chapter 2. The term 'left behind', like 'ordinary people', is implicated in power relations of both marginalisation and privilege, particularly around race, class, gender and age. This equally recalls Sara Ahmed's questioning about how some bodies are constructed as emotional (2004, 4) – and I would add – who are seen to be so emotional that their feelings need to be assuaged by policy interventions. It also recalls my further question in the introduction to this book about who speaks to these emotions, or claims to act on behalf of emotional subjects.

CAN THE PUBLIC MOOD BE SHIFTED?

I do not claim to offer any easy answers to what is a difficult, complex and continually evolving situation, and, as I have suggested, am wary of those who do. However, it is clear that progressive gains cannot be taken for granted anymore. At the time of writing, we are in a situation of having to defend the limited gains which are the legacy of new social movements and the labour movement, while being aware that such gains do not go far enough and are not radical enough. We are also having to defend the gains of official multiculturalism against racist right populism. As Ghassan Hage has argued, we cannot be overly critical of the liberal white nationalist's slogans of 'long live hospitality to the stranger' in the face of xenophobic intolerance, but we need to simultaneously be aware of the legitimate critiques that have been made of official multiculturalism for not challenging white power structures (Hage 2017).

One urgent task at hand is to challenge the triumphalism of Right populist claims to represent a groundswell of public opinion, and to speak to the public mood. As Judith Butler pointed out, Trump was actually elected by a minority of the American public due to the outmoded nature of the electoral system (particularly the Electoral College), the disenfranchisement of young, poor and ethnic minority voters, and widespread disillusionment with electoral politics (2016). Those who supported Trump (or, to a lesser extent, those who voted for Brexit) should not be left unchallenged to speak and act as if they are the absolute majority. Therefore, we need to be wary of guilty hand-wringing and self-censorship because of feeling like an unpopular minority who is out of step with the public mood. We also should not apologise about challenging prejudice, from politicians and anyone else – in the street, on social media and in other public forums, lest prejudice become even more entrenched as common sense and people become even more fearful about going against the public mood. It is especially important to publicly question the legitimation of prejudice through claims to speak for 'ordinary people', or invocations of 'the people' that imply a rejection of entire sections of society as undesirables, or to make easy claims about who is left behind without considering how there might be others who are even more marginalised, and whose concerns are not seen to matter.

As I have suggested, it is also necessary to open questions about the power relations in the use of such language. As this is highly emotive language which performatively includes some and excludes others, it is also important to examine how the use of it makes us feel, either as speakers or as objects, and how it can construct a public mood. What does it mean to feel like we belong to 'the people', or that we do not? Do we feel our everyday experience fits Right populist conceptions of the 'ordinary'? Part of unpacking these concepts is about challenging the melancholic and nostalgic narratives I have discussed throughout this book. The invocations of 'ordinary people' and the 'people', as they are articulated by Right populists, are connected to the implicit belief that we once lived in harmonious and close-knit communities which have since become atomised and fragmented; that multiculturalism has destroyed social cohesion and is incompatible with a functioning welfare state. The implication is that we must return to a simpler conception of 'the people' which is uncomfortably close to Appadurai's 'fear of small numbers' (where ethnicity becomes synonymous with national identity, minus the complexities of immigration, globalisation or the legacy of colonialism) as discussed in chapter 4. It is also important to challenge nostalgic narratives because of how they undermine a sense of agency, and because of how they produce individualised guilt and shame. This includes the perception that present-day experiences of poverty and hardship lack the gravity of experiences of the past because they do not match common conceptions of poverty as virtuous deprivation (because people might own smartphones, flat-screen televisions and other gadgets, for example) – meaning they must just be the result of individual failures. Another common narrative is that a full-time job, home ownership and stable living arrangements are easily attainable, and that those who do not achieve these, or do so only through indebtedness, are failures in life. In chapter 7, I have discussed just how difficult it has become for many people to achieve these norms (particularly in relation to the work of PAH and Debt Collective).

If the narratives I have described are the bad stories we have continually told ourselves, the 'bad stories which make bad politics' (Grossberg 2017), then we need to come up with better ones. But doing so will take some patient work. This is the patient work of trying to understand why such narratives continue to have such a strong hold on people (this book represents, in part, an attempt to do so). But there is also the patient work to be done of creating spaces, inspired by legacies of feminism, where people can discuss the effects of austerity on their lives, how austerity makes them feel, and recognise that they are not alone. Such spaces and the discussions they engender can hopefully form the starting point for questioning the bad stories and the power they have over us, and imagine, and begin to tell, and ultimately enact better ones. The discussion spaces created by the PAH, the Debt Collective and, to a lesser extent, Focus E15 can serve as a model. The trade union movement also can provide such spaces, but needs to move beyond some of the organisational conservatism discussed in chapter 6 and take on more imaginative approaches.

In order to resist narrow and nationalistic ideas of 'the people', solidarity as an imaginative act (as I have discussed in chapter 4) also becomes important. This includes being able to consider the everyday experiences of people who live very different lives, and, in particular, outside the national context as equally 'ordinary'. Solidarity is also a practice of bringing people together and feeling a connection. History has given us examples in which transversal links were made across communities and social struggles. In the 1980s, Gays and Lesbians Support the Miners brought together two very different communities in solidarity. In 'Blind Pessimism and the Sociology of Hope' (2015), Les Back reflects on the collections to support the 1980s miners' strike by the Indian Workers' Association as well as by local residents in the multicultural areas of Lozells and Handsworth, Birmingham (ibid.). Such examples show how imaginative links could be made. Some of the accounts in this book also could be seen as imaginative acts of solidarity: Louise's story in chapter 6 about the woman who did not work with her showing that she cared about her, or Debt Collective's proposal of bringing together people in very different conditions of debt, or the PAH's collective support sessions. The task is now to make such acts of solidarity much more common, and much more widespread, and, in doing so, shift the public mood.

As this book goes to press, there is a sense that the public mood may be starting to shift. The 2017 general election result was one that confounded the expectation of pollsters, politicians and pundits, who were predicting a Conservative landslide victory, on the scale of Thatcher's 1983 election victory, whereby the Labour Party was brought down to historically low levels of electoral support. Two horrific terrorist attacks took place in Manchester and London immediately before the vote. However, attempts by both PM Theresa May and the tabloid press to capitalise on the attacks and smear Jeremy Corbyn (leader of the Labour Party) as a terrorist sympathiser had limited success in changing people's minds. Although the Labour Party did not win the election, they won 40% of the popular vote, which was a remarkable achievement, coming close to Blair's 2001 election victory. The Conservatives were denied a majority, forcing them to cobble together a potential alliance with the Democratic Unionist Party (DUP), a Protestant extremist party from Northern Ireland which is anti-abortion, anti-LGBT rights and has historical links with sectarian paramilitary groups. It was assumed that young people were apathetic and disengaged with electoral politics and so they did not matter. Despite this, 2 million people registered to vote, particularly those aged under twenty-five (BBC 2017). There are accounts of high numbers of young people turning out to vote, and in particular for the Labour Party. The outcome of the 2017 election therefore represents some cautious optimism around the shifting of the public mood. It raises questions around the construction of the public by austerity policies and rhetoric, and who this excludes, particularly the young. The situation is still fluid, and much depends on what sorts of mobilisations will happen in the months to come. It also depends on how much critical reflection takes place about what we see to be the public mood and who we think of as the public. However, there is a sense that space could be potentially be opening up to shift the public mood, and create alternatives to austerity.

NOTES

1. The Tea Party is a Right populist faction within the US Republican Party. Their activities declined after 2010, but they exercised a strong influence on the Republican Party. https://www.teaparty.org/.

2. See *Miller vs. Secretary of State* 2016 for the full legal transcript at https://www.judiciary.gov.uk/judgments/r-miller-v-secretary-of-state-for-exiting-the-euro pean-union-accessible/.

3. The audio can be accessed at https://www.youtube.com/watch?v=8wM248 Wo54U.

Bibliography

Ahmed, Sara. 2004. *The cultural politics of emotion*. Abingdon: Routledge.

Aldridge, Hannah, Theo Barry Borne, Ada Tinson and Tom MacInnes. 2015. *London's Poverty Profile 2015*. London: New Policy Institute. Accessed 15 December 2016. http://www.londonspovertyprofile.org.uk/2015_LPP_Document_01.7-web%202.pdf

Allsopp, Kirstie. 2015. 'Why do the chattering classes think it's smug and middle class to hate litter?' *Daily Mail*, 30 January 2015. Accessed 10 October 2015. http://www.dailymail.co.uk/news/article-2933829/KIRSTIE-ALLSOPP-chattering-classes-think-s-smug-middle-class-hate-litter.html

Anderson, Bridget. 2007. 'Battles in time: The relation between global and labour mobilities'. *COMPAS Working Paper* #55. Accessed 10 October 2015. https://www.compas.ox.ac.uk/fileadmin/files/Publications/working_papers/WP_2007/WP0755%20Bridget%20Anderson.pdf

Anderson, Bridget. 2013. *Us vs. them? The dangerous politics of immigration control*. Oxford: Oxford University Press.

Anstice, Ian. 2015. 'PERC paper 11: Public libraries in the age of austerity'. *Political Economy Research Centre*, 20 October. Accessed 10 January 2017. http://www.perc.org.uk/project_posts/perc-paper-11-public-libraries-in-the-age-of-austerity/

Appadurai, Arjun. 2006. *Fear of small numbers: An essay on a geography of anger*. Durham, NC: Duke University Press.

Ashcroft, Michael. 2016. 'How the United Kingdom voted on Thursday . . . and why'. *Lord Ashcroft Polling*, 24 June. Accessed 10 January 2017. http://lordashcroftpolls.com/2016/06/how-the-united-kingdom-voted-and-why/

Back, Les. 2015. 'Blind pessimism and the sociology of hope'. *Discover Society* Issue 27, 15 December 2015. Accessed 5 January 2017. http://discoversociety.org/2015/12/01/blind-pessimism-and-the-sociology-of-hope/

Bagguley, Paul. 1995. 'Middle-class radicalism revisited'. In *Social Change and the Middle Classes*, edited by Tim Butler and Mike Savage, 293–309. London: UCL Press.

Banet-Weiser, Sarah and Kate Miltner. 2016. '#MasculinitySoFragile: Culture, structure, and networked misogyny'. *Feminist Media Studies* 16 (1), 171–174.

Bartholomew, James. 2015. 'The reclassification of poverty was a con-trick by the Left'. *The Telegraph*, 26 May. Accessed 10 October 2015. http://www.telegraph.co.uk/finance/economics/11629120/The-reclassification-of-poverty-was-a-con-trick-by-the-Left.html

BBC News. 1999. 'Blair defends welfare cuts'. BBC News, 19 May. Accessed 10 October 2015. http://news.bbc.co.uk/1/hi/uk_politics/347747.stm

BBC News. 2012. 'Immigrants have to earn £35,000 to settle'. Accessed 10 October 2015. http://www.bbc.co.uk/news/uk-politics-17204297

BBC News. 2013. 'In quotes: Margaret Thatcher'. Accessed 10 October 2015. http://www.bbc.co.uk/news/uk-politics-10377842

BBC News. 2015a. 'Labour won't oppose Welfare Bill'. Accessed 10 October 2015. http://www.bbc.co.uk/news/uk-33498110

BBC News. 2015b. 'Harriet Harman: Labour to back child benefit curbs'. Accessed 10 October 2015. http://www.bbc.co.uk/news/uk-politics-33497441

BBC News. 2015c. 'Newham tops best house price performers for 2015'. BBC News, 28 December. http://www.bbc.co.uk/news/business-35188806

BBC News. 2016. 'EU Referendum: David Cameron's benefit ban options'. BBC News, 29 January. Accessed 20 January 2017. http://www.bbc.co.uk/news/uk-politics-35101437

BBC News. 2017. 'General Election 2017: How many people are registering to vote?'. *BBC News* 20 May 2017. Accessed 10 June 2017. http://www.bbc.co.uk/news/uk-politics-39678859

Beatty, Christina and Steve Fothergill. 2013. *Hitting the poorest hardest: The local and regional impact of welfare reform*, April 2013. Accessed 10 January 2017. http://www4.shu.ac.uk/research/cresr/sites/shu.ac.uk/files/hitting-poorest-places-hardest_0.pdf

Beck, Ulrich. 2000. *The brave new world of work*. Cambridge: Polity.

Beck, Ulrich and Elizabeth Beck-Gernsheim. 2002. *Individualization: Institutionalized individualism and its social and political consequences*. London: Sage.

Belfield, Chris, Jonathan Cribb, Andrew Hood and Robert Joyce. 2016. 'Living standards, poverty and inequality in the UK 2016'. *Institute for Fiscal Studies*, 19 July. Accessed 25 November 2016. http://www.ifs.org.uk/uploads/publications/comms/R117.pdf

Belgrave, Kate. 2014. 'Focus E15: The young mothers' struggle for universal housing'. OpenDemocracy, 21 February. Accessed 5 January 2017. https://www.opendemocracy.net/opensecurity/kate-belgrave/focus-e15-young-mothers-struggle-for-universal-housing

Berezin, Mabel. 2013. 'The normalisation of the Right in post-security Europe'. In *The politics of austerity*, edited by Armin Schäfer and Wolfgang Streeck, 239–261. Cambridge: Polity Press.

Berlant, Lauren. 2011. *Cruel optimism*. Durham, NC: Duke University Press.

Bey, Hakim. 1991. *The temporary autonomous zone*. New York: Autonomedia.

Bhandar, Brenda and Denise Ferreira Da Silva. 2013. 'White Feminist Fatigue Syndrome'. *Critical Legal Thinking*, 21 October 2013. Accessed 15 August 2015. http://criticallegalthinking.com/2013/10/21/white-feminist-fatigue-syndrome/

BIS. 2016. 'Trade union membership 2015: Statistical bulletin'. *Department of Business, Innovation and Skills.* Accessed 1 August 2016. https://www.gov.uk/government/uploads/system/uploads/attachment_data/file/525938/Trade_Union_Membership_2015_-_Statistical_Bulletin.pdf

Black Triangle Campaign. 2016. 'Iain Duncan Smith legacy'. *Black Triangle Campaign*, 15 May. http://blacktrianglecampaign.org/2016/05/15/iain-duncan-smith-legacy/

Blair, Olivia. 2016. 'Gina Miller: I can no longer travel on public transport because of threats over my Brexit legal challenge'. *Independent*, 5 December. Accessed 10 January 2017. http://www.independent.co.uk/news/people/gina-miller-brexit-legal-challenge-threats-no-longer-safe-public-interview-a7456446.html

Blond, Phillip. 2009. *Red Tory: How the Left and Right have broken Britain and how we can fix it.* London: Faber & Faber.

Blyth, Mark. 2013a. *Austerity: The history of a dangerous idea.* Oxford: OUP Press.

Blyth, Mark. 2013b. 'The austerity delusion: Why a bad idea won over the West'. *Foreign Affairs*, May/June 2013, 41–56.

Boltanski, Luc and Eve Chiapello. 2005. *The new spirit of capitalism.* London: Verso.

Booth, Robert. 2010. 'The spirit level: How "ideas wreckers" turned a book into political punchbag'. *Guardian*, 14 August. https://www.theguardian.com/books/2010/aug/14/the-spirit-level-equality-thinktanks

Boston, Sally. 2015. *Women workers & the trade unions.* London: Lawrence & Wishart.

Bowcott, Owen. 2016. 'G4S equality contract helpline raises serious concern, high court told'. *Guardian*, 29 September. Accessed 30 November 2016. https://www.theguardian.com/society/2016/sep/29/g4s-equality-helpline-contract-raises-serious-concern-high-court-told

Bowditch, Gillian. 2006. 'Comment: Gillian Bowditch: The cure for poverty is wealth'. *Sunday Times*, 26 November. Accessed 10 October 2015. http://www.thesundaytimes.co.uk/sto/news/uk_news/article173529.ece

Brady, Fern. 2013. 'Who takes the harshest anti-welfare line? Those on state benefits'. *Guardian*, 12 February. Accessed 10 July 2014. http://www.theguardian.com/commentisfree/2013/feb/12/anti-welfare-rhetoric-families

Bramall, Rebecca. 2013. *The cultural politics of austerity: Past and present in austere times.* Basingstoke: Palgrave-MacMillan.

Bramall, Rebecca. 2016. 'Introduction: The future of austerity'. *New Formations* 87, 1–10.

British Social Attitudes. 2013. 'Changing attitudes towards the role of the state'. *British Social Attitudes 30: Key Findings.* Accessed 10 October 2015. http://www.bsa.natcen.ac.uk/latest-report/british-social-attitudes-30/spending-and-welfare/introduction.aspx

British Social Attitudes. 2015. 'Benefits and welfare: short term trends or long-term reactions?' *National Centre for Social Research.* http://www.bsa.natcen.ac.uk/latest-report/british-social-attitudes-32/welfare.aspx

Brown, Gordon. 2007. 'Open remarks/early challenges [speech to Labour Party conference]'. BBC News, 24 September. Accessed 10 January 2017. http://news.bbc.co.uk/1/hi/uk_politics/7010664.stm

Brown, Wendy. 1999. 'Resisting Left Melancholy'. *Boundary* 2, 26(3), 19–27.

Bruff, Ian. 2012. 'Authoritarian neoliberalism, the Occupy Movements, and the future of IPE'. *Critical Globalisation Studies* 5, 114–116.

Bruff, Ian. 2014. 'The rise of authoritarian neoliberalism'. *Rethinking Marxism* 26, 113–129.

Burrell, Ian. 2014. 'Grimsby residents attempt to stop Channel 4 from filming 'poverty porn' series in their city'. *Independent*, 20 January. Accessed 15 April 2015. http://www.independent.co.uk/news/media/tv-radio/grimsby-residents-attempt-to-stop-channel-4-from-filming-poverty-porn-series-in-their-city-9073054.html

Burton-Cartledge, Phil. 2015. 'How the Conservatives can win again'. *All That Is Solid*, 7 June. Accessed 10 October 2015. http://averypublicsociologist.blogspot.co.uk/2015/06/how-conservatives-can-win-again.html.

Bush, Stephen. 2015. 'Labour's anti-immigration mug: the worst part is, it isn't a gaffe'. *New Statesman*, 28 March. Accessed 1 February 2017. http://www.newstatesman.com/politics/2015/03/labours-anti-immigrant-mug-worst-part-it-isnt-gaffe

Bush, Stephen. 2016. 'Westminster has yet to come to terms with the consequences of Brexit'. *New Statesman*, 2 July. Accessed 10 November 2016. http://www.newstatesman.com/politics/uk/2016/07/westminster-has-yet-come-terms-consequences-brexit

Butler, Judith. 2015. *Notes toward a performative theory of assembly*. Cambridge, MA: Harvard University Press.

Butler, Judith. 2016. Interviewed by Christian Salmon. 'Trump, fascism, and the construction of "the people": An interview with Judith Butler'. *Verso*, 29 December. Accessed 10 January 2017. http://www.versobooks.com/blogs/3025-trump-fascism-and-the-construction-of-the-people-an-interview-with-judith-butler

Butler, Judith and Athena Athanasiou. 2013. *Dispossession: The performative in the political*. Cambridge: Polity Press.

Butler, Patrick and George Arnett. 2015. 'Lower benefit caps "will exclude poor families from large parts of England". *Guardian*, 20 July. Accessed 10 October 2015. http://www.theguardian.com/society/2015/jul/20/lower-benefit-caps-exclude-poor-families-make-cities-unaffordable

Castells, Manuel. 2007. 'Communication power, power and counter-power in the network society'. *International Journal of Communication* 1, 238–266.

Child Poverty Action Group. 2012. *Universal credit: What we know and what we don't yet know*. Accessed 10 October 2015. http://www.cpag.org.uk/content/universal-credit-what-we-know-and-don%E2%80%99t-yet-know

Chorley, Matt. 2015. 'Nigel Farage says that he would rather I'd rather Britain was poorer with fewer people, says Farage as he blames migrants for children in towns like Boston and Peterborough not playing outside'. *Daily Mail*, 2 April. Accessed 10 January 2017. http://www.dailymail.co.uk/news/article-3022780/Farage-says-person-Britain-poorer-means-cutting-immigration.html

Clark, Malcolm. 2010. 'Debunking the Right's attacks on *The Spirit Level*'. *Left Foot Forward*, 19 July. Accessed 10 October 2015. http://leftfootforward.org/2010/07/debunking-the-rights-attacks-on-the-spirit-level/

Clarke, John and Sharon Gewirtz. 2001. *Comparing welfare states*. London: Sage.

Clarke, John and Janet Newman. 1997. *The managerial state: Power, politics and ideology in the remaking of social welfare*. London: Sage.

Clarke, John and Janet Newman. 2015. 'States of imagination'. In *Kilburn manifesto*. London: Lawrence and Wishart.

Coates, Andrew. 2013. 'Stuart Hall, Thatcherism and Marxism today'. *Tendance Coatesy*, 21 June. Accessed 10 December 2016. https://tendancecoatesy.word press.com/2013/06/21/stuart-hall-thatcherism-and-marxism-today/

Coates, Andrew. 2014. 'The legacy of Stuart Hall (dies aged 82)'. *Tendance Coatesy*, 10 February. Accessed 10 December 2016. https://tendancecoatesy.wordpress. com/2014/02/10/the-legacy-of-stuart-hall/

Cocco, Federica. 2015. 'Farage and UKIP lose momentum as the election approaches'. *Mirror*, 26 March. Accessed 10 October 2015. http://www.mirror.co.uk/news/ ampp3d/farage-ukip-lose-momentum-election-5399486

Colau, Ada and Adrià Alemany. 2015. *Mortgaged lives: From the housing bubble to the right to housing*. Los Angeles/Leipzig/London: Journal of Aesthetics and Protest Press.

Colgan, Fiona and Sue Ledwith. 2000. 'Diversity, identities, and strategies of women trade union activists'. *Gender, Work and Organization* 7, 242–257.

Colligan, Philip. 2014. 'People powered public services in practice'. *Nesta*, 13 February. http://www.nesta.org.uk/blog/people-powered-public-services-practice

Collins, Michael. 2004. *The likes of us: A biography of the white working class*. London: Granta Books.

Connolly, William. 2013. *The fragility of things: Self-organising processes, neoliberal fantasies and democratic activism*. Durham, NC: Duke University Press.

Coote, Anna and Beatrix Campbell. 1987. *Sweet freedom*. Oxford: Basil Blackwell.

Couldry, Nick. 2002. *Media rituals: A critical approach*. Abingdon: Routledge.

CPEC. 2013. 'Part 1: Synthesis of findings'. *The over-indebtedness of European households: Updated mapping of the situation, nature and causes, effects and initiatives for alleviating its impact*. Report for the European Commission Directorate General Health and Consumers, 4 December. Accessed 10 October 2016. http:// ec.europa.eu/consumers/financial_services/reference_studies_documents/docs/ part_1_synthesis_of_findings_en.pdf

Cross, Steve and Jo Littler. 2010. 'Celebrity and schadenfreude: The cultural economy of fame in freefall. *Cultural Studies* 24(3), 395–417.

Crossley, Nick. 2003. 'From reproduction to transformation: Social movement fields and the radical habitus'. *Theory, Culture & Society* 20(6), 43–68.

Dathan, Matt. 2015. 'David Cameron announces new crackdown on non-EU immigration'. *Independent*, 10 June. Accessed 10 October 2015. http://www. independent.co.uk/news/uk/politics/david-cameron-announces-new-crackdown-on-noneu-immigrants-10310192.html

Davenport, Coral. 2016. 'Donald Trump, in Pittsburgh, pledges to boost both coal and gas'. *New York Times*, 22 September. Accessed 5 January 2017. http://www. nytimes.com/2016/09/23/us/politics/donald-trump-fracking.html

Davies, Will. 2012. 'The emerging neo-communitarianism'. *The Political Quarterly* 82(4), 767–776.

Davies, Will. 2016. 'Home office rules'. *London Review of Books* 38(21), 3 November. Accessed 15 December 2016. http://www.lrb.co.uk/v38/n21/william-davies/ home-office-rules

Davies, Philip. 2014. 'Oral answers to questions (work and pensions debate)'. *Hansard*, 13 January, Column 561. Accessed 16 January 2015. http://www.publica tions.parliament.uk/pa/cm201314/cmhansrd/cm140113/debtext/140113-0001.htm

Davis, Rowenna. 2011. *Tangled up in blue: Blue Labour and the struggle for Labour's soul*. London: Short Books.

Davison, Sally and George Shire. 2015. 'Race, migration and neoliberalism'. *Soundings* 59, 81–95.

de Certeau, Michel. 2011. *The practice of everyday life*. Berkeley: University of California Press.

De Filippis, James. 2004. *Unmaking Goliath: Community control in the face of Capitalism*. Abingdon: Routledge.

De Filippis, James, Robert Fisher and Eric Shragge. 2007. 'What's left in the community? Oppositional politics in contemporary practice', *Community Development Journal* 44(1), 38–52.

De Santos, Robbie. 2015. 'Navigating the new normal: Why working families fall into problem debt and why we need to respond'. *Report produced for the Foundation for Credit Counselling*. Accessed 5 October 2016. https://www.stepchange. org/Portals/0/documents/media/reports/StepChange%20Debt%20Charity%20 New%20Normal%20report.pdf

Dean, Jodi. 2016. *Crowd and party*. London: Verso.

Deans, Jason. 2014. 'Benefits street ending pulls in 4.5 million'. *Guardian*, 11 February. Accessed 15 March 2015. http://www.theguardian.com/media/2014/feb/11/ benefits-street-tv-ratings-channel-4-love-production

Dearden, Lizzie. 2016. '"Authoritarian populism" behind Donald Trump's victory and Brexit becoming driving force in European politics'. *Independent*, 21 November. Accessed 5 January 2017. http://www.independent.co.uk/news/world/ europe/donald-trump-nigel-farage-europe-politics-le-pen-ukip-afd-authoritarian-populism-yougov-defining-a7430341.html

Debt Collective. n.d. https://www.debtcollective.org/

Deleuze, Gilles. 1978. 'Lecture transcripts on Spinoza's concept of affect'. Lecture delivered at *Cours Vincennes*. Accessed 3 March 2017. http://www.gold.ac.uk/ media/images-by-section/departments/research-centres-and-units/research-centres/ centre-for-the-study-of-invention/deleuze_spinoza_affect.pdf

Denham, John and Michael Kenny. 2016. 'Introduction'. In *Who speaks to England? Labour's English challenge* edited by John Denham and Michael Kenny. London: Fabian Society.

Derbyshire, Jonathan. 2012. 'We have to talk about Englishness'. *New Statesman* 23 August 2012. Accessed 15 August 2015. http://www.newstatesman.com/politics/ uk-politics/2012/08/stuart-hall-we-need-talk-about-englishness

Deutscher, Isaac. 1967. *On Socialist Man*. New York: Merit Publishers.

Deville, Joe and Gregory Siegworth. 2014. 'Everyday debt and credit'. *Cultural Studies* 29(5–6), 616–629.

Dhaliwal, Sukhwant and Mina Patel. 2015. 'Hostility and dissent: Resisting anti-immigrant messaging'. *New Left Project*, 14 July. Accessed 10 January 2017. http://www.newleftproject.org/index.php/site/article_comments/hostility_and_ dissent_resisting_anti_immigrant_messaging

Disability News Service. 2016. 'Government set to slash equality watchdog's budget . . . again'. *Disability News Service*, 28 April. Accessed 5 September 2016. http://www.disabilitynewsservice.com/government-set-to-slash-equality-watchdogs-budget-again/

Disability Rights. 2016. *Independent living fund replacement schemes*. 8 February 2016. http://www.disabilityrightsuk.org/independent-living-fund

Dominiczak, Peter. 2014. 'Iain Duncan Smith: I'll stop Benefits Street Britain'. *Telegraph*, 22 January. Accessed 15 January 2015. http://www.telegraph.co.uk/news/politics/conservative/10590933/Iain-Duncan-Smith-Ill-stop-Benefits-Street-Britain.html

Dorling, Danny. 2013. 'How social mobility got stuck'. *New Statesman*, 16 May. Accessed 15 March 2015. http://www.newstatesman.com/politics/2013/05/how-social-mobility-got-stuck

Du Gay, Paul. 2000. *In praise of bureaucracy: Weber, organisation, ethics*. London: Sage.

Dustmann, Christian and Tommaso Frattini. 2013. 'The fiscal effects of immigration to the UK'. *Centre for Research and Analysis of Migration*. Discussion Paper 22/3, November 2013. http://www.cream-migration.org/publ_uploads/CDP_22_13.pdf

Dyer-Witheford, Nick. 2005. 'Cognitive capitalism and the contested campus'. *European Journal of Higher Arts Education* 2, 71–93.

Ebbinghaus, Bernard. 1995. 'The Siamese twins: Citizenship rights, cleavage formation, and party-union relations in Western Europe'. *International Review of Social History* 40(S3), 51–89.

Ehrenreich, Barbara. 1989. *Fear of falling: The inner life of the middle class*. London: HarperPerennial.

E-Inclusion Europe. 2015. 'Disability hate prosecutions increase by 213%'. 15 January. Accessed 10 October 2015. http://www.e-include.eu/news/245-disability-hate-prosecutions-increase-by-213

Elliot, Larry. 2010. 'Alistair Darling: We will cut deeper than Margaret Thatcher'. *Guardian*, 25 March. Accessed 10 January 2017. https://www.theguardian.com/politics/2010/mar/25/alistair-darling-cut-deeper-margaret-thatcher

England, Charlotte. 2016. 'Former KKK leader David Duke: "We won it for Donald Trump"'. *Independent*, 9 November. Accessed 5 January 2017. http://www.independent.co.uk/news/world/americas/us-elections/donald-trump-wins-kkk-david-duke-leader-we-did-it-a7406966.html

European Services Strategy Unit. 2008. 'The Case against Leisure Trusts'. Accessed 1 August 2015. http://www.european-services-strategy.org.uk/news/2008/leisure-trusts-briefing/leisure-trusts-briefing.pdf

Evans, Dean. 'What's happening to all the CRT TVs?' *TechRadar*, 6 February 2009. Accessed 10 October 2015. http://www.techradar.com/news/television/whats-happening-to-all-the-crt-tvs-525649

Faus, Pau. 2014. *Si Se Puede! Seven days at PAH Barcelona*. Directed by Pau Faus. Uploaded 2015; Barcelona: Commando Video, 2014. MP4. Accessed 10 August 2016. http://www.paufaus.net/comandovideo/SISEPUEDE-Film-English.mp4

Feasey, Rebecca. 2011. 'Mothers on the naughty step: *Supernanny* and reality parenting television'. *FlowTV Journal*, 13 November 2011. Accessed 3 March 2017. http://www.flowjournal.org/2011/11/mothers-on-the-naughty-step/

Federici, Silvia. 2012. 'Putting feminism back on its feet'. In *Revolution at point zero: Housework, reproduction and feminist struggle*, 28–40. Oakland, CA: PM Press.

Federici, Silvia and Nicole Cox. 2012. 'Counter-planning from the kitchen'. In *Revolution at Point Zero: Housework, reproduction and feminist struggle*, 54–62. Oakland, CA: PM Press.

Felstead, Alan, Duncan Gallie and Frances Green. 2015. *Skills and Employment Survey 2012* [data collection]. UK Data Service 2015. Accessed 10 October 2015. http://discover.ukdataservice.ac.uk/catalogue?sn=7466

Finchett-Maddock, Lucy. 2016. *Protest, property and the commons: Performances of law and resistance*. Abington: Routledge.

Fiske, John. 1989. 'Shopping for pleasure'. In *Reading popular culture*. London: Unwin-Hyman, 13–42.

Florida, Richard. 2002. *The rise of the creative class and how it's changing work, leisure, community and everyday life*. New York: Basic Books.

Focus E15. 2014a. *Focus E15 vs. Robin Wales and Newham Council*. YouTube video. Posted by Focus E15 Mothers and Residents Campaign, 14 July 2014. Accessed 10 January 2017. https://www.youtube.com/watch?v=gsPxancNiqk&feature=youtu.be

Focus E15. 2014b. E15 Open House Occupation. *Focus E15: Social housing not social cleansing*. 14 November 2014. Accessed 10 January 2017. https://focuse15.org/e15-open-house-occupation/

Focus E15. n.d. 'About us'. *Focus E15: Social housing not social cleansing*. Accessed 5 September 2015. https://focuse15.org/about/

Focus E15. 2016. '3 years of resistance: how we did it'. *Focus E15: Social housing not social cleansing*. Accessed 10 December 2016. https://focuse15.org/2016/09/23/3-years-of-resistance-how-we-did-it/

Forkert, Kirsten, Emma Jackson and Hannah Jones. 2017. 'Whose feelings count? Performance politics, emotion and government immigration control'. In *Emotional states: Sites and spaces of affective governance*, edited by Eleanor Jupp, Jessica Pykett and Fiona Smith, 177–190. Abingdon: Routledge.

Frank, Thomas. 2004. *What's the matter with Kansas? How Conservatives won the heart of America*. London: Picador.

Fraser, Nancy. 2013. 'How feminism became capitalism's handmaiden – and how to reclaim it'. *The Guardian* 14 October 2013. Accessed 15 August 2015. https://www.theguardian.com/commentisfree/2013/oct/14/feminism-capitalist-handmaiden-neoliberal

FullFact. 2013. 'How much does the NHS lose from foreign "health tourists"?'. *FullFact*, 2 August. Accessed 15 January 2017. https://fullfact.org/health/how-much-does-nhs-lose-foreign-health-tourists/

FullFact. 2015. 'Some immigration facts…factchecked'. *FullFact*, 25 August. Accessed 15 January 2017. https://fullfact.org/immigration/some-immigration-facts-fact checked/

FullFact. 2016. 'The Daily Mail, "enemies of the people", and a Nazi Newspaper'. *FullFact*, 8 November 2016. Accessed 19 March 2017. https://fullfact.org/law/daily-mail-headine-comparison-to-nazis/

Gall, Gregor. 2016. 'How relevant are the TUC and unions today?' *The Conversation*, 12 September. Accessed 1 October 2016. https://theconversation.com/how-relevant-are-the-tuc-and-unions-today-65183

Garnham, Nicholas. 2005. 'From cultural to creative industries'. *International Journal of Cultural Policy* 11 (1), 15–29.

Garton Ash, Timothy. 2016. 'England can be true to itself, if liberals reclaim patriotism'. *Guardian*, 15 April. https://www.theguardian.com/commentisfree/2016/apr/15/england-liberals-patriotism-nationalism-flag-st-george-right

Gavin, Mike. 2011. 'Are we unfit to survive a bad economy?' *Wall Street Journal*, 4 November. Accessed 10 October 2015. http://blogs.wsj.com/wsjam/2011/11/04/are-we-unfit-to-survive-a-bad-economy/

Gayle, Damien. 2016. 'Home office requested schools' census data on nearly 2,500 children'. *Guardian*, 29 October. Accessed 15 January 2017. https://www.the guardian.com/uk-news/2016/oct/29/national-pupil-database-home-office-immi gration-children-lords

Geary, Ian and Adrian. 2015. *Blue Labour: Forging a new politics*. London: IB Tauris.

Gentleman, Amelia. 2015. 'Labour vows to reduce reliance on food banks if it comes to power'. *Guardian*, 17 March 2015. Accessed 22 February 2017. https://www.the guardian.com/society/2015/mar/17/labour-vows-to-reduce-reliance-on-food-banks-if-it-comes-to-power

Geuntner, Simon, Sue Lukes, Richard Stanton, Bastian A. Vollmer and Jo Wilding. 2016. 'Bordering practices in the UK welfare system'. *Critical Social Policy* 36(3), 1–21.

Gilbert, Jeremy. 2013. *Common ground: Democracy and collectivity in an age of neoliberalism*. London: Pluto.

Gilbert, Jeremy. 2014. 'The urgent legacy of Stuart Hall'. *Red Pepper*, February 2014. Accessed 10 August. http://www.redpepper.org.uk/the-urgent-legacy-of-stuart-hall/

Gill, Rosalind. 2002. 'Cool, creative and egalitarian? Exploring gender in project-based new media work in Europe'. *Information, Communication and Society* 5 (1), 70–89.

Gill, Rosalind. 2007. 'Postfeminist media culture: Elements of a sensibility'. *European Journal of Cultural Studies* 10(2), 147–166.

Gilroy, Paul. 2004. *After empire: Melancholy or convivial culture?* London: Routledge.

Gilroy, Paul, Angela McRobbie and Lawrence Grossberg. (eds.). 2000. *Without guarantees: In honour of Stuart Hall*. London: Verso.

GLA. 2015. 'London Housing Market Report'. *Greater London Authority*, 18 March. Accessed 9 September 2016. https://data.london.gov.uk/housingmarket/

Glasman, Maurice, Jonathan Rutherford, Marc Stears and Stuart White. (eds). 2011. *The Labour tradition and the politics of paradox*. London: Lawrence & Wishart.

Goodhart, David. 2004. 'The discomfort of strangers'. *Guardian*, 24 February. Accessed 20 January 2017. Part 1: http://www.theguardian.com/politics/2004/feb/24/race.eu#; Part 2: http://www.theguardian.com/politics/2004/feb/24/immi grationandpublicservices.eu

Goodhart, David. 2013. *British dream: Successes and failures of post-war immigration*. London: Atlantic Books.

Goodhart, David. 2014. 'A post-liberal future?'. *Demos Quarterly* 1, 17 January. Accessed 10 January 2017. http://quarterly.demos.co.uk/article/issue-1/a-postliberal-future/

Goodwin, Matthew and Rob Ford. 2014. *Revolt on the Right: Explaining support for the radical right in Britain*. London: Routledge.

Gordon, David. 2011. 'Consultation response: social mobility and child poverty review'. Policy response series No. 2, *Poverty and Social Exclusion in the UK*. Accessed 15 May 2015. http://www.poverty.ac.uk/sites/default/files/WP%20Policy%20Response%20No.%202%20Consultation%20Resp%20Social%20Mobility%20%26%20Child%20Poverty%20(Gordon%20Oct%202011).pdf

Gorz, Andre. 1987. *Farewell to the working class: An essay on post-industrial Socialism*. London: Verso.

Gov.UK. 2016. 'Statement from the new Prime Minister Theresa May'. *GOV.UK*, 13 July. Accessed 15 August 2015. https://www.gov.uk/government/speeches/statement-from-the-new-prime-minister-theresa-may

Graeber, David. 2011a. 'Interview by Ellen Evans and John Moses'. *The White Review*, December. Accessed 1 August 2016. http://www.thewhitereview.org/interviews/interview-with-david-graeber/

Graeber, David. 2011b. *Debt: The first 5,000 years*. New York: Melville House Publishing.

Graeber, David. 2013. 'On the phenomenon of bullshit jobs'. *Strike Magazine*, 17 August. http://strikemag.org/bullshit-jobs/

Graeber, David. 2015. *The democracy project: A history, a crisis, a movement*. London: Penguin.

Graefer, Anne. 2017. ' "Actually we should be growing up": Neoliberalism and austerity in NEON'. In *Popular culture and the austerity myth*, edited by Peter Bennett and Julie McDougall. London: Routledge.

Grisiola, Francesco and Emmanuele Ferragina. 2015. 'Social innovation on the rise: Yet another buzzword in the time of austerity?' *Salute e Societa* 1, 169–179.

Grossberg, Lawrence. 2017. 'There are no guarantees in history: A cultural studies perspective on the current crisis'. *Truthout*, 1 January. http://www.truth-out.org/opinion/item/38906-there-are-no-guarantees-in-history-a-cultural-studies-perspective-on-the-current-crisis

Guardian editorial. 2016. ' "Property is a better bet than a pension" says Bank of England economist'. *Guardian*, 28 August. Accessed 10 October 2016. https://www.theguardian.com/money/2016/aug/28/property-is-better-bet-than-a-pension-says-bank-of-england-economist

Gumy, Julia. 2013. 'Country report: Spain'. In: 'Part 2: Country Reports'. *The over-indebtedness of European households: Updated mapping of the situation, nature and causes, effects and initiatives for alleviating its impact*. Report for the European Commission Directorate General Health and Consumers, 4 December, 457–477. Accessed 1 August 2016. http://ec.europa.eu/consumers/financial_services/reference_studies_documents/docs/part_2_synthesis_of_findings_en.pdf

Hage, Ghassan. 2017. 'Tolerance, acceptance, enrichment . . . once again'. *Hage Ba'a*, 2 February. Accessed 10 February 2017. http://hageba2a.blogspot.co.uk/2017/02/tolerance-acceptance-enrichment-once.html?spref=fb

Hall, Stuart. 1981. 'Notes on deconstructing the popular'. In *People's History and Socialist Theory*, edited by Raphael Samuel, 227–243. Abingdon: Routledge.

Hall, Stuart. 1985. 'Authoritarian populism: A reply to Jessop et al.' *New Left Review* 1(151), 115–124.

Hall, Stuart. 1988a. 'Living with the crisis'. In *The hard road to renewal: Thatcherism and the crisis of the Left*, 19–38. London: Verso.

Hall, Stuart. 1988b. 'The great moving right show'. In *The hard road to renewal: Thatcherism and the crisis of the Left*, 39–56. London: Verso.

Hall, Stuart. 1988c. 'Popular democratic vs. Authoritarian populism: Two ways of taking democracy seriously'. In *The hard road to renewal: Thatcherism and the crisis of the Left*, 123–149. London: Verso.

Hall, Stuart. 1988d. 'No light at the end of the tunnel'. In *The hard road to renewal: Thatcherism and the crisis of the Left*, 80–92. London: Verso.

Hall, Stuart. 1988e. 'Gramsci and Us'. In *The hard road to renewal: Thatcherism and the crisis of the Left*, 161–174. London: Verso.

Hall, Stuart. 1988f. 'The battle for socialist ideas in the 1980s'. *The hard road to renewal: Thatcherism and the crisis of the Left*, 177–195. London: Verso.

Hall, Stuart. 1990. 'Cultural identity and diaspora'. In *Identity, community, culture, difference*, edited by Jonathan Rutherford, 222–237. London: Lawrence and Wishart.

Hall, Stuart. 1992. 'The question of cultural identity'. In *Modernity and its futures*, edited by Stuart Hall, David Held and Tony McGrew, 274–316. Cambridge: Polity.

Hall, Stuart. 1993. 'Culture, community, nation'. *Cultural Studies* 7, 349–363.

Hall, Stuart. 1998. 'The great moving nowhere show'. *Marxism Today*, November/ December 9–14. Accessed 10 January 2017. http://users.sussex.ac.uk/~ssfa2/hall nowhere.pdf

Hall, Stuart. 2005. 'New Labour's double shuffle'. *The Review of Education, Pedagogy, and Cultural Studies* 27, 319–335.

Hall, Stuart. 2011. 'The neoliberal revolution'. *Cultural Studies* 25(6), 705–728.

Hall, Stuart. 2012. 'We need to talk about Englishness'. *New Statesman*, 23 August. Accessed 15 August 2016. http://www.newstatesman.com/politics/uk-politics/2012/ 08/stuart-hall-we-need-talk-about-englishness

Hall, Stuart and Tony Jefferson. 1993. *Resistance through ritual: Youth subcultures in post-war Britain*. Abingdon: Routledge.

Hall, Stuart, Brian Roberts, John Clarke, Tony Jefferson and Chas Critcher. 1978. *Policing the crisis: Mugging, the state and law and order*. Basingstoke: Palgrave-Macmillan.

Hanley, Lynsey. 2008. 'This white working class stuff is a media invention'. *Guardian* 30 May 2008. Accessed 1 May 2016. https://www.theguardian.com/ commentisfree/2008/may/30/thefarright

Hanretty, Chris. 2016. 'Most Labour MPs represent a constituency that voted Leave'. Medium.com, 30 June. Accessed 10 October 2016. https://medium.com/@ chrishanretty/most-labour-mps-represent-a-constituency-that-voted-leave-36f13 210f5c6#.afpe0l2zv

Harcourt, Bernard. 2013. 'Political disobedience'. In *Occupy: Three inquiries in disobedience*. Chicago: University of Chicago Press.

Hardy, Kate and Tom Gillespie. 2016. *Homelessness, health and housing: Participatory action research in East London*. December 2016. Accessed 20 January 2017.

http://www.e15report.org.uk/Resources/Downloads/E15_Final_report_PAR_in_East_London.pdf

Harris, John. 2016. 'The lesson of Trump and Brexit: A society too complex for its people risks everything'. *Guardian*, 29 December 2016. Accessed 10 January 2017. https://www.theguardian.com/commentisfree/2016/dec/29/trump-brexit-society-complex-people-populists

Harvey, David. 2012. *Rebel cities: From the right to the city to the urban revolution*. London: Verso.

Hatherley, Owen. 2016. *The ministry of nostalgia*. London: Verso.

Hay, Colin 2007. *Why we hate politics*. Cambridge: Polity Press.

Heery, Edmund, Melanie Simms, Dave Simpson, Rick Delbridge and John Salmon. 2000. 'Organizing unionism comes to the UK'. *Employee Relations* 22(1), 38–57.

Helm, Toby and Philip Inman. 'Theresa May's "just managing" families set to be worse off'. *Guardian*, 29 October. Accessed 10 December 2016. https://www.theguardian.com/politics/2016/oct/29/theresa-may-just-managing-families-worse-off-brexit

Hewison, Robert. 2014. *Creative capital: The rise and fall of Creative Britain*. London: Verso.

Higgin, Tamar. 2014. '/b/lack up: What trolls can teach us about race'. *Fibreculture* 22. Accessed 25 January 2015. http://twentytwo.fibreculturejournal.org/fcj-159-black-up-what-trolls-can-teach-us-about-race/

Himmelblau, Sophia. 2011. '#riotcleanup or #riotwhitewash?'. *University of Strategic Optimism*, 11 August. Accessed 10 October 2015. https://universityforstrategicoptimism.wordpress.com/2011/08/10/riotcleanup-or-riotwhitewash/

Hobolt, Sara. 2016. '"A victory for ordinary people": Why did voters choose Brexit?' *Policy Network*, 29 June. Accessed 10 December 106. http://www.policy-network.net/pno_detail.aspx?ID=5109&title=%E2%80%9CA-victory-for-ordinary-people%E2%80%9D-Why-did-the-voters-chose-Brexit

Hobsbawm, Eric. 1996. 'Identity politics and the left'. *New Left Review* 1(217), 39–47.

Howkins, John. 2007. *The Creative Economy: How people make money from ideas*. London: Penguin Books.

Huyssen, Andreas. 1986. *After the great divide: Modernism, mass culture, postmodernism*. Bloomington: Indiana University Press.

Intergenerational Foundation. 2015. *Intergenerational Fairness Index 2015*. Accessed 10 October 2015. http://www.if.org.uk/archives/6909/2015-intergenerational-fairness-index

Jane, Emma. 2014. 'You're an ugly whorish slut: Understanding e-bile'. *Feminist Media Studies* 14(4), 531–546.

JCWI. 2015. 'No passport = no home: An independent evaluation of the "Right to Rent" Scheme'. *Joint Council for the Welfare of Immigrants*, 3 September. https://www.jcwi.org.uk/sites/default/files/documets/No%20Passport%20Equals%20No%20Home%20Right%20to%20Rent%20Independent%20Evaluation_0.pdf

Jender, Ren. 2013. 'When the stupidity about rape wouldn't stop, I quit a movement I loved'. *XOJane*, 14 January. Accessed 15 July 2016. http://www.xojane.com/issues/sexism-rape-occupy-movement

Jensen, Tracey. 2013. 'Austerity parenting'. *Soundings: A Journal of Politics and Culture* 55, 60–70.

Jensen, Tracey. 2014. 'Welfare commonsense, poverty porn and doxosophy'. *Sociological Research Online* 19(3)3, 1–7.

Jessop, Bob. 2002. 'Liberalism, neoliberalism and urban governance: A state-theoretical perspective'. *Antipode* 34(3), 452–472.

Jessop, Bob, Kevin Bonnett, Simon Bromley and Tom Ling. 1984. 'Authoritarian populism, two nations and Thatcherism'. *New Left Review* 1(147), 32–60.

Jessop, Bob, Kevin Bonnett, Simon Bromley and Tom Ling. 1985. 'Thatcherism and the politics of hegemony'. *New Left Review* 1(153), 87–101.

Jessop, Bob, et al. 1987. 'Popular Capitalism, flexible accumulation, and left strategy'. *New Left Review* 1(165), 104–122.

Joe, interviewed by Kirsten Forkert, 13 February 2015.

Jonathan, interviewed by Kirsten Forkert, 13 February 2015.

Jones, Hannah, et al. 2017. *Go home? The politics of immigration controversies*. University of Manchester Press.

Jones, Owen. 2015. 'Syriza's victory: This is what the politics of hope looks like'. *Guardian*, 26 January. Accessed 15 August 2015. http://www.theguardian.com/commentisfree/2015/jan/26/syriza-victory-lifted-greek-politics-cynicism-hope

Jones, Owen. 2016. 'Is there anything more patriotic than the Left's tradition of protest?'. *Guardian*, 9 October. Accessed 10 December 2015. https://www.theguardian.com/commentisfree/2015/oct/09/left-labour-protest-patriotic

Jones, Owen. 2017. *Chavs: The demonization of the working class*. London: Verso.

Joseph, Miranda. 2002. *Against the romance of community*. Minneapolis: University of Minnesota Press.

Katwala, Sunder, Steve Ballinger and Matthew Rhodes. 2014. 'How to talk about immigration'. *British Future*. Accessed 10 January 2017. http://www.britishfuture.org/wp-content/uploads/2014/11/How-To-Talk-About-Immigration-FINAL.pdf

Katwala, Sunder, Jill Rutter and Matthew Rhodes. 2016. 'Disbanding the tribes: What the referendum told us about Britain (and what it didn't)'. *British Future*, July 2016. Accessed 10 January 2017. http://www.britishfuture.org/wp-content/uploads/2016/08/Disbanding-the-tribes-report.27-July-2016.pdf

Keen, Richard and Ross Turner. 2016. 'Statistically driven information on migrants and benefits'. *House of Commons Briefing Paper* CBP 7445, 8 February. Accessed 15 January 2017. http://researchbriefings.files.parliament.uk/documents/SN06955/SN06955.pdf

Kehr, Jemima. 2014. 'Biopolitical nostalgia in times of austerity'. Paper presented at Kings College London, 30 April.

Kelly, John. 1998. *Rethinking industrial relations: Mobilisation, collectivisation and long waves*. Abingdon: Routledge.

Kircup, James and Robert Winnett. 2012. 'We're going to give illegal migrants a really hostile reception'. *Telegraph*, 25 May. Accessed 15 January 2017. http://www.telegraph.co.uk/news/uknews/immigration/9291483/Theresa-May-interview-Were-going-to-give-illegal-migrants-a-really-hostile-reception.html

Kirton, Gill and Anne-Marie Greene. 2002. 'The dynamics of positive action in UK trade unions: The case of women and black members'. *Industrial Relations Journal* 33(2), 157–172.

Kirton, Gill and Geraldine Healy. 2012. 'Lift as you rise: Union women's leadership talk'. *Human Relations* 68(7), 979–999.

Klein, Naomi. 2008. *The shock doctrine: The rise of disaster capitalism*. London: Penguin Books.

Komaromi, Priska, Karissa Singh, Jennifer Vallis, Hazma Beg and Isobel Wilson-Cleary. 2016. 'Post-referendum racism and xenophobia: The role of social media activism in challenging the normalisation of xeno-racist narratives'. *Institute for Race Relations* 2016. Accessed 10 October 2016. http://www.irr.org.uk/wp-content/uploads/2016/07/PRRX-Report-Final.pdf

Krugman, Paul. 2003. 'Lumps of labor'. *New York Times*, 7 October 2003. Accessed 10 October 2015. http://www.nytimes.com/2003/10/07/opinion/lumps-of-labor.html?scp=1&sq=lumps%20of%20labor&st=cse

Lansley, Stewart and Joanna Mack. 2015. *Breadline Britain: The rise of mass poverty*. London: Oneworld Publications.

Lash, Scott and John Urry. 1987. *The end of organised capitalism*. Cambridge: Polity.

Lavalette, Michael and Mooney, Gerry. 1999. 'New Labour, new moralism: The welfare politics and ideology of New Labour under Blair'. *International Socialism Journal*, Winter 1999.

Law Gazette. 2016. 'Truss urged so speak out amid press onslaught on Brexit judges'. *Law Gazette*, 4 November. https://www.lawgazette.co.uk/news/brexit-judges-are-enemies-of-the-people-media-onslaught-follows-article-50-ruling/5058655.article

Leadbeater, Charles. 1999. *Living on thin air: The new economy*. London: Penguin Books.

Lentin, Alana and Gavan Titley. 2011. *The crises of multiculturalism: Racism in a neoliberal age*. London: Zed Books.

Levitas, Ruth. 2012. 'The Just's umbrella: Austerity and the Big Society in Coalition Policy and beyond'. *Critical Social Policy* 32(3), 320–342.

Lewis, Jane. 2015. 'New Labour's approach to the voluntary sector: Independence and the meaning of partnership'. *Social Policy and Society* 4(2005), 121–131.

Lewisham Council. 2011. 'Meeting minutes'. *Library Service – Asset transfer proposals and provision of community library facilities*, 6 May. Accessed 10 September 2016. http://councilmeetings.lewisham.gov.uk/mgAi.aspx?ID=1427.

Lewisham Council. 2012. '2011 Census Second Release'. Accessed 10 September 2016. http://www.lewisham.gov.uk/inmyarea/Documents/2011CensusSecondReleaseDec2012.pdf

Lewisham Joint Strategic Needs Assessment. c. 2010. *Index of multiple deprivation*. Accessed 10 October 2016. http://www.lewishamjsna.org.uk/health-inequalities/index-of-multiple-deprivation.

Lewisham Joint Strategic Needs Assessment. c. 2012. *Ethnicity*. Accessed 10 September 2016. http://www.lewishamjsna.org.uk/a-profile-of-lewisham/social-and-environmental-context/ethnicity

Lewisham Strategic Partnership. n.d. *About the Borough*. Accessed 10 September 2016. http://www.lewishamstrategicpartnership.org.uk/borough.asp

Lieseman, Steve. 2016. 'US household debt climbs to $12.25 trillion in first quarter'. *MSNBC*, 24 May. Accessed 15 August 2016. http://www.cnbc.com/2016/05/24/household-debt-climbs-to-1225-trillion-in-first-quarter.html

Lilla, Mark. 'The end of identity liberalism'. *New York Times*, 18 November. Accessed 10 December 2016. http://www.nytimes.com/2016/11/20/opinion/sunday/the-end-of-identity-liberalism.html

Littler, Jo. 2013. 'Meritocracy as plutocracy: The marketing of "equality" under neo-liberalism'. *New Formations: A Journal of Culture/Theory/Politics* 80/81, 52–72.

Littler, Jo, Nina Power and members of the Precarious Workers' Brigade. 2014. 'Life after work'. *New Left Project*, 20 May. Accessed 1 August 2016. http://www.new leftproject.org/index.php/site/article_comments/life_after_work

Lomax, Tamar. 2011. 'Occupy rape culture'. *The Feminist Wire*, 5 November. Accessed 15 May 2015. http://www.thefeministwire.com/2011/11/occupy-rape-culture/

London Councils. 2014. '2014 Borough election results: London'. Accessed 5 May 2015. http://www.londoncouncils.gov.uk/londonfacts/elections2014/boroughs/lewisham

Lorey, Isabell. 2015. *The state of insecurity: Government of the precarious*. London: Verso.

Louise, interviewed by Kirsten Forkert, 23 May 2016.

Lovink, Geert and Ned Rossiter. 2007. *MyCreativity Reader*. Amsterdam: Institute of Network Cultures.

Lyons, James. 2012. 'Sickening indignity: Terminally ill patients face repeat fit-to-work tests'. *Mirror*, 3 March. Accessed 10 January 2017. http://www.mirror.co.uk/news/uk-news/sickening-indignity-terminally-ill-patients-750517

Mahony, Nick and John Clarke. 2013. 'Public crises, public futures'. *Cultural Studies* 26(14), 933–954.

Mason, Paul. 2016. 'Don't complain about the strikers – they're only doing what we all should in 2017'. *Guardian*, 16 December. Accessed 20 December 2016. https://www.theguardian.com/commentisfree/2016/dec/19/dont-complain-about-the-strikers-theyre-only-doing-what-we-all-should-in-2017

May, Theresa. 2015. 'Theresa May's speech to the Conservative Party Conference in full'. *Independent*, 6 October. Accessed 10 January 2017. http://www.inde pendent.co.uk/news/uk/politics/theresa-may-s-speech-to-the-conservative-party-conference-in-full-a6681901.html

May, Theresa. 2016. 'Theresa May's Conference speech in full'. *The Telegraph*, 5 October. Accessed 10 December 2016. http://www.telegraph.co.uk/news/2016/10/05/theresa-mays-conference-speech-in-full/

McCarthy, Tom. 2017. 'Everything you need to know about the legal showdown over Trump's travel ban'. *Guardian*, 6 February. Accessed 10 February 2017. https://www.theguardian.com/us-news/2017/feb/06/trump-travel-ban-court-battle-everything-you-need-to-know

McInerny, Laura. 2012. 'Things rich people never understand'. *Laura McInerny*, 23 October. Accessed 10 October 2015. http://lauramcinerney.com/2012/10/23/things-rich-people-never-understand/

McKinney, Emma. 2014. 'White Dee quits benefits street after race abuse about kids'. *Birmingham Mail*, 14 September. 1 March 2015. http://www.birminghammail.co.uk/whats-on/whats-on-news/white-dee-quits-benefits-street-7769031

McKnight, Abigail. 2015. 'Downward mobility, opportunity hoarding and the "glass floor"'. *Social Mobility and Child Poverty Commission*, June 2015. Accessed 1 August 2016. https://www.gov.uk/government/uploads/system/uploads/attachment_data/file/447575/Downward_mobility_opportunity_hoarding_and_the_glass_floor.pdf

McNeal, Ian. 2014. 'Benefits street: Political and community leaders condemn decision to film second series in Stockton'. *GazetteLive*, 26 August. Accessed 26 May 2015. http://www.gazettelive.co.uk/news/teesside-news/benefits-street-political-comm unity-leaders-7668372

McRobbie, Angela. 2008. *The aftermath of feminism*. London: SAGE Publications.

McRobbie, Angela. 2013. 'Feminism, the family and the new mediated maternalism'. *New Formations: A Journal of Culture/Theory/Politics* 80, 119–137.

McVegas, Craig. 2014. '4 reflections on the anti-austerity movement'. *Novara Media*, 4 June. Accessed 10 October 2015. http://wire.novaramedia.com/2014/06/4-reflections-on-the-anti-austerity-movement/

McVeigh, Tracy and Toby Helm. 2015. 'UK "failing its young" as gulf grows between generations'. *Guardian*, 11 July. Accessed 10 October 2015. http://www.theguardian.com/society/2015/jul/11/uk-young-fairness-george-osborne-budget

Melrose, Jamie interviewed by Kirsten Forkert, 15 May 2016.

Methven, Nicola. 2014. 'Labour MP slams Channel 4 for making "misery telly" such as *Skint* and *Benefits Street*'. *Mirror*, 17 November. Accessed 15 August 2015. http://www.mirror.co.uk/tv/tv-news/labour-mp-slams-channel-4-4646231

Mezzadra, Sandro and Brett Nielson. 2013. *Border as method or the multiplication of labour*. Durham, NC: Duke University Press.

Migrants Rights Network. 2016. 'Motion passed! BMA to stand against the Immigration Act!'. *Migrants Rights Network*, 23 June. Accessed 17 January 2017. http://mrnlondonprojects.org.uk/wp/news/motion-passed-bma-stand-immigration-act/

Miguel, interviewed by Kirsten Forkert, 20 February 2015.

Milkman, Ruth. 2014. 'Millennial movements: Occupy Wall Street and the dreamers'. *Dissent* 61(3), 55–59.

Mirowski, Philip. 2013. *Never let a serious crisis go to waste: How neoliberalism survived the financial meltdown*. London: Verso.

Montgomerie, Johanna and Liam Stanley. 2015. 'The UK's everyday debt economy'. *Sheffield Political Economy Research Institute*, 30 January 2015. Accessed 20 October 2016. https://www.gold.ac.uk/media/documents-by-section/departments/politics-and-international-relations/PoliticsofDebtinUK_FINAL.pdf

Moore, Peter. 2016. 'How Britain voted'. *YouGov*, 27 June. Accessed 10 August 2016. https://yougov.co.uk/news/2016/06/27/how-britain-voted/

Morley, David and Kuan-Hsing Chen (eds.). 1996 *Stuart Hall: Critical dialogues in cultural studies*. Abingdon: Routledge.

Morrissey, Belinda and Susan Yell. 2016. 'Performative trolling: Szubanski, Gillard, Dawson and the nature of the utterance'. *Persona Studies* 2(1), 27–40.

Mouffe, Chantal. 2005. *On the political*. Abingdon: Routledge.

Mouffe, Chantal and Inigo Erejon. 2016. *Podemos: In the name of the people*. London: Lawrence & Wishart.

Nakamura, Lisa. 2013. 'Glitch racism: Networks as actors within vernacular internet theory'. *Culture digitally*, 10 December. Accessed 1 August 2015. http://culturedigitally.org/2013/12/glitch-racism-networks-as-actors-within-vernacular-internet-theory/

National Centre for Social Research. 2015. 'Paper summary: Benefits and welfare 202'. *British Social Attitudes Survey*. Accessed 15 January 2017. http://www.bsa.natcen.ac.uk/latest-report/british-social-attitudes-32/welfare.aspx

National Coalition for Independent Action. 2015. *Fight or fright: Voluntary services in 2015*. Accessed 10 September 2016. http://www.independentaction.net/wp-content/uploads/2015/02/NCIA-Inquiry-summary-report-final.pdf

Negri, Antonio. 1989. *The politics of subversion: A manifesto for the twenty-first century*. Cambridge: Polity.

Nesta, n.d. 'Centre for Social Action Innovation Fund'. Accessed 10 October 2015. http://www.nesta.org.uk/project/centre-social-action-innovation-fund.

New Cross Learning. 2013. 'Learning New Cross'. YouTube video, 15:10, posted by mffj, 15 December 2015. http://www.youtube.com/watch?v=CdMy7GrmlME.

Newham Council. 2011. *A strong community: Building resilience in Newham*. May 2011. Accessed 10 October 2015. https://www.newham.gov.uk/Docu ments/Council%20and%20Democracy/AStrongCommunityBuildingResiliencein Newham.pdf

Newham Council. 2012. 'Armed services and people in employment to be prioritised for social housing'. *Newham Council*, 28 September. Accessed 10 September 2016. https://www.newham.gov.uk/Pages/News/Armed%20services%20 and%20people%20in%20employment%20to%20be%20prioritised%20for%20 social%20housing.aspx

Newham Council. 2014. 'Newham council election – Thursday 22nd May 2014'. *Newham Council*, 22 May. https://mgov.newham.gov.uk/mgElectionResults. aspx?ID=2&V=1&RPID=12765227

Newman, Janet and John Clarke. 2014. 'States of imagination'. *Soundings* 57, 153–169.

News Shopper. 2010. 'Lewisham: Library futures to be discussed at meeting', *News Shopper*, 21 July 2010. http://www.newsshopper.co.uk/archive/2010/07/21/8284279. LEWISHAM__Library_futures_to_be_discussed_at_meetings/

Ngai, Sianne. 2005. *Ugly Feelings*. Cambridge, MA: Harvard University Press.

Nominet Trust. 2012. *Employment and the internet*. May 2012. Accessed 10 October 2015. http://www.nominettrust.org.uk/sites/default/files/NT%20SoA%20 4%20-%20Employment%20and%20the%20internet.pdf

NUS. 2016. 'International students'. *National Union of Students*. Accessed 15 January 2017. https://www.nus.org.uk/en/who-we-are/how-we-work/international-students/

Nye, Catrin. 2012. 'Naturalising Newham: Radical plan to boost integration'. BBC News, 20 September. Accessed 10 October 2015. http://www.bbc.co.uk/news/ uk-24146572

Oakley, Kate. 2009. 'The disappearing arts: Creativity and innovation after the creative industries'. *International Journal of Cultural Policy* 15(4), 403–413.

Oakley, Kate, David Hesmondhalgh, David Lee and Melissa Nesbitt. 2014. 'The national trust for talent? NESTA and New Labour's cultural policy'. *British Politics* 9, 297–317.

O'Connor, Justin. 2007. 'The cultural and creative industries: A review of the literature'. *Report for Creative Partnerships*, Arts Council England. Accessed 15 June 2015. http://kulturekonomi.se/uploads/cp_litrev4.pdf

O'Connor, Justin. 2015. 'Intermediaries and imaginaries in the cultural and creative industries'. *Regional Studies* 49(3), 374–387.

Office of National Statistics. 2013a. 'Government deficit and debt under the Maastricht Treaty, Calendar Year 2012'. *Statistical Bulletin*, 3 April. Accessed 10 January 2017.

https://www.ons.gov.uk/economy/governmentpublicsectorandtaxes/publicsector finance/bulletins/eugovernmentdeficitanddebtreturn/2013-10-02

Office of National Statistics. 2013b. 'Who owns businesses in the UK?'. *Business ownership in the UK 2013*. Accessed 10 October 2015. http://webarchive.nation alarchives.gov.uk/20160105160709/http://www.ons.gov.uk/ons/rel/abs/annual-business-survey/ownership-in-the-uk—2013/sty-abs-bus-own.html

Office of National Statistics. 2014. 'Large increase in 20 to 34-year-olds living with parents since 1996'. *Population*, 21 January 2014. http://www.ons.gov.uk/ons/rel/ family-demography/young-adults-living-with-parents/2013/sty-young-adults.html

Office of National Statistics. 2015. 'House price index'. *Office of National Statistics*, 13 December. Accessed 10 January 2017. https://www.ons.gov.uk/economy/ inflationandpriceindices/bulletins/housepriceindex/oct2016

Office of National Statistics. 2016a. *Migration Statistics Quarterly Report February 2016*. Accessed 15 January 2017. http://www.ons.gov.uk/peoplepopulation andcommunity/populationandmigration/internationalmigration/bulletins/migra tionstatisticsquarterlyreport/february2016

Office of National Statistics. 2016b. 'Labour disputes in the UK: 2015'. *Office of National Statistics*, 2 August. Accessed 1 November 2016. https://www.ons.gov.uk/employ mentandlabourmarket/peopleinwork/workplacedisputesandworkingconditions/ articles/labourdisputes/2015

O'Hara, Saskia, interviewed by Kirsten Forkert, 14 January 2017.

O'Leary, Duncan. 2014. 'Why the young favour pensioner benefits over those for the unemployed'. *New Statesman*, 6 January. http://www.newstatesman.com/ politics/2014/01/why-young-favour-pensioner-benefits-over-those-unemployed

Olma, Sebastian. 2014. 'Rethinking social innovation between imitation and invention'. *Institute of Network Cultures*. Accessed 10 March 2015. http://networkcultures. org/mycreativity/2014/08/18/rethinking-social-innovation-between-invention-and-imitation

Oxfam. 2013. *The true cost of austerity and inequality: A UK case study*. September 2013. Accessed 10 January 2017. https://www.oxfam.org/sites/www.oxfam. org/files/cs-true-cost-austerity-inequality-uk-120913-en.pdf

Panayi, Panikos. 2014. *An immigration history of Britain: Multicultural racism since 1800*. Abingdon: Routledge.

Parker, Sophia and Charles Leadbeater. 2013. 'A call for action: Ten lessons for local authority innovators'. *Nesta/ LGA Creative Councils*. Accessed 10 March 2015. http://www.nesta.org.uk/sites/default/files/creative_councils_10_lessons.pdf

Peck, Jamie, 2005. 'Struggling with the creative class'. *International Journal of Urban and Regional Research* 29 (4), 740–770.

Penny, Laurie. 2014. *Unspeakable things: Sex, lies and revolution*. London: Bloomsbury Press.

Phil, interviewed by Kirsten Forkert, 17 June 2014.

Phillips, Whitney. 2015. *This is why we can't have nice things: Mapping the relationship between online trolling and mainstream culture*. Cambridge, MA: MIT Press.

Pickerill, Jenny and John Krinsky. 2012. 'Why does Occupy matter?'. *Social Movement Studies* 11(3–4), 1–9.

Piketty, Thomas. 2014. *Capital in the twenty-first century*. Cambridge, MA: Harvard University Press.

Piore, Michael and Charles Sabel. 1984. *The second industrial divide: Possibilities for prosperity*. New York: Basic Books.

Poulantzas, Nicos. 2000. *State, power, socialism*. London: Verso.

Pratt, Andy and Paul Jefcutt. 2009. 'Creativity, innovation and the cultural economy: Snake oil for the 21st century?'. In *Creativity, innovation in the cultural economy, London*, edited by Andy Pratt and Paul Jefcutt, 3–19. Abingdon: Routledge.

Press Association. 2015. 'Benefits Street's White Dee: We've lost everything'. *Guardian*, 30 March. Accessed 1 June 2016. http://www.theguardian.com/media/2015/mar/30/benefits-street-white-dee-channel-4

PressTV. 2013. 'Young mothers in London face eviction over budget cuts'. YouTube video, 2:52, posted by PressTV on 13 October 2013. Accessed 27 February 2017. https://www.youtube.com/watch?v=_DuWouCeVDw

PSE. 2012. 'PSE reports'. Accessed 1 October 2015. http://www.poverty.ac.uk/pse-research/pseuk-reports

Puar, Jasbir. 2007. *Terrorist assemblages: Homonationalism in queer times*. Durham, NC: Duke University Press.

Public Libraries News, n.d. 'List of volunteer run libraries'. Accessed 10 September 2016. http://www.publiclibrariesnews.com/about-public-libraries-news/list-of-uk-volunteer-run-libraries.

Reeves, Rachel. 2016. 'Rachel Reeves MP: Ending free movement should be a red line for Labour post-Brexit'. *New Statesman*, 19 September. Accessed 15 November 2016. http://www.newstatesman.com/politics/economy/2016/09/rachel-reeves-mp-ending-free-movement-should-be-red-line-labour-post-brexit

Rhodes, Chris. 2015. 'Manufacturing: Statistics and policy'. *Report for the House of Commons Library, Briefing Paper 01942*, 6 August 2015. Accessed 1 September 2016. researchbriefings.files.parliament.uk/documents/SN01942/SN01942.pdf

Robert, interviewed by Kirsten Forkert, 1 June 2016.

Rojek, Chris. 2003. *Stuart Hall*. Cambridge: Polity.

Rolling Jubilee. 2013. http://rollingjubilee.org/

Rootes, Christopher. 1986. 'The politics of the higher educated'. *Melbourne Journal of Politics* 18, 184–200.

Rose, Hilary. 1994. *Love, power and knowledge: Towards a feminist transformation of the sciences*. Cambridge: Polity Press.

Rose, Nikolas. 1998. *Inventing ourselves: Psychology, power and personhood*. Cambridge: Cambridge University Press.

Ross, Andrew. 2004. *No collar: The humane workplace and its hidden costs*. Philadelphia: Temple University Press.

Ross, Andrew. 2009. *Nice work if you can get it: Life and labour in precarious times*. New York: NYU Press.

Ross, Andrew. 2014. *Creditocracy: And the case for debt refusal*. New York: New York University Press.

Rothenbuhler, Eric. 2009. 'From media events to ritual to communicative form'. In *Media events in a global age*, edited by Nick Couldry, Andreas Hepp and Friedrich Krotz, 61–75. Abingdon: Routledge.

Rucht, Dieter. 2013. 'Protest movements and their media usages'. In *Mediation and protest movements*, edited by Bart Cammaerts, Alice Mattoni and Patrick McCurdy, 249–268. Bristol: Intellect Books.

Runnymede Trust. 2015. *The 2015 budget: Effects on black and minority ethnic people*. July 2015. Accessed 10 January 2017. http://www.runnymedetrust.org/uploads/The%202015%20Budget%20Effect%20on%20BME%20Runnymede-Trust%2027thJuly2015.pdf

Rustin, Michael. 1989. 'The politics of post-Fordism: Or, the trouble with "New Times"'. *New Left Review*, 54–78.

Rustin, Michael. 2016. 'The neoliberal university and its alternatives'. *Soundings* 63, 147–170.

Ryan, Frances. 2015. 'Inflicting suffering on those in need is now at the heart of our benefits system'. *Guardian*, 10 March 2015. Accessed 1 April 2016. http://www.theguardian.com/commentisfree/2015/mar/10/inflicting-suffering-heart-benefits-system-unemployed-disabled.

Saggar, Shamit. 1992. *Race and politics in Britain*. Saddle River, NJ: Prentice-Hall.

Saggar, Shamit. 2004. 'Immigration and the politics of public opinion'. *The Political Quarterly*, 74(s1):178–194.

Saul, Heather. 2014. 'Working couple filmed 'extensively' cut from final episodes'. *The Independent*, 16 January. Accessed 1 March 2016. http://www.independent.co.uk/arts-entertainment/tv/news/benefits-street-working-couple-filmed-extensively-were-cut-from-final-episodes-9063637.html

Seabrook, Jeremy. 2014. 'Why shame is the most dominant feature of modern poverty'. *Guardian*, 30 September. Accessed 1 March 2015. http://www.theguardian.com/commentisfree/2014/sep/30/shame-modern-poverty-poor-people-tory-welfare-cuts

Sennett, Richard. 2004. *Respect: The formation of character in an age of inequality*. New York: W.W. Norton.

Sharma, Nandita. 2015. 'Terror and mercy at the border'. In *Nothing to lose but our fear*, edited by Fiona Jefferies. London: Zed Books.

Sharzer, Greg. 2012. *No local: Why small-scale alternatives won't change the world*. Winchester: Zero Books.

Shelter. 2016. 'Bedroom tax: Are you affected?' 25 April 2016. Accessed 10 January 2017. http://england.shelter.org.uk/get_advice/housing_benefit_and_local_housing_allowance/changes_to_housing_benefit/bedroom_tax

Sherwin, Adam. 2015. 'Immigration street: Protesters force controversial TV show to be cut from six to one episode'. *Independent*, 12 February. Accessed 1 August 2015. http://www.independent.co.uk/arts-entertainment/tv/news/immigration-street-protesters-force-controversial-tv-show-to-be-cut-from-six-to-one-episode-10042791.html

Silver, Nate. 2016. 'The mythology of Trump's "working-class" support'. *Five Thirty Eight*, 3 May. Accessed 10 December 2016. http://fivethirtyeight.com/features/the-mythology-of-trumps-working-class-support/

Sims, Alexandra. 2016. 'Theresa May defends freedom of the press after High Court Brexit ruling attacked by media'. *Independent*, 6 November. http://www.independent.co.uk/news/uk/politics/theresa-may-responds-high-court-brexit-ruling-media-coverage-a7401346.html

Skeggs, Beverley. 1997. *Formations of class and gender: Becoming respectable*. London: Sage.

Skeggs, Beverley. 2012. 'Feeling class: Affect and culture in the making of class relations'. In *The Wiley-Blackwell companion to sociology*, edited by G. Ritzer. Chichester, UK: John Wiley.

Skeggs, Beverley and Helen Wood. 2012. *Reacting to reality television: Audience, performance and value*. Abingdon: Routledge.

Slimstone, Sun. 2014. 'Benefits-land?'. *The musings of Sun Slimstone*, 22 January. Accessed 1 August 2014. https://slimstone.wordpress.com/tag/benefits-street/

Smale, Kelly. 2011. 'Group occupy New Cross Library in protest over closure threats'. *News Shopper*, 5 February. Accessed 20 September 2016. http://www.news shopper.co.uk/news/8835838.NEW_CROSS__Group_occupy_library_in_protest_ over_threatened_closure

Snow, David, E. Burke Rochford Jr., Steven K. Worden and Robert D. Benford. 1986. 'Frame alignment processes, micromobilization, and movement participation'. *American Sociological Review* 51(4), 464–481.

Social Enterprise London. 2011. 'Libraries in transition: Are there creative alternatives?'. *Public Service Hub 2020 at the RSA*. Accessed 10 September 2014. http://www. rsa2020publicservices.org.uk/publications/libraries-in-transition-are-there-crea tive-alternatives/

Social Enterprise UK. 2013. 'Out of the shadows'. October 2013. Accessed 10 September 2014. http://www.socialenterprise.org.uk/uploads/files/2013/10/out_of_ the_shadows_report.pdf

Social Security Advisory Committee. 2014. *Occasional paper #12: The cumulative impact of welfare reform: A commentary*. April 2014. Accessed 10 January 2017. https://www.gov.uk/government/uploads/system/uploads/attachment_data/ file/324059/ssac_occasional_paper_12_report.pdf

Southall Black Sisters. 2016. 'Recourse to public funds – History'. Accessed 15 January 2017. http://www.southallblacksisters.org.uk/campaigns/abolish-no-recourse-to-public-funds/#history

Spencer, Ian. 2002. *British Immigration Policy since 1939: The making of multi-racial Britain*. Abingdon: Routledge.

Spencer, Sarah. 2012. *The migration debate*. Bristol: Policy Press.

Srnicek, Nick and Alex Williams. 2015. *Inventing the future: Post-capitalism and a world without work*. London: Verso.

Standing, Guy. 2011. *The Precariat: The new dangerous class*. London: Bloomsbury.

Stone, Jasmin. 2014. 'Why I'm occupying a boarded-up East London council house'. *Guardian*, 23 September. Accessed 2 January 2017. https://www.theguardian. com/commentisfree/2014/sep/23/why-occupying-boarded-up-east-london-council-house-social-housing

Strangleman, Tim. 2007. 'Nostalgia for permanence at work: The end of work and its commentators'. *The Sociological Review* 55(1), 81–103.

Strike Debt. 2012a. 'The debt resistor's organising kit'. http://strikedebt.org/Strike-Debt-Organizing-Kit.pdf

Strike Debt. 2012b. 'Debt soapbox in Washington Square Park'. Online video. 48:28. 2012b. Posted by StopMotionsolo. http://www.ustream.tv/recorded/23229223#utm

Strike Debt, n.d. *Strike debt: Debt resistance for the 99%*. http://strikedebt.org/

Stuart, Paul. 2014. 'Benefits Street TV show lied to us, say Winson Green Residents'. *Birmingham Mail*, 6 January. Accessed 1 September 2014. http://www.birming hammail.co.uk/news/local-news/benefits-street-tv-show-lied-6470342

Summers, Deborah. 2009. 'David Cameron warns of new "age of austerity"'. *Guardian*, 26 April. Accessed 10 January 2017. https://www.theguardian.com/politics/2009/apr/26/david-cameron-conservative-economic-policy1

Sweeney, Mark. 2014. 'Benefits Street cleared of breaching rules on welfare of child participants'. *Guardian*, 30 June. Accessed 1 September 2014. http://www.theguardian.com/media/2014/jun/30/benefits-street-cleared-child-participants-channel-4-ofcom

Syal, Ryal. 2016. 'Amber Rudd's plan to force firms to reveal foreign staff numbers abandoned'. *Guardian*, 10 October. Accessed 15 January. https://www.theguardian.com/uk-news/2016/oct/09/plan-to-force-firms-to-reveal-foreign-staff-numbers-abandoned

Taylor, David. 1989. 'Citizenship and social power'. *Critical Social Policy* 26, 19–31.

Taylor, Jim. 2011. 'What effect has scrapping EMA had?'. *BBC Newsbeat*, 13 October. Accessed 10 January 2017. http://www.bbc.co.uk/newsbeat/article/15272526/what-impact-has-scrapping-ema-had

Townsend, Mark. 2016. 'Homophobic attacks in UK rose 147% in three months after Brexit vote'. *Guardian*, 8 November. https://www.theguardian.com/society/2016/oct/08/homophobic-attacks-double-after-brexit-vote

Touraine, Alain, Michel Wieviorka and Francois Dubet. 1987. *The workers' movement*. Cambridge: Cambridge University Press.

Travis, Alan. 2013. 'New migrants to face £1,000 healthcare levy'. *Guardian*, 3 July. Accessed 15 January 2017. https://www.theguardian.com/uk-news/2013/jul/03/immigrants-levy-healthcare

Trentmann, Frank. 2016. *Empire of things: How we became a world of consumers, between the fifteenth century to the twenty-first*. London: Allen Lane.

Tronti, Mario. 1962. 'Factory and society'. *Quaderni Rossi* 2, 1–31.

Tronti, Mario. 1966. *Workers and capital*. Turin: Einaudi.

Trump, Donald. 2016. 'Full transcript: Donald Trump's jobs plan speech'. *Politico*, 28 June. Accessed 10 December 2016. http://www.politico.com/story/2016/06/full-transcript-trump-job-plan-speech-224891

TUC. 2013. 'Involuntary part-time work driving rising employment'. 9 August. Accessed 10 November 2016. https://www.tuc.org.uk/economic-issues/labour-market/labour-market-and-economic-reports/involuntary-temporary-jobs-driving

TUC. 2014a. 'Trade unions and disabled people fighting austerity; a TUC briefing'. *Trades Union Congress*, January 2014. Accessed 10 January 2017. https://www.tuc.org.uk/sites/default/files/DisabledPeopleFightingAusterity.pdf

TUC. 2014b. 'More than two in five new jobs created since mid-2010 have been self-employed'. 14 April. https://www.tuc.org.uk/economic-issues/economic-analysis/labour-market/labour-market-and-economic-reports/more-two-five-new

TUC. 2014c. 'Tax credits and benefits play crucial role in preventing working people falling into poverty, says TUC'. *Trades Union Congress*, 14 February. Accessed 1 March 2015. https://www.tuc.org.uk/social-issues/welfare-and-benefits/tax-credits/tax-credits-and-benefits-play-crucial-role-preventing

TUC. 2015a. 'The impact on women of recession and austerity'. *Trades Union Congress*, March 2015. Accessed 10 January 2017. https://www.tuc.org.uk/sites/default/files/WomenRecession.pdf

TUC. 2015b. *The impact on women of recession and austerity*. March 2015. Accessed 16 September 2016. https://www.tuc.org.uk/sites/default/files/WomenRecession.pdf

TUC. 2016. 'Living on the edge: The rise of job insecurity in modern Britain'. *Trades Union Congress*. Accessed 1 November 2016. https://www.tuc.org.uk/sites/default/files/TUCLivingOnTheEdge.pdf

Turner, Victor. 1967. *Forest of symbols: Aspects of Ndembu ritual*. Ithaca, NY: Cornell University Press.

Tyler, Imogen. 2013. *Revolting subjects: Social abject and resistance in neoliberal Britain*. London: Zed Books.

UCU. 2016. 'Precarious work in higher education'. *University and College Union*. Accessed 10 November 2016. https://www.ucu.org.uk/media/7995/Precarious-work-in-higher-education-a-snapshot-of-insecure-contracts-and-institutional-attitudes-Apr-16/pdf/ucu_precariouscontract_hereport_apr16.pdf

UCU and CLASS. 2014. *Why immigration is good for all of us*. Accessed 15 January 2017. http://www.ucu.org.uk/media/6865/Why-immigration-is-good-for-us-all-UCU—CLASS-Oct-14/pdf/whyimmigrationisgoodforallofus_oct14.pdf

UK Government. 2011. *Budget 2011: Britain open for Business*. 23 January. Accessed 10 December 2015. https://www.gov.uk/government/news/2011-budget-britain-open-for-business

UK Government. 2012. *Health and Social Care Act 2012*. Accessed 10 January 2017. http://www.legislation.gov.uk/ukpga/2012/7/contents/enacted

UK Government. 2013. 'David Cameron's immigration speech'. *GOV.UK*, 25 March. Accessed 15 January 2017. https://www.gov.uk/government/speeches/david-camerons-immigration-speech.

UK Government. 2014a. *Code of practice in preventing illegal working*, May. Accessed 15 January 2017. https://www.gov.uk/government/uploads/system/uploads/attachment_data/file/311668/Code_of_practice_on_preventing_illegal_working.pdf

UK Government. 2014b. *Transparency of Lobbying, Non-Party Campaigning and Trade Union Administration Act 2014*, 15 September 2015. http://www.legislation.gov.uk/ukpga/2014/4/contents/enacted/data.htm

UK Government. 2016. *Trade Union Act*. Accessed 20 November 2016. http://www.legislation.gov.uk/ukpga/2016/15/contents/enacted/data.htm

UK Legislation. 2014. *Immigration Act 2014*. Accessed 15 January 2017. http://www.legislation.gov.uk/ukpga/2014/22/contents/enacted

Underground. 2014. *Parasite Street*. http://www.parasite-street.co.uk/

Under-occupied. 2013. 'On benefits and working?'. *Under-Occupied*, 22 November. Accessed 1 August 2014. http://underoccupied.net/2013/11/22/on-benefits-and-working/

United Kingdom. 2010. 'Parliamentary debates', 9 December. Accessed 10 November 2016. http://www.publications.parliament.uk/pa/cm201011/cmhansrd/cm101209/debtext/101209-0004.htm#column_624

United Kingdom. 2011. 'Localism Act 2011, Part 7, Chapter 1: Homelessness'. *UK Legislation*. http://www.legislation.gov.uk/ukpga/2011/20/part/7/chapter/1/crossheading/homelessness/enacted

Valios, Natalie. 2015. 'Stockton-on-Tees residents fight back over Benefits Street series'. *CommunityCare*, 11 May. Accessed 1 June 2015. http://www.communitycare.co.uk/2015/05/11/stockton-tees-residents-fight-back-benefits-street-series/

Vance, JD. 2016. 'How Donald Trump seduced America's white working class'. *Guardian*, 11 September. Accessed 10 December 2016. https://www.theguardian.com/commentisfree/2016/sep/10/jd-vance-hillbilly-elegy-donald-trump-us-white-poor-working-class

Virdee, Satnam. 2014. *Race, class and the racialised outsider*. Basingstoke: Palgrave MacMillan.

Wadsworth, Jonathan. 2014. 'Immigration and the UK Labour Market'. *London School of Economics* Working Paper EA019. Accessed 15 January 2017. http://cep.lse.ac.uk/pubs/download/ea019.pdf

Walker, Peter. 2016. 'Sure start closures almost doubled last year'. *Guardian*, 8 December. Accessed 10 January 2017. https://www.theguardian.com/society/2016/dec/08/sure-start-closures-almost-doubled-last-year-figures-show

Walkerdine, Valerie. 2010. 'Communal beingness and affect: An exploration of trauma in an ex-industrial community'. *Body and Society* 16(1), 91–116.

Walkerdine, Valerie and Luis Jimenez. 2012. *Gender, work and community after de-industrialisation*. Basingstoke: Palgrave MacMillan.

Walters, William. 2004. 'Secure borders, safe haven, domopolitics'. *Citizenship Studies* 8(93), 237–260.

Ware, Vron. 2008. 'Towards a sociology of resentment: A debate on class and whiteness'. *Sociological Research Online* 13 (5) 9. Accessed 1 March 2016. http://socresonline.org.uk/13/5/9.html

Weeks, Kathi. 2011. *The problem with work: Feminism, Marxism, anti-work politics and post-work imaginaries*. Durham, NC: Duke University Press.

Williams, Raymond. 2011. *The long revolution*. Cardigan: Parthian Books.

Williams, Rowan. 2015. 'Foreword'. In *Blue Labour: Forging a new politics*, edited by Ian Geary and Adrian Pabst, ix–xii. London: IB Tauris.

Williams, Zoe. 2015. 'Let's ditch the nostalgia that has invaded our TV and our politics'. *The Guardian*, 30 April. Accessed 10 October 2015. http://www.theguardian.com/commentisfree/2015/apr/30/ditch-nostalgia-television-politics-austerity-bake-off

Wintour, Patrick. 2014. 'Benefits Street reveals "ghetto reality", says Iain Duncan Smith'. *Guardian*, 22 January. Accessed 10 February 2017. http://www.theguardian.com/politics/2014/jan/22/duncan-smith-benefits-street-shock

Wintour, Patrick. 2015. 'Cameron's immigration bill to include a crackdown on illegal workers'. *Guardian*, 21 May. http://www.theguardian.com/uk-news/2015/may/20/immigration-bill-to-include-crackdown-on-illegal-foreign-workers

Women's Budget Group. 2016. *A cumulative gender impact assessment of ten years of austerity policies*. March 2016. Accessed 10 October 2016. http://wbg.org.uk/wp-content/uploads/2016/03/De_HenauReed_WBG_GIAtaxben_briefing_2016_03_06.pdf

Wood, Helen. 2014. 'Benefits Britain live debate: Hiding in the light'. *CSTOnline*, 21 February. Accessed 10 August 2015. http://cstonline.tv/benefits-britain-the-live-debate-hiding-in-the-light

World Bank. 2011. *Migration and Remittances Factbook 2011*. Accessed 10 October 2015. http://siteresources.worldbank.org/INTLAC/Resources/Factbook2011-Ebook.pdf

Wynne-Jones, Ros. 2015. 'Gloating Tories don't care that people are dying of poverty on the real-life Benefits Street'. *Mirror*, 15 January. Accessed 1 April 2015. http://www.mirror.co.uk/news/uk-news/gloating-tories-dont-care-people-3022783

Yuval-Davis, Nira. 2013. 'A situated intersectional approach to the study of everyday bordering'. *EU Borderscapes Working Paper #2.* http://www.euborderscapes.eu/fileadmin/user_upload/Working_Papers/EUBORDERSCAPES_Working_Paper_2_Yuval-Davis.pdf

Index

Note: page numbers in italics indicate photos.

213

About the Author

A researcher, teacher and activist, **Kirsten Forkert** is based in the School of Media at BCU in Birmingham, where she is Associate Director of the Birmingham Centre for Media and Cultural Research. She is the author of *Artistic Lives* (2013), and is a co-author of *Go Home: The Politics of Immigration Controversies* (2017) and the forthcoming *Media, War and the Making of Migrants*. She is a member of the editorial collective of *Soundings*.

Printed in Great Britain
by Amazon